THE FOLKLORE SOCIETY

MISTLETOE SERIES

Animals in Folklore

This important collection of essays on one of the most perennially fascinating themes of folklore, marks the centenary of the Folklore Society, whose history is surveyed by Katherine Briggs in an introductory essay. The papers, contributed by distinguished specialists, fall into four groups: animal motifs; studies of animals in local folklore (including essays on the black dog in English folklore and animals in Yorkshire accounts of witchcraft); shape changing (including folklore about werewolves) and animal images. The essays cover both western and oriental folklore, and the time span is equally wide-ranging.

Other titles in the Mistletoe Series

THE LAST OF THE ASTROLOGERS: THE AUTOBIOGRAPHY OF WILLIAM LILLY
ed. K. M. Briggs

THE JOURNEY TO THE OTHER WORLD
ed. H. R. E. Davidson

A COLLECTION OF HIGHLAND RITES AND CUSTOMES
ed. J. L. Campbell

LEGENDS OF ICELANDIC MAGICIANS
ed. and tr. Jacqueline Simpson

THE SECRET COMMON-WEALTH
Robert Kirk,
ed. Stewart Sanderson

BALLAD STUDIES
ed. E. B. Lyle

RITUAL ANIMAL DISGUISE
E. C. Cawte

In preparation

THE JACK IN THE GREEN
Roy Judge

FRONTISPIECE

A painted wooden bead from India, carved in the form of a fossil brachiopod shell. Length 5 cm. The bead appears to be modelled on the Jurassic (Vesulian) species *Terebratula phillipsiana* Walker, now referred to *Morrisithyris*.

The bead has been gilded and painted using the decorative motif known as the cone form (or *buta* pattern). It was probably the central bead of a Kashmiri necklace, the silk cord of which passed through a loop of copper wire inserted into the replica of the shell's umbo; mid-19th century.

Fossil Brachiopoda Collection, British Museum (Nat. Hist.). Photograph by Colin Keates. Reproduced by permission of the Trustees.

(See pp. 214 and 280.)

ANIMALS IN FOLKLORE

Edited by

J. R. Porter and W. M. S. Russell

Published by D. S. Brewer Ltd and Rowman & Littlefield
for The Folklore Society
1978

Published by D. S. Brewer Ltd, PO Box 24, Ipswich IP1 1JJ
and 240 Hills Road, Cambridge

First published 1978

First published in the United States of America 1978
by Rowman & Littlefield, 81 Adams Drive,
Totowa, N.J. 07512

British Library Cataloguing in Publication Data

Animals in folklore. – (Mistletoe series).
1. Animal lore
I. Porter, Joshua Roy II. Russell, William
Moy Stratton III. Series
389′.369 GR705

ISBN 0-85991-034-2

ISBN (US) 0 8476 6065 6

Filmset in 'Monophoto' Ehrhardt 11 on 12 pt by
Richard Clay (The Chaucer Press) Ltd, Bungay, Suffolk
and printed in Great Britain by
Fletcher & Son Ltd, Norwich

Contents

Preface

This volume is published to mark the Centenary of the Folklore Society, which occurs in 1978. Its nucleus is a series of papers read at a joint conference of the Folklore Society and the Department of Sociology of the University of Reading on *Witchcraft, Magic and the Animal World*, held at Reading in April 1976, by courtesy of the Head of the Department, Professor S. L. Andreski; but the scope has been widened and further contributions on the same general theme have been added. There is also an introductory essay on the history of the Folklore Society during its first hundred years.

INTRODUCTION

The Folklore Society and its Beginnings

KATHARINE M. BRIGGS

The Eighteenth and the Nineteenth Centuries were the great periods of the amateur scholars. Young gentlemen of scholarly tastes, who had lingered at the University or extended the Grand Tour to meet foreign savants, returned to their country houses to build up a library already several generations old, and to correspond with like-minded contemporaries in the intervals of performing their local duties. In London the learned amateurs would meet at clubs and coffee-houses to discuss their special interests and form associations for research. Already in Restoration England the Royal Society for the Promotion of Science had been founded under the patronage of Charles II. In the country these associations were emulated, and societies for the promotion of Archaeology, of Local History, of Heraldry and other kindred subjects sprang up all over the country. The Folk-Lore Society was founded rather late—not until 1878, but it had a long ancestry of Antiquarians behind it—Leland, Camden, Aubrey, Glanvil, Bovet, Hearne. Then at the end of the eighteenth century and the beginning of the nineteenth the Romantic Revival encouraged the collectors of tales, ballads and popular antiquities, which included Calendar Customs. Douce, Crofton Croker, Keightley, Strutt, Hone, Brand, Chambers, Cunningham, Hogg, Scott, all took their part in these researches.

The Nineteenth Century showed no abatement of interest in Popular Antiquities. Robert Southey, working as a man of letters rather than an antiquarian, took a lively interest in popular traditions. He was the first to publish the now famous story of The Three Bears, then so little known that it was supposed by Jacobs to have originated with Southey, though a manuscript version of the story written before its publication in *The Doctor* has finally established it as a folk-tale. It was Southey who encouraged Mrs. Bray to pursue her researches into the folk-beliefs of the district of Devon in which she lived.

W. J. Thoms, born at the beginning of the nineteenth century, was the first person to suggest 'Folk-Lore' as a more appropriate name for the study of traditional beliefs and customs than the cumbrous 'Popular Antiquities'. The suggestion was made in an article in *The Athenaeum* on the 22nd of August 1841. It was a time when there was a great enthusiasm for the Anglo-Saxon strain in our language, and the suggestion was enthusiastically adopted, and soon gained international currency. Thoms lived till 1885, and so was able to see the formation of the Society which he had christened. In an open correspondence with Lawrence Gomme in *Notes and Queries*, which had been originated by Thoms and was edited by him until 1872, he discussed and urged the foundation of a Folk-Lore Society. He insisted that 'not a day must be lost in organizing such a society' and two years after the correspondence began the Folk-Lore Society was founded, with Thoms as its Director, an office which he held until his death in 1885.

The whole century was marked by an increasing interest in Folklore Studies and a gradual shift of focus towards a more scientific approach to field studies. The literary folklorists who edited and drew their conclusions from early literature, pamphlets and magical manuscripts, or from legal documents, do not show such a change of attitude. Thomas Wright and W. J. Thoms have much in common in their treatment of their material, but when we come to those who are collecting and publishing oral traditions we are aware of an increasing conscientiousness about verbal accuracy. In the time of the Romantic Revival there was a great interest in traditional matter, people were eager for tales of the supernatural—ghosts, witches and fairies, and there were many writers who were themselves countrymen and were directly in touch with the rural traditions. The trouble was that they found it impossible to believe that their educated readers would tolerate a plain transcription of a tale as it was actually told at the fireside, it must be given poetic and decorative embroidery before it could be acceptable. We find this particularly in the Lowland Scots and the English Borderers. Hogg and Cunningham knew all that was to be known about local traditions, but they could not reproduce them without re-furbishing them. John Roby is a particularly glaring example. His *Traditions of Lancashire* was first published in 1829, and the kernel of each story contained an actual piece of tradition, but each one was re-written as a kind of novelette, with so much decoration as to make it quite difficult to understand what was supposed to have happened. Horace Walpole's *Castle of Otranto* seems quite calm and well-motivated by comparison. Hardwick, who covered something of the same ground in 1872, rightly criticizes Roby's work, saying: 'When put forth as "traditions", in the true acceptation of the term, they are worse than useless, for they are calculated equally to mislead both the antiquary and the collector of folk lore'.

As the century went on this attitude became more general. Mrs. Balfour's 'Legends of the Cars', published in *Folklore* 2, 1891 is sometimes suspect because her reproduction of the Fen Country dialect contains a sprinkling of Lowland Scots which came too readily to her tongue, but that she made a real effort to preserve the essential shape of the story is shown by the reproduction of the notes which she took as each one was told. William Henderson made a most admirable collection of *Folklore of the Northern Counties*, first published as early as 1866; Robert Hunt had collected the materials for his *Popular Romances of the West of England* some twenty years before its publication in 1865. In 1895 Addy gave careful particulars of the narrators of his tales, and everywhere respect for the verbal accuracy of reproduction was growing. In *Folk-Lore Record*, No. 1, 1878, which celebrated the founding of The Folk-Lore Society, W. R. S. Ralston (*Folk-Lore Record*, I pp. 72–3) besides moving towards a classification of folk tales, emphasizes the importance of this accuracy. 'It is impossible to impress too strongly on collectors', he says, 'the absolute necessity of accurately recording the stories they hear, and of accompanying them by ample references for the sake of verification. The temptation to alter, to piece together, and to improve, is one which many minds find extremely seductive; but yielding to it deprives the result of any value, except for the purpose of mere amusement.'

The time for a scientific approach to folklore was drawing nearer, and the general interest in folk traditions was strengthening at the same time. The principles underlying Mythology and Folk-Lore were exerting an ever-widening interest. The twenty-five years before the foundation of The Folk-Lore Society were occupied by a lively and prolonged battle about these principles, which is admirably described by R. M. Dorson in his monumental work, *The British Folklorists*, indispensable to anyone interested in the history of Folklore.

Max Müller was a German philologist, who, after studying in Liepzig, Berlin and Paris, settled in England in 1846 at the age of twenty-eight and became a Professor at Oxford University. He had early turned his attention from the Classics to the new study of Sanskrit, and he became convinced that Philology was the most necessary tool for the study of Mythology and Folklore. He had long been puzzled by the survival of savage and primitive myths among the highly civilized and sophisticated Greeks and also by the similarity of the names of the supreme god in Sanskrit, Indian, Greek and Roman languages. The solution that occurred to him was that Dyaus, Zeus and Deus were all one word, meaning in the ancient Vedic, the earliest written Indo-Germanic language, 'Brightness' or 'The Sky'. The main foundation of all mythology became to him Sun-Worship, and the strange accretions and aberrations of later myths were due to what he rather infelicitously called 'a disease of language', meaning variations due to forgetfulness, and misunderstanding. He expounded this theory in 1856 in *Oxford Essays*, presenting it most lucidly and persuasively, so that it made an immediate appeal to the scholarship of the day, ripe for the reception of such a theory. For more than ten years the school of Linguistic Mythology held the field almost undisputed, but during that time the Science of Ethnology gathered strength, the study of living men, who reasoned and behaved as primitive man might be thought to have done. A new concept of beliefs sprang up with the discovery of totemism, fetishism and allied savage practices, and these were to a certain extent reinforced by Archaeology, with its evidence of practices and beliefs parallel to those found among modern primitive races. The weakness of the ethnological argument was that so-called primitive men had behind them as long a train of ancestors as civilized men, and might be an example of degeneration rather than retarded development. This objection might to a certain extent be refuted by the discoveries of archaeologists.

In 1873 Andrew Lang launched a full-scale attack against the theories of Max Müller from the general standpoint of Ethnology. Lang was a brilliant polemist, equipped with a tremendous range of knowledge, an agile mind and an impish sense of humour. He danced round Müller, attacking him from all sides, and Müller stood four-square to the attack, and never gave ground. He refused to regard seriously the arguments of a scholar who knew no Sanskrit and would not even attempt to learn it. Andrew Lang occasionally conceded a point, but Müller continued the argument indomitably and without concession until his death in 1900. Müller stood high in public estimation. In 1875, when several European governments were trying to persuade him to return to the Continent, Dean Liddell of Christ Church prevailed on him to stay in Oxford by the unprecedented offer of a Chair free from all teaching duties.

In spite of this, when the Folk-Lore Society was founded in 1878 the Ethnologists were in the ascendant. Perhaps Professor Müller had not been helped by the extravagances of his disciples, Sir George Cox, who tended to sweep the heroes of all myths into one net, claiming King Arthur and Grettur the Strong as solar deities as well as Odysseus, Achilles, Heracles, Theseus, Bellerophon and Meleagros, or Robert Brown, who was more catholic; he included moon goddesses as well as sungods into the myths, and even a god of the sea. He traced his mythology to Semitic rather than Vedic sources, but remained an ardent disciple of Max Müller.

The brilliance, wit and range of scholarship displayed by the two great opponents and their supporters engaged the attention of informed readers everywhere in Britain. It is surprising to find how many folklore themes occur in literature at that time, and the impact which the controversy made. At least one school for girls, that attended by Juliana Horatia Gatty—afterwards Mrs. Ewing—included the study of Sanskrit in its syllabus. Charlotte Yonge's novel *Magnum Bonum* contains a reference to the Müller–Lang controversy in a holiday magazine written by the family.

'The magazine contained a series of notes on the nursery rhymes where "The Song of Sixpence" was proved to be a solar myth. The pocketful of rye was the yield of the earth, and the twenty-four blackbirds sang at sunrise while the King counted the golden drops of the rain, and the Queen ate the produce, while the Maid's performance in the garden was, beyond all doubt, symbolic of the clouds suddenly broken in upon by the lightning!'

This skit, which is similar to one published in Dublin Trinity

College Magazine in 1870, makes no attempt to reproduce a philological argument, but the interpretation is no more extravagant than that of 'Jack and the Beanstalk' by Professor Angelo de Gubernatis, an Italian philologist who was converted to Müller's theöry in *Zoological Mythology* (1872). Professor Dorson, however, draws our attention to an even more eccentric interpretation of it by modern psychology. We moderns also have our aberrations.

The first volume of *The Folk-Lore Record* is of special interest in the history of the Folk-Lore Society because it gives a clear picture of the Constitution and membership of the Society. The object of the Folk-Lore Society is laid down as 'The preservation and publication of Popular Traditions, Legendary Ballads, Local Proverbial Sayings, Superstitions and Old Customs (British and foreign) and all subjects relating to them.'

Curiously enough Folk-Tales and Legends have been omitted from this list, though the first volume itself contains two articles on Folk-Tales, and they became immediately of importance to the work of the Society. Neither were Games, Sports or Nursery Rhymes expressly mentioned. It was some time before artifacts and crafts were included in the area of study, in fact they were expressly excluded in Charlotte Burne's *Handbook of Folk-Lore* (1913). For the first ten years of the Society the custom, common to many of the learned Societies, was to choose a noble patron as President, who took little part in the day-to-day running of the Society. The practical Chairman of the Council was called 'The Director' and this office was held by W. J. Thoms while the President was The Earl of Verulam, F.R.G.S. The Council was an impressive one. Among its members were James Britten, Henry C. Coote, Laurence Gomme, Andrew Lang, Max Müller, W. R. S. Ralston, Edward Solly and Edward Tylor. Sophia Burne and Marian Raolfe Cox, who were to make valuable contributions to the literature of the Society were not yet on the list of members of the Society, nor has the great figure of Sir James Frazer loomed on the horizon.

From 1878 until the middle of the First Great War 'The Great Team', as Professor Dorson calls them, were in full vigour, and were joined by many helpers and eminent scholars. The six 'giants' named by Professor Dorson were Andrew Lang, George Laurence Gomme, Alfred Nutt, Edwin Sidney Hartland, Edward Clodd and

W. A. Clouston. Each of these had a notable contribution to make, and was a character in his own right. Broadly speaking all were ethnological in their theories, but each had a different approach to the subject, though they were truly a team. They met, debated, corresponded, and helped each other with information, proof-reading and criticism. At the same time they were not afraid to differ, and the Society was kept lively with their discussions and debates.

Andrew Lang, who had entered Folklore through the gate of the classics with his translation of The Odyssey, ranged far through the folktales of all countries and races, became deeply involved in the study of savage practices and myths and later showed himself ready to investigate psychic phenomena as a contributory factor to folklore beliefs. He was an accomplished man of letters, a brilliant debater and a man of wide learning. Like James Frazer he was not himself a collector, but gained his material from the researches of others. He was a popularizer whose various coloured fairy books have won the hearts of generations of children, though they were looked at askance by the purists.

Sir Laurence Gomme wrote the first handbook on the study of Folk-Lore and outlined the views of the Ethnological school in his book *Ethnology in Folklore*. His second interest was in the History of London, on which he wrote a number of books. His interest in both History and Folk-Lore finds expression in *Folklore as an Historical Science* (1908).

Alfred Nutt was not only the publisher for the Folklore Society but was a leading Celtic Scholar who introduced many of the Irish Legends and Romances to the world in such books as *The Voyage of Bran*. His publication for the Society was a labour of love, and sometimes entailed some financial loss. Sidney Hartland's most important contributions to the literature of Folk-Lore were *The Science of Fairy Tales*, which exhibits a considerable range of learning in a compact space, and his *English Fairy and Folk Tales*, a selection of well-chosen materials from early books, manuscripts and chap-books. An even more important contribution to the theory of Folk-Lore—the earliest of the monographs written on a Tale-Type—is *The Legend of Perseus* in which Hartland traces back the various motifs which make up the legend to primitive and barbarous beliefs. Hartland outlived most of his contemporaries and wrote the obituaries of W. A. Clouston, Walter

Gregor, Mr. Gladstone, Sir John Rhys, Paul Sebillot and Charlotte Burne and did not himself die until 1927.

Edward Clodd survived Hartland by three years. He was a genial and popular man who was host to a great many members of literary society as well as to the leading folklorists. He was also a convinced atheist who believed that the chief function of Folk-Lore was to explore the savage beliefs and practices underlying established religion. His Presidential Address in 1896 rocked the Society to its foundations and lost it the support of many of its members, including Mr. Gladstone. Nevertheless the Society survived, and a fresh direction of research, which might be symbolized by the work of W. A. Clouston, became important. The Ethnologists, under the seminal influences of Edward Tylor, had held the field—not undisputed but supremely influential—for the first eight years of the Society's life, now Clouston's translations from Indian, Persian and Arabic sources opened the door to a new theory of the origins of Folk-Tales, that of the Diffusionists, and the Indo-Germanic theory of origin began to be fashionable. Clouston was geographically a little removed from the rest of The Great Team. He was an Orcadian living in Glasgow, but his literary contributions to Folk-Lore were as considerable as his learning. He wrote many valuable articles and translations from the oriental languages, but the two books by which he is most remembered are *Popular Tales and Fictions, Their Migrations and Transformations*, published in New York in 1887 and *The Book of Noodles* (1888), an important monograph about the follies of simpletons which were popular in medieval times both in East and West, and trickled down through Jest Books and oral narratives from the 16th century onwards.

From this time the Society was reinforced by other Diffusionists, notable among them Joseph Jacobs, whose work on Jewish History would have been enough to make him famous and who had much to add to the study of Folk-Lore as well. He was the editor of *Folk-Lore* from 1889 to 1900. He took a particular interest in Fables, and in 1888 edited *The Earliest English Version of the Fables of Bidpai* in a series published by Nutt. In 1889 he edited, again for Nutt, the Caxton version of *The Fables Of Aesop*, of which Volume I was devoted to The History of Aesopic Fable. In modern times his fame chiefly rests on the five books of folk-tales retold to children, *English Fairy Tales*, *More English Fairy Tales*, *Celtic*

Fairy Tales, *More Celtic Fairy Tales* and *Indian Fairy Tales*. The first four have lately been reprinted. Though the Tales have been re-written, and in some cases unnecessary alterations have been made, they are a model for the recent adaptors of Folk Stories because of the valuable notes to be found at the end of each book. The source of the stories is always given and every alteration is acknowledged. Many interesting points are also raised. The children who choose to read the notes are already half-way to being folklorists.

Another Jewish authority was drawn into the fold of Folk-Lore, the Rumanian exile, Moses Gaster, who arrived in England in 1885, already the author of a definitive work on *Rumanian Popular Culture*. Almost at once he was invited to deliver the Ilchester Lectures at Oxford, which were published in 1887. In these lectures Gaster examined and discussed both the Ethnological and the Mythological theories, particularly for Folk-Tales, more literary and articulate than fragmentary survivals and beliefs, and praised the work of the German, Theodor Benfey, who first advanced the theory of the Indic origin and subsequent transmission of folk-tales. The Folk-Lore Society, which was not afraid of controversy, gladly welcomed both Moses Gaster and James Frazer into their ranks, and in 1887 Gaster's article, 'The Modern Origin of Fairy Tales', appeared in *Folk Lore Journal*, V. In 1907 he was elected as President of the Folk-Lore Society. At that time the office was held for two years only. Gaster lived till 1934 and collected three volumes of his scattered articles between 1925 and 1928, but the book by which he is now best known is *Rumanian Bird and Beast Stories*, published in 1915. Towards the end of his life he concentrated increasingly on Hebraic Studies. He was not a man who dedicated himself as so many did to one society alone. He also served as an officer in the Jewish Historical Society and the Royal Asiatic Society.

If Gaster strengthened the Diffusionists, Sir James Frazer's membership of the Society kept the Ethnologists in good heart. From 1900 to 1914 the Society was not likely to sink into sloth. It was a time when many contributions from the outlying fringes of the Empire supplied material for theoretical work. Scholars and theologians of the calibre of Professor Samuel Hooke and Professor James took office in the Society. Sir John Rhys who held the Chair of Celtic Studies in Oxford was Chairman of the International Congress of 1891, an important milestone in the history of the Society.

Before we pass on to beyond the orbit of the Great Team let us recall the lesser team of the Women Folklorists, not so eminent, perhaps, but many of them performing great service, particularly in the collection of material. There was the dynamic Charlotte Burne, the first woman to be President of the Folklore Society, whose book on *Shropshire Folklore* put together from the notes of Georgina F. Jackson, is perhaps the best County Folklore book we possess as well as the most monumental. Beside her we may place Marian Roalfe Cox, whose *Introduction to Folk-Lore* was inspired by Edward Clodd and was strictly loyal to the Ethnological school. Paradoxically her *Cinderella*, one of the early monographs on a tale-type, was unintentionally a prime source of material to the Diffusionists. Then we have Eleanor Hull, who wrote an attractive and distinguished book, *Folk-Lore of the British Isles*, and contributed a number of articles on Irish Folk Beliefs to *Folk-Lore*. Her obituary was written by Professor Marrett in 1935. Lady Gomme, a loyal wife to Sir Laurence, was a pioneer in the collection of children's games, a forerunner of the splendid work done by Iona and Peter Opie.

Sir Laurence Gomme was collecting material for *A Dictionary of British Folklore*, and his wife, Alice Gomme, brought out the First Part, *The Traditional Games of England Scotland and Ireland* in two volumes (1894–8). She collected some of the games personally, the greater part from a large number of correspondents, well documented. The work covers an enormous scope of all types of popular games, and is still invaluable. The only drawback in adapting the singing games for use is that occasionally the tunes and the words are assembled from different informants and are not easy to combine. Lady Gomme put them to practical use, however, for she taught a selection of them to a group of children and demonstrated them at the 1891 Folklore Congress, where they were an outstanding success. The accompanying notes, introductions and memoir are a marked feature of a monumental work. Another important County Folklore book, based on first-hand research was produced by Mary E. Leather in 1913, *The Folk-Lore of Herefordshire*. Old people can still remember how she travelled about in her little pony-cart collecting material. If we are to match the men's team perhaps we should give the sixth place to Mrs. Balfour, whom I have already mentioned, whose 'Legends of the

Cars' appeared in *Folklore* in 1891. Two notable tales from them, 'Tattercoats' and 'The Buried Moon', were included by Joseph Jacobs in his Collections of Fairy Tales, as well as one which he received orally. Mrs. Eliza Gutch, Mabel Peacock, Lady E. C. Gurdon and Charlotte Latham were compilers of The County Folk-Lore Series published from time to time from 1895 onwards. These are compilations from printed matter and not original research, except for Volume 8 which does not belong to the early history of the Society.

The outbreak of the First World War brought an epoch in Britain's history to an end. Even before 1914 many of the founder members had died and 1918 found a great many gaps in the ranks. Professor Marrett of Oxford had done a brave holding operation as President during the four years of the War, but when it was over Peace dawned on a different world. The leisured, educated amateurs who had formed the rank and file of the Folklore Society were gone. What was worse was the fading of academic recognition. Sociology and Anthropology ranked as scholarly disciplines; Folk Lore could count a number of Professors among its private members, but its status was still amateur. Still the Society carried on bravely in a world which seemed no longer to take a keen interest in the problems which once stirred the folklorists to the core and awakened lively participation in the surrounding public. Some first-rate elder statesmen still survived: I have already mentioned Professor James and Professor Hooke with their deep theological discipline.

Professor S. H. Hooke died in 1967 at the age of ninety-three. Though his deafness made conversation difficult for him his mind was fully alert and his conversation was pleasantly humorous. He was at work almost to the last on a deep mystical interpretation of the Book of Revelation. One of his latest books on *Middle Eastern Mythology* was first published in 1963 and reprinted in 1966. In 1932 he launched what was called The Myth and Ritual School. He was President of The Folk-Lore Society in the years 1936 and 1937 and gave two notable presidential addresses, 'The Siege Perilous' and 'Time and Custom'. He was a distinguished Hebraic and Biblical Scholar and held a Chair of Oriental Studies in Toronto and the Davidson Professorship of Old Testament Studies at the University of London as well as having been the Speaker's Lecturer at Oxford.

Professor E. O. James was President in 1931 and 1932, with only Professor Rose, another distinguished Scholar, between them. It will be seen that there was no lack of learned men to take official positions in the Society, even in those comparatively lean times. Professor James also undertook the onerous work of editing *Folklore* for many years, until he was relieved of it by Christina Hole in 1956. It is amazing to think that this quarterly periodical has been edited by one person—a professional writer without office staff or secretarial help for over twenty years. This is an example, though an extreme one, of the voluntary help given by members of the Society. Articles are donated to *Folklore*, books printed by the Society earn no royalties for the authors; until recently books were reviewed without charge and returned to the Library. For some years now it has been admitted that reviewers have the right to keep the books if they wish to do so, but this has been a recent concession. In the past the Society received many legacies and handsome donations from members, but these are more stringent times and all Societies are feeling the pinch. It is still true to say that a tremendous amount of free help and work is given by all the committed members of the Society.

Another notable Scholar who added lustre to the Folklore Society was Professor R. M. Dawkins, who was its President in 1929 and 1930, and contributed a paper to the Jubilee Congress of 1928. Fourteen of his articles were published in Folklore between 1904 and 1953. Dawkins was a brilliant scholar of modern Greek, a Fellow of the British Academy, Director of the British School of Archaeology in Athens from 1906 to 1914 and Bywater and Sotheby Professor of Byzantine and Modern Greek Language and Literature in Oxford from 1920 to 1937. He is best remembered for his translations of Modern Greek Folktales. His best-known books are *Forty-five Stories from the Dodecanese* (1950), *Modern Greek Folktales* (1953), *More Greek Folktales* (1955). He was an admirable translator with a mastery of simple unaffected English, and a great interest in the meaning that lay behind the tales, particularly the insight into human psychology that they display.

Two notable lectures of his delivered to the Folklore Society deserve the attention of all students of Folktales. 'The Silent Princess' was read to a meeting of the Society in December 1951 and is to be found in *Folklore* 63 (1952) and 'Some remarks on Greek Folk' is in Volume 59 (1948). His sensible and critical attitude to the subject of Folklore is to be found in his treatment of the question of origins, a subject of hot controversy since the Society was founded. R. A. Georges, in a most excellent article to the memory of Richard Dawkins (*Folklore* 76, 1965), quotes a passage from the Introduction to *Modern Greek Folktales* (p. xix):

> 'It is here the place to say that I cannot regard any one country or any one culture as the exclusive or even as the predominant source of the stories in this book; neither India nor the gypsies or any other place or people. Stories with a defined plot have, we may be pretty sure, been invented in some one place where there is a taste for this kind of art; yet as a rule the evidence is not sufficient to say where ... Each story has to be judged on its own merits and only too often the evidence can give us no clear answer.'

His critical remarks on the stories and the methods of story-telling are always of great pregnancy.

These three admirable scholars who survived the stresses of two World Wars and continued to serve their specialized branches of knowledge and to make their individual contributions to the work of the Society until they died are a sample of the quality that was still left to carry the study of Folklore from the past to the future.

There is one other person who should be mentioned, a character and an eccentric, but one who made more impact on the young people of today than any of our careful, reasonable and learned scholars. Dr. Margaret Murray was born in 1863 in Calcutta and lived to be able to call her Autobiography *My First Hundred Years*, a privilege perhaps unique to an author. After she returned from India at the age of six she received the excellent Victorian home education. In 1894 she went to University College, London, to train as an Egyptologist, for this was the best centre of training in Egyptology at that time. She had never sat an examination in her life but within six years she had passed her Doctorate and had been appointed by Flinders Petrie as a part-time lecturer to the Department. By the end of the century she was teaching hieroglyphs and Coptic, giving classes and public lectures on Egyptian history, language and culture besides doing a good deal of administration for the College and supervising the work of post-graduate students. In 1904 she went with Flinders Petrie on his excavations at Abydos and was subsequently left in complete charge of the work at Osirsion. She was called back by the First

World War and by the increasing pressure of work at University College, and was subsequently only able to dig in vacation time. Various academic orders were awarded to her. She received her D. Litt. from University College, was made a Fellow of the Society of Antiquaries of Scotland and a Fellow of University College, London. She was requested to catalogue the Collections of Egyptian Antiquities in the Museums of Dublin, Edinburgh and Manchester and in the Ashmolean in Oxford. Her reputation as an Egyptologist could hardly have stood higher.

She began to look further afield, for she was a woman of boundless energy. In 1917 she contributed an article to *Folklore*, 'Organisations of Witches in Great Britain' and began to interest herself in The Folk-Lore Society. In 1920 she contributed another article on 'Witches and the Number Thirteen', and in 1921 her book *The Witch-Cult in Western Europe* appeared and made an immediate and deep impression. Up till that time the witchcraft beliefs had been treated as pure, unfounded superstitions. The Ethnological School of the Folklorists had indeed regarded spells and rustic ritual practices as remnants of an earlier, buried religion, a relic of primitive paganism, and Margaret Murray continued her researches in this subject, as a branch of anthropology. Here she broke new ground. In general the educated person in the 19th century regarded the belief in Witchcraft as a delusion: the result of ignorance and superstition on the part of the prosecutors and of hysteria and misery on that of the witches. The confession of Major Weir, for example, was regarded as a mad outburst of fanaticism and melancholia, fostered by his exaggerated Puritanism, while the extreme poverty, misery and loneliness of some of the old women led them to levy a kind of blackmail upon their neighbours and in the end, perhaps, deceive themselves with their own pretences. Some Satanists thoroughly believed in Witchcraft, Montague Summers as its opponent and Aleister Crowley as a practitioner of Black Magic. Both were generally considered equally unhealthy. Margaret Murray, with her anthropological approach to stimulate her, embarked on a careful study of the many records of Witchcraft trials which had been preserved, and relying on their evidence advanced the thesis that Witchcraft really existed as the last remnant of a prehistoric religion, which she described as the *Dianic Cult*, a primitive fertility cult dating from a pastoral rather than an agricultural society and with a priesthood, officers and a horned god. She divided Witchcraft into two types, 'Operative' and 'Ritualistic'. The first dealt with charms, spells and imitative magic and about the effectiveness of this she was entirely sceptical, the second was a natural religion, and here she was sympathetic. Her first book *The Witch-Cult in Western Europe* (1921) made an enormous impact and was followed by a re-appraisal of the Witchcraft Case both in Europe and America. Such books as Aarne Runeberg's *Witches, Demons and Fertility Magic* (Helsinki 1947), Kittredge's *Witchcraft in Old and New England* (Cambridge, Mass. 1928) and Henry C. Lea's monumental collection of *Materials towards a study of Witchcraft*, edited and published posthumously by A. C. Howland in 1939, would hardly have been undertaken without the initial stimulus of Margaret Murray's book. There were of course objections made to it. The most valid were that she was too apt to jump over several stages in reaching her conclusions, that she did not make sufficient use of the discoveries of modern anthropologists about savage witch beliefs and practices and that she did not make allowance for the effect of torture in extorted confessions. But these are criticisms of a pioneering work and one of enormous importance which changed the whole structure of witchcraft research for the next few decades. Unfortunately as she proceeded in her next books Dr. Murray omitted to check her conclusions by the discoveries of later research, revealed, for instance, in the evidence produced by H. C. Lea. On the contrary she advanced boldly to make less warrantable assumptions. In *The God of the Witches* (1933) she claimed William Rufus, Robin Hood, Joan of Arc and Gilles de Rais as willing sacrificial victims, representatives of the God of the Witches. *The Divine King in England* went even further. Arithmetic as well as common sense was outraged in it. The vigour and persuasiveness of Margaret Murray's writing, however, took effect not only in the number of books on the subject that were inspired by it, but on the young people of Britain and America, uneasy and frightened at the complexity and danger of modern life, who embraced a form of Witchcraft, largely of their own invention but founded vaguely on the views of Margaret Murray as they understood them. The movement is founded on a spiritual hunger, probably symptomatic of the present disorders of Society and is the last effect which Dr. Murray would have foreseen from her researches.

Except for what one might suppose to be a certain waning in her powers of judgement Dr. Margaret Murray retained her faculties to the full and published her last book, *The Genesis of Religion*, at the age of one hundred and one, the year of her death. It is the record of a remarkable life.

Devoted service was given to the Society during the difficult times following the Second World War. Mrs. Lake-Barnett found the finances in a perilous state when she became Hon. Treasurer in 1947. She gradually built them up again, not, one suspects, without some generous donations from the family purse from her sister and herself. She left the finances in a prosperous state when she retired in 1971. Many new members had joined the Society by this time who were well fitted to face the changing face of the world. In the 1960's it became clear that a new Constitution was needed and through 1968 informal meetings of the Committee were held to hammer it out. Mr. J. R. Peal of Oxford, a solicitor who had had considerable experience in framing Constitutions, gave invaluable advice and on January 8th, 1969, a special General Meeting of the Society was held at which the Constitution was read, explained and adopted. It will be found in full in Volume 80 of *Folklore* pp. 74–8.

In the years after the War, as the British Empire gradually melted away, contributions of administrators of the Empire naturally lessened, but there continued to be many contributions to International Folklore. In 1959 the International Institute of Folk Narrative Research was founded under the Presidency of Professor Kurt Ranke of Göttingen and held its first meeting in September of that year in Kiel and Copenhagen. Participants came from all over the world—a specially strong contingent from the U.S.A.—and England, Scotland, Ireland and Canada were all represented. The Conference was well run and very pleasant because the numbers were not too large to allow all the lectures to be in common. Since that time a meeting has been held every seven years in different cities, Athens, Bukharest and Helsinki, and though they have paid the penalty of success by becoming too large, they have always been pleasant and instructive occasions.

There have been small Conferences held in England in the last few years, a small joint meeting of English and American Folklorists held at Ditchley Park Anglo-American Conference Centre in 1969, a very successful Conference at Exeter on Other World

Journeys, another at Cambridge and yet a third at Lancaster, which have been both useful in themselves and valuable also for allowing local folklorists, who are debarred by distance from visiting the London meetings, to get to know fellow-folklorists from other parts of the country and to hear papers and lectures.

In 1971 the Diamond Jubilee of the English Folk Dance and Song Society was held. There has always been cordial affiliation between the Folk Dance and Folk-Lore Societies. We have many members in common, Douglas Kennedy who was our President from 1965 to 1967, the late Dame Maud Karpeles who was long a most useful member of our Council, Miss Violet Alford and Miss Dean-Smith, to name only a few. Some of our publications were of special interest to the Folk Dance and Song Society, especially *English Ritual Drama* published in 1968 by Alex Helm with the collaboration of Christopher Cawte and Norman Peacock. Years of devoted work had been put into this index by Alex Helm and it is likely to be the definitive work on its subject for many years to come. Alex Helm's death in 1970 was a loss to both Societies. I have already mentioned the work of Iona and Peter Opie, indefatigable both in research and the production of outstanding books. Our able and tirelessly energetic Honorary Secretary is sedulous to procure lecturers of high academic quality for our meetings and to keep world contacts everywhere open. She gives a constant dedication to the interests of the Society unrivalled even amongst the most devoted members in the past. The new modelling of *Folklore* promises to be an actual improvement although it was primarily undertaken in the interests of economy. So much for our internal affairs. As for our contacts with the outside world, an independent but very valuable auxiliary to folk knowledge has arisen in the Folk Life Society, a fairly recent foundation which specializes in the work of Folk Museums. St. Faggan's Castle Museum in South Wales is a shining example of what can be done in this line.

The most important academic centre of Folklore, however, is to be found at Leeds University under the directorship of Mr. Stewart Sanderson. The Department of Theology in Exeter University has appointed Miss Theo Brown as their Folklore Adviser and it is to be hoped that other Universities may do something of the same kind. Dr. Ellis Davidson, Dr. Carmen

Blacker and Dr. Michael Loewe have by right of their specialist knowledge close contacts with Cambridge University.

If the Society can weather the country's present economic crisis there is good hope that it may move into its second century with every prospect of expansion.

ANIMAL MOTIFS

Historical Dragon-Slayers

JOHN ANDREW BOYLE

The story of Perseus and Andromeda is, in the words of Frazer[1], a 'type of folk-tale of which versions have been found from Japan and Annam in the East to Senegambia, Scandinavia and Scotland in the West. The story varies in details from people to people but as commonly told it runs thus. A certain country is infested by a many-headed serpent, dragon, or other monster, which would destroy the whole people if a human victim, generally a virgin, were not delivered up to him periodically. Many victims have perished, and at last it has fallen to the lot of the king's own daughter to be sacrificed. She is exposed to the monster but the hero of the tale, generally a young man of humble birth, interposes in her behalf, slays the monster, and receives the hand of the princess as his reward. In many of the tales the monster, who is sometimes described as a serpent, inhabits the waters of a sea, a lake, or a fountain. In other versions, he is a serpent or dragon who takes possession of the springs of water, and only allows the water to flow or the people to make use of it on condition of receiving a human victim'.

Of this last-named type, in which the reptile figures as the guardian of a spring or well, neither Frazer nor Hartland[2] mentions the most ancient version: the Indo-Iranian myth of the serpent—Vṛtra or Ahi in the Veda, Azhi Dahāka[3] in the Avesta—slain by the Indian war god Indra or the Iranian hero Thraetaona. The monster is represented in the Veda as lying hidden in the waters, encompassing them and preventing their flow: by killing it the god or hero releases the waters and liberates two women held captive in its stronghold.[4] The sea monsters from which Perseus rescues Andromeda and Hercules Hesione are clearly borrowed from a different tradition and recall the Mesopotamian Tiamat or the Canaanite Leviathan. On the other hand the serpent or dragon slain by Cadmus before the founding of Thebes was, like Vṛtra, the guardian of a spring. In his commentary on this story Frazer cites folk-tales from many parts of the world reflecting the belief that 'water, especially the water of a spring, is guarded by a dragon or serpent...' His final example is a modern Greek tale telling 'how a spring was guarded by a twelve-headed serpent, who devoured a human being once a week and then kindly allowed people to draw water at the spring.'[5] An Armenian version, unknown to Frazer, approaches much closer to the Indo-Iranian myth. In the popular epic known as 'The Daredevils of Sassoun' Sanassar, the founder of the House of Sassoun, comes with his twin brother Balthasar to a town called Green City and they are told by an old woman who befriends them that there is no water in the town: 'All the fountains are dry. There is a spring on top of that mountain but a dragon sits there and will not let anybody have water. We can't go near it, we are afraid. Every year we have to take a beautiful virgin to that mountain spring and let the dragon eat her to get some water. Tomorrow it's the turn of another girl to be eaten by the dragon...' The twins kill the dragon by smashing its ribs and crushing its head with the two round stones of an olive press. No sooner was it dead than 'water flowed out of the fountains in the city and people rushed to fill their vessels. There was plenty of water now for everybody'.[6]

Dragons or serpents (the terms are interchangeable) stand guard not only over water but over treasure, either buried treasure in the literal sense or, in the words of Eliade, 'every symbol embodying the sacred or able to bestow *power*, *life* or *omniscience*.'[7] Thus in Greek mythology the golden apples in the garden of the Hesperides were guarded by a dragon; so was the Golden Fleece. The earliest reference to the function in the literal sense occurs in the fabulist Phaedrus, who flourished in Rome in the first half of the first century AD. In one of his fables he tells of a burrowing fox who came upon a cave in which a dragon was guarding hidden treasure. He asks the dragon: 'What profit do you get from this toil, or what reward does it bring so great as to induce you to go without sleep and wear away your life in the dark?' 'No reward at all,' replies the dragon, 'but the task has been assigned to me by Jupiter the most high.'[8] So too the dragon in *Beowulf* is said to be 'doomed to seek out hoards in the ground and guard for an age there the heathen gold...' Having found such a treasure he guards it for 300 years, sleeping in the cave where it was hidden by day and flying out by night.[9] Much better known is Fafnir, the dragon slain by Sigurd in the *Völsunga Saga*; the brother of Sigurd's foster-father Regin, he murdered his father for the gold of the dwarf Andvari and 'went off to live in the wilds and allowed none but himself to have pleasure in the riches, and later on he turned into a terrible dragon and now he lies on the treasure'.[10] In Persia the snake as guardian of hidden treasure is proverbial for the disagreeable concomitant of something agreeable. The poet Sa'dī (d. 1294) in his *Gulistān* tells the story of a man whose beautiful wife had died; 'but the mother, a decrepit old dotard, remained a fixture in his house because of the dowry.' His friends come to condole with him, and one of them asks: 'How is it with you, since the loss of that dear friend?' And he replies: 'The absence of my wife is not so intolerable as the presence of her mother: "They plucked the rose and left me the thorn; they plundered the treasure, and let the snake remain!"'[11]

Beowulf and Sigurd, like Perseus and Hercules and Indra and Thraetaona, are mythical dragon-slayers, but historical persons in ancient and medieval times have also been credited with the killing of such monsters. One thinks in the first place of saints of the Church, and leaving aside the most famous instance of all, St. George, who may not have been an historical person, it seems almost that in the Middle Ages, and particularly in France, no bishop or abbot achieved sainthood, without first having slain a dragon.[12] However, in such cases a plausible explanation has been suggested to account for the legends. In the early days of the Church the dragon was a symbol of the Devil; and statues and other representations of the saint triumphing over the Prince of Darkness were taken by a later and more literal-minded generation to depict the actual slaying of a real-life reptile.[13] This explanation does not account for similar legends attached in the Middle Ages to non-clerical figures. The historian of religions Eliade cites a number of such instances in which an 'historical personage is assimilated to his mythical model (hero, etc.) while the event is identified with the category of mythical actions (fight with a monster, enemy brothers, etc.)'[14] Of these, the first, and from our point of view the most interesting, is the legend of Dieudonné de Gozon, third Grand Master (1346–53) of the Knights of St. John at Rhodes, and his slaying of the great dragon of Malpasso. The earliest record of the legend is the version set down by a German pilgrim who visited Rhodes in 1521, two centuries after de Gozon's birth. The best-known version is that of Giacomo Bosio, the historian of the Order of St. John, who wrote some seventy years later, i.e. after the expulsion of the Knights from Rhodes by the Ottomans. Bosio's account, as summarized by Hasluck,[15] is as follows:

> 'The dragon lived in a cave, from which a spring flowed, at the roots of St. Stephen's hill, sone two miles from the city, at a place called Malpasso. Everyone was forbidden to fight with it. De Gozon, however, resolved to defy the prohibition. He retired to the castle of Gozon in Gascony, where his elder brother ruled, and made a dummy dragon of canvas stuffed with tow, resembling the real dragon in every particular, and so devised that it could be moved mechanically, making hideous noises as it did so. Having trained his horse and dogs to attack the dummy monster, he returned to Rhodes and set out to Malpasso by a roundabout route, sending his dogs with the servants to wait for him at the church of St. Stephen. Thence he made his attack in the dragon's cave and after a terrible combat, slew it by a stroke in the under part of its body. In its last agonies it fell upon him and he was with difficulty rescued from under it by his servants.'

Eliade makes no mention of the dragon-slayers in British folklore,[16] who are extremely numerous and one of whom, like Dieudonné de Gozon, was a knight of Rhodes. This was Sir John Lambton, the ancestor[17] of the Earls of Durham and the present Lord Lambton, who flourished in the fifteenth century, and who, according to a legend that survives in ballads to the present day,[18] slew the dragon known as the Lambton Worm. The story runs as follows.[19] The scene was the park of Lambton, still the seat of the family, on the banks of the River Wear, to the north of Lumley in County Durham. As a young man John Lambton led a profane and godless life: he used to spend his Sunday mornings fishing in the Wear when he should have been attending Mass. One Sunday he had cast his line into the river many times without any success, and he gave vent to his disappointment in loud curses which caused great offence to the servants and tenants passing by on their way to the chapel at Brugeford. Soon afterwards he felt something tugging at his line and pulling it in, he found he had caught, not a fish, but a strange-looking worm. Filled with disgust he tore it from the hook and flung it into a near-by well.

A stranger, who happened to pass by, looked at the creature in the well. It was, he said, in appearance like a newt, only with nine holes on either side of its mouth; and he thought it boded no good. In this he was a true prophet. The worm soon emerged from the well, which was now too small to contain it. It used to spend the daytime coiled round a rock in the middle of the river and at night made its way to a neighbouring hill and twined itself round its base; it grew so fast that it could soon encircle the hill three times. This hill, on the north side of the Wear, about a mile and a half from Old Lambton Hall, is still called Worm Hill. The Worm now began to terrorize the whole countryside, sucking the cows' milk, worrying the cattle, devouring the lambs and committing every kind of depredation on the peasantry. After laying waste the region to the north of the Wear it recrossed the river and approached Lambton Hall, where the old lord lived alone, his son John, the young heir,[20] having repented of his sins and gone to the crusades. As the creature drew closer, the household held a council of war and it was decided to fill a large trough that stood in the courtyard with milk. The Worm drank the milk and without doing any further harm went back across the Wear and coiled itself around the hill. It returned the next day and was appeased once again by refilling the trough with milk. It was found that it took the milk of nine cows to fill the trough and that if it was not replenished every day the Worm would vent its rage by winding its tail around the trees in the park and wrenching them up by the roots.[21] By now the Worm had become a menace to the whole of the North Country; and many knights rode out to battle with it, but all in vain, since it possessed the miraculous power of reuniting itself when cut asunder. Finally, after seven years' absence, John Lambton, the young heir, returned from the wars, and consulting a sybil or wise woman, was advised to have his best coat of mail studded with spear-heads[22] and, having donned it, to await his enemy on the rock in the middle of the river. She charged him, however, before going to meet his adversary, to take a vow that if he was successful he would kill the first living creature that he met on his way back.[23] If he failed to observe this vow, so the sybil warned him, then for nine generations no Lord of Lambton would die in his bed. The young heir, having followed the sybil's advice to the letter, came to blows with the Worm as it swam across the river, close to the rock where he had taken his stand. The creature, by coiling itself tightly around him, was weakened by self-inflicted wounds, and Lambton was able to cut it in half with his sword; and one half being carried off by the swift current the Worm was unable to reunite itself and so finally perished. It had been pre-arranged that in the event of victory young Lambton was to blow on his bugle as a signal for the release of his favourite hound, which he intended to sacrifice in fulfilment of his vow. The bugle was duly sounded but the old lord, forgetting everything but his son's safety, rushed out to meet and embrace him. In this cruel dilemma the young man blew a second blast; the dog bounded up to him and he plunged his sword into its heart. However, the vow had been broken, and the curse is said to have really been laid upon the family for nine generations, as the sybil had prophesied. Certain it is that two Lambtons, father and son, fell in battle in the Civil War and that Henry Lambton, M.P., the ninth in succession from John Lambton, knight of Rhodes, died in his carriage when crossing the new bridge of Lambton on the 26th June, 1761.

But long before the time of Dieudonné de Gozon and Sir John Lambton the slaying of a dragon had been attributed to no less a personage than Alexander the Great. The story is not to be found in the Greek recensions of the Alexander Romance, but in the Syriac version composed in the seventh century there is incorporated a long account, apparently based on a Greek original, of a journey made by Alexander from India across Central Asia to China. The dragon-slaying episode, which occurs at the very beginning of this account, is reproduced below in full from Budge's translation.[24] The account is apparently a continuation of the letter to Aristotle on the wonders of India, and Alexander is speaking in the first person:

> 'Then we set out from the country of Prasiakê,[25] and set our faces straight for the east. And when we had gone a journey of ten days along the road, we came to a high mountain; and some of the people that lived on the mountain said to us, "King Alexander, thou art not able to cross over this mountain, for a great god in the form of a dragon lives in it, who protects this country from enemies." And I said to them, "In what place is the god?". They said to me, "He is a journey of three days from here by yon river." And I said to them, "Does this god change himself into another form?" And they said to me, "Enemies never dare to come to this country through fear of him." And I said to them, "Is he able to keep off enemies from all your coasts?" And they said, "No, only on

that side where his dwelling is." And I said to them, "Has this god a temple? and do ye go to his presence and know him?" And they said, "Who can go near unto him that can swallow an elephant by drawing in his breath?" And I said, "Whence know ye this since ye go not near him?" And they said, "We know that a number of people are swallowed up by him every year, besides two oxen which they give to him regularly every day for food from our land, and he also kills men." And I said, "How do ye give him these two oxen to eat?" They said, "He that is set apart for the service of the god selects oxen from the land and takes two of them each day in the morning, when as yet he has not come forth from his temple, and goes down to the bank of the river; and he ties the legs of the oxen and throws them upon the bank of the river, and he goes up to the top of the mountain; and when the god comes forth from his temple, he crosses over that horrible river, and swallows up those oxen." And I said to them, "Has this god one place for crossing, or does he cross wherever he pleases?" And they said, "He has but one place for crossing." Then I bethought me that it was not a god but a phantasy of wicked demons. I took some of the people of the land (with me), and set out from thence, and came to the bank of that river. And I commanded them to place the oxen as they were accustomed to do, and I and my troops stood upon the top of the mountain. And we saw when the beast came forth from his den and came to the bank of the river. When I saw the beast, I thought that it was a black cloud which was standing upon the bank of the river, and the smoke which went forth from its mouth was like unto the thick darkness which comes in a fog. And we saw it crossing the river, and when as yet it had not reached the oxen, it sucked them into its mouth by the drawing in of its breath, as (if cast) by a sling, and swallowed them. When I had seen this, I gave orders next day that they should put two very small calves instead of the two big oxen, that the beast might be the more hungry on the following day. After it had found the two calves, it was obliged to cross over again on that day; and when it had crossed over for the second time, by reason of its hunger, it went wandering from this side to that but found nothing. And when the beast desired to come on towards the mountain, all my troops with one voice raised a shout against it; and when it heard the shout, it turned and crossed the river. Then I straightway gave orders to bring two oxen of huge bulk, and to kill them, and to strip off their hides, and to take away their flesh, and to fill their skins with gypsum and pitch and lead and sulphur, and to place them on that spot. When they had done this, the beast according to its wont crossed the river again, and when it came to them,

> it suddenly drew both of the skins into its mouth by its breath and swallowed them. As soon as the gypsum entered its belly, we saw that its head fell upon the ground, and it opened its mouth, and uprooted a number of trees with its tail.[26] And when I saw that it had fallen down, I ordered a smith's bellows to be brought and balls of brass to be heated in the fire and to be thrown into the beast's mouth; and when they had thrown five balls into its mouth, the beast shut its mouth, and died.'

Another historical dragon-slayer is Ardashīr, the first (AD 225–40) of the Sassanians, the national dynasty that succeeded the Parthians as rulers of Persia. The story bears in certain respects a remarkable resemblance to that of the Lambton Worm: it is told in the greatest detail in the *Shāh-nāma* or 'Book of Kings' of Firdausī.[27] In a city in the South of Persia on the shores of the Persian Gulf there lived a man called Haftavād—so called because, as the name indicates in the Persian language, he had seven sons.[28] He had also one daughter, who, along with the other girls of the town, used to go up every day on to a mountain to pass the whole day spinning cotton. One day, when they stopped work for their meal, this young woman took a bite in an apple which she had picked up on the way: she found a worm inside it which she gently placed in her spindle-holder. The worm brought her luck and she spun twice as much cotton as she had ever spun before. It caused her father's fortune to flourish also. The creature began to increase in size; the spindle-holder became too small for it and the girl made a beautiful casket for it to nestle in. Her father Haftavād was now a man of wealth and influence: leagued with the chief men of the town he overthrew and slew the ruler and then leaving the town built a citadel on the mountainside. The Worm had by this time outgrown the casket and a pool was constructed for it inside the citadel and a custodian appointed to feed it each day with a potful of rice. Years passed by, and the Worm grew to the size of an elephant. Haftavād now ruled over a vast region as the Worm's commander-in-chief or major-domo, and Ardashīr, seeing his own position threatened by this rival, marched out against him but was driven back by the Worm's army. In the end he had to resort to guile and, gaining entrance to the citadel disguised as a jewel merchant, persuaded the Worm's attendants to allow him to feed it. He then had boiling solder poured down the creature's throat instead of the rice and milk[29] to which it was accustomed; and it gave out a great roar and burst into two pieces. With the death of the Worm the overthrow of its master or protégé, Haftavād, was only a matter of time.

What are we to make of these historical dragon-slayers? Eliade, as we have seen, accounts for the creation of such myths by the theory that popular memory, disregarding a man's real exploits, equips him with a mythical biography in which a battle with a snake or dragon plays an inevitable part. Whether we accept his explanation or not, he has produced a number of instances in which such transformations of biography into myth have actually taken place; and in this paper further such instances, unknown, I think, to Eliade, have been adduced and would seem to confirm his argument. Leaving that aspect of the phenomenon on one side, however, let us examine a circumstance common to many of these legends. It would seem that to kill the monster required more than a simple blow struck at a vital point: the creature needed in fact to be disintegrated. The Lambton Worm, it will be remembered, had the power of reuniting itself. The Hydra slain by Hercules had nine heads, of which the central one was immortal, and the remainder, on being lopped off, were each replaced by two new ones. So too the two snakes on Ḍaḥḥāk's shoulders in the Persian National Epic[30] had the power of reproducing themselves. To destroy the monster therefore it was necessary to resort to drastic means. In the case of the Lambton Worm recourse was had to hydraulics, one half of the creature being carried away by the force of the stream.[31] Another method was to use some kind of explosive to blow the animal to pieces. This is how Alexander disposed of the mountain dragon and Ardashīr of Haftavād's worm. We read in the Apocrypha how Daniel destroyed a dragon in a similar fashion;[32] so too in Rhodes, where de Gozon slew his dragon, there was in modern times a Turkish legend of a dervish who killed a dragon by causing it to swallow forty donkeys laden with quicklime.[33] In Roxburghshire not too far from Lambton, the laird of Lariston slew the Worme of Linton, by thrusting down its throat 'a peat dipped in scalding pitch and fixed on his lance'[34]; in this case, it is true, the creature seems to have died rather of asphyxiation. Yet another method of destroying the monster was to attack it from within. Thus Hercules, when delivering Hesione, daughter of Laomedon, King of Troy, from the sea-monster sent by Neptune, plunged fully armed down the creature's throat, from which he hacked his way out again after three days' imprisonment, having lost all his hair in the process. A story is told by Andrew Lang,[35] apparently based on oral tradition at Balmaclellan in Kirkcudbright, how a great snake that used to lie twined round a tumulus at Dalry and, in addition to other depredations, used to dig up and devour the newly dead in the nearby churchyard, finally met its end at the hands of a smith, who had fashioned a suit of armour covered with long sharp retractable spikes. Wearing this armour he was swallowed by the snake, and then shooting out the spikes tore his way out through the animal's carcase. He found the snake quite dead; and for three days after the Water of Ken, by which the carcase lay, is said to have run red with its blood.

If these dragons are equated with the Vṛtra of the Veda, destroyed in equally drastic fashion by Indra's thunderbolt, then we have of course to do with an Indo-European myth, reflecting perhaps a prehistoric ritual in which a snake—not a dragon[36] or even, in the Northern regions where we may assume the rite to have been performed, a large serpent—was lifted out of its hiding-place in a mountain spring, hacked to pieces and its *disjecta membra* scattered far and wide in the belief that such action would promote a downfall of rain. Alternatively we can compare these imaginary creatures with the sea monsters that threatened Andromeda and Hesione and trace their descent to the Babylonian Tiamat, the personification of the primeval deep. We are told in the *Enuma elish* how Marduk, having already encompassed the monster's death,

> . . . trod upon the legs of Tiamat,
> With his unsparing mace he crushed her skull,
> When the arteries of her blood he had severed,
> The North wind bore (it) to places undisclosed,
> . . . .
> . . . .
> Then the lord paused to view her dead body,
> That he might divide the monster and do artful works,
> He split her like a shellfish into two parts:
> Half of her he set up and ceiled it as the sky. . . .[37]

Perhaps in these medieval legends, as in some of the Greek tales, we have a blending of both traditions: in bisecting the Worm Sir John is re-enacting the rôles both of Marduk and of Indra; he is at once a demiurge and a rain-god.

Animals as Threatening Figures in Systems of Traditional Social Control

J. D. A. WIDDOWSON

Traditional modes of verbal social control apparently exist in all cultures and have attracted the attention of linguists, folklorists, anthropologists, psychologists and others.[1] Among these traditional usages the threats employed by adults in controlling the behaviour of children have emerged as a focal point of recent research. Although there is strong evidence for the widespread use of such threats in numerous cultures it is only in the last two decades that they have been the subject of systematic research in English-speaking countries. The pioneering work of Professor Herbert Halpert on traditional threats in North America and the British Isles[2] has paved the way for several subsequent studies[3] and over a period of some twenty years he has assembled a very substantial body of data on this topic from many parts of the world, utilizing both printed and oral sources. Professor Halpert has also devised a basic classification scheme for the figure of fear used in the threats, and has encouraged his colleagues and students, including myself, to pursue research into the subject, while generously making available his own data which constitutes the only major collection in the English-speaking world.

Studies of these traditional threats have concentrated for the most part on the identification and classification of the figures used. In the late nineteenth and early twentieth centuries Grimm, Mannhardt, Ploss, Chamberlain, Kidd[4] and others noted the wide range of supernatural and mythological figures of fear and their apparent preponderance in the threats, and the Mannhardtian school emphasized the degree of belief which adults were thought to have in the existence of such figures. The imbalance of this emphasis was corrected by Von Sydow[5] who argued convincingly that most of these supernatural figures were merely 'pedagogical fikts' invented by adults for the purpose of controlling children's behaviour, often with little or no measure of belief in their existence on the part of the adult. Although in redressing the balance Von Sydow may have overstated his case somewhat, evidence from subsequent research[6] corroborates his contention that many of these threatening figures are constructs utilized in the context of social control but not believed in by adults.

In more recent studies[7] the linguistic structure and social function of the threats have been the focus of attention. Linguistically threats have a restricted structural patterning which, as with other traditional forms, gives them a distinct status in the language and has particular significance for their memorability and hence their tenacity in culture. The typical structural patterns include affirmative statements ('The —— will get you'; '—— is coming'), conditions and consequences ('If you do/don't (*do that*), —— will happen/come/take you etc.'), and imperatives[8] ('Shut up!'; Be good or ——'; 'Go to sleep, because ——'; 'Eat your dinner, and ——'). In terms of structural linguistics the slots in these examples may be filled by a variety of appropriate forms, the nominal slots including the names of threatening figures from the stock of such names within each culture, and the verbal slots including details of the threatened retribution. The typical structural pattern may also be seen in transformational/generative terms in which a given threat (T) may be generated by the application of the following rewrite rules:[9]

$$T\left\{\begin{array}{l}\text{AFFIRMATION}\\ \text{CONDITION}\\ \text{IMPERATIVE}\end{array}\right.\left.\begin{array}{l}+(\text{CONSEQUENCE})\\ +(\text{ALTERNATIVE})\\ +(\text{REASON})\\ +(\text{RESULT})\end{array}\right\}(++T)$$

It will be noted that one or more threats may be added to each structure to form a series of composites, allowing considerable variation whilst preserving the basic structures typical of the genre.

The function of such threats is obviously to influence and/or control children's behaviour. It operates in several contexts of social control, including sanctions against disobedience/naughtiness/misbehaviour, 'bad habits', going to dangerous or forbidden places, doing dangerous things, interfering with animals, crops, implements etc., going/staying out after dark, not going to bed/to sleep, neglecting personal hygiene, not dressing properly, quarrelling, getting in the way of adults, showing off, being bad mannered, not eating food, touching or eating poisonous or undesirable plants or substances, vandalism, mischief, trickery etc.

In using a threat of this kind adults employ a traditional device designed to avoid the meting out of physical punishment to a child. At the same time they transfer the onus of responsibility for correction and punishment to some external agency, supernatural, imaginary or real. At the interface between adult and child this often absolves the adult from taking upon himself the punitive role and indeed he may present himself as the protector of the child against the external agencies which he himself employs in the threats. On the other hand one may use an adult's own power and status to threaten the child as when a mother says, 'You just wait till your father gets home!'

The utterance of threats also has the function of releasing the adult's anger, irritation or frustration, acting as a safety-valve for pent-up emotions which often accompany the mixture of responsibility and guilt which adults may feel at the interface. In such cases the very utterance of the threat, often with specific vocal quality and gestures, helps to relieve the tension felt by the adult and at the same time communicates his displeasure to the child in no uncertain terms.

The figures which occupy the nominal slots in the threats may be divided into three main groups:

1. Supernatural/mythological/invented.
2. Living people.
3. Animals, objects, locations and natural phenomena.

Group 1 includes supernatural beings such as gods, angels, devils, figures of myth and legend, and such invented constructs as the bogeyman. Group 2 consists of living people, including those in authority (e.g. priest, policeman, father), those who are strange or unusual in some way (e.g. foreigners, strangers, tramps, eccentrics, recluses, people suffering from a variety of physical deformity or mental abnormality). Group 3 includes animals, birds and fish, various objects (some of which, such as the strap and slipper, are used in physical punishment), frightening places (e.g. dark rooms, places associated with death) and natural phenomena such as thunder. All have intrinsically frightening qualities which are capitalized upon and often emphasized or exaggerated by the adult in the threatening context so that they appear even more fearsome.

In this paper I should like to take up the subject of animals in such threats and specifically to point out which animals are typical of them, posing at the same time the question of why these particular animals are chosen to serve this function. This inevitably has wider implications concerning our views of and attitudes towards animals in general, and also with regard to the cultural specificity of such attitudes. The primary data on which I shall draw was collected in Newfoundland in the years 1963–8.[10] For the purposes of comparison data from a pilot study of threats collected in England 1969–76 will also be utilized.[11]

In the Newfoundland corpus the threatening figures in group 3 form a comparatively small section, groups 1 and 2 being numerically very much larger. The same proportions are equally evident in the material from the pilot study in England. Within group 3, however, living animals constitute the largest sub-group and merit further consideration.

Certain animals are chosen for use in threats whereas others are not. Animals which are wild, rather than tame or domestic, are obviously more likely to be used, especially if they are fierce, dangerous, voracious or regarded as in some way unpleasant for a variety of reasons. In Newfoundland the bear, lynx, fox, beaver and shark, together with birds of prey such as the eagle and the hawk are natural choices. Smaller wild animals are also prominent in the Newfoundland material, especially rodents, reptiles and certain insects which often arouse a disproportionate amount of dislike, disgust and even fear,[12] on the part of both children and adults.

The use of tame and domestic animals in threats is more surprising, especially when they live in close proximity to man and are often children's pets. Reasons for the apparent ambivalence of attitudes here are not far to seek. Even domestic animals may be frightening, especially to children, by virtue of their size (in the case of horses, cows etc., bulls being obviously dangerous), or their dual nature (cats and dogs acting in a domesticated way at one moment and killing and eating small animals and birds at another). Encountering animals, especially at night, may also be a frightening experience. Still more important is the fact that a dog, cat, horse etc. tends to be used to threaten a child of a household other than that to which the animal belongs. It thus has the qualities of strangeness and unpredictability.

Characteristics such as the size and voracity of such animals are deliberately stressed and exaggerated by adults in the threats. Dogs and even fish, for example, are presented as much larger than life and therefore take on some of the frightening qualities of their supernatural counterparts. Indeed in many of the threats real animals are endowed with supernatural characteristics in such a way that they become more fearsome to the child but indicate a corresponding lack of belief in such characteristics on the part of the adults.

In a corpus of 1870 threats in the Newfoundland material, 132 include animals as threatening figures. Of these 3 refer to animals in general, warning children not to go near or touch an animal or it would bite or eat them. An unspecified fish appears in one report to keep children away from a river, and 11 threats use a 'big fish' to warn children away from wharves, docks, harbours and other places where they might fall into the sea, and from beaches and ponds. Unspecified insects occur in 2 threats and on both occasions are associated with a dark cellar in which the naughty or annoying child is threatened to be put, where the insects (and rats) will eat them.

Specific animals are found in 115 citations and are listed below in order of frequency, the general references to animals, fish and insects being included in brackets for comparison.

	Occurrences
bear	30
rat	26
(fish, big fish)	12
dog	9
moose	6
mouse	5
shark	4
(animal, gen.) goat owl	3
(insects, gen.) bat bull fox horse wolf	2

Animal	Citations each
beaver bugs cat conger eel cow frog greep (eagle) hawk jay lice mole mountain cat (lynx) sparrow spider tansy wasp weasel whale worm	} 1
	132

It will be seen from this table that mammals and reptiles form the largest sub-section (100 citations), followed by fish (19 citations), birds (7 citations), and insects and spiders (6 citations). Animals also predominate in the English study, followed by insects and spiders, with fish and birds occurring only once.

From a total of 32 Newfoundland animals used as threatening figures, the vast majority (26) are wild, only 6 being tame or domestic. This demonstrates the overwhelming preponderance of wild animals in this sub-group within the Newfoundland corpus, a tendency corroborated by the evidence from England.

The dominance of the bear in the Newfoundland threats is explained at least partially by the fact that bears are not infrequently seen, both in the woods and also on the outskirts of settlements where they have learned to scavenge. They thus pose a real threat in that children may actually see them and know that they are perhaps nearby. The threats involving bears are used to discourage children from going into the woods (berrypicking etc.), to get them indoors before dark and discourage them from going out after dark, to prevent them from going to other dangerous or forbidden places, to encourage obedience and good behaviour in general and to dissuade them from making fun of bald-headed men! In this latter citation the threat was said to stem from an Old Testament reference to a bear carrying away children 'who were making fun of one of the bald-headed prophets'.[13] The bear's voracity, a characteristic which it shares with sharks, rats and many of the other creatures used, is referred to frequently in the threats. For various reasons at least one-third of the creatures cited are noted for their voracity and powerful teeth or beak, and if one includes the dog, goat and whale, let alone the biting power of bugs and lice, this characteristic is even more important. Incidentally it is shared with many figures in groups 1 and 2, but is subservient there to the supposed power of supernatural, invented and human figures to take the child away. The bear is one of only two animals which are said to have this power and this additional link with the figures in groups 1 and 2 may help to account for its frequency of occurrence.

The apparently universal dislike and fear of certain rodents, particularly rats, is clearly reflected in the inventory of figures and also appears in the English material where rats, mice and bats are each reported once. The mouse ranks much higher in the Newfoundland reports and, if we include the bat and beaver, rodents account for 34 of the 132 citations, the mole and the weasel also having obvious similarities with this sub-set.[14] Rats are used in threats to encourage obedience and good behaviour, ('I've got rats stored up in my attic for naughty little boys like you'), to keep children out of the cellar and dark, dangerous or forbidden places, to get them to bed and to sleep, and to discourage them from eating food in bed. Mice are used for similar reasons, but 2 out of the 5 citations refer to encouraging children to eat. The beaver deters children from going near a brook, while the bat, mole and weasel are used for unspecified misbehaviour.

Among the other wild animals the moose seems a rather surprising choice, but its size and large antlers, allied to its habitat in the woods are sufficient to give it frightening qualities. By contrast the shy, swift-moving caribou does not appear as a threatening figure in the corpus and attitudes towards it are benevolent, notwithstanding the fact that, like the moose, it is hunted for meat. The fox and wolf, on the other hand, are regarded with malevolence and although the wolf is extinct on the island of Newfoundland and exists only in the mainland Labrador section of the province, it is still used in threats. Interestingly enough, the wolf also appears in one of the English citations. Both the fox and the wolf are used to deter Newfoundland children from going or staying out in the dark, the fox also being used for general misbehaviour and the wolf to keep children from the woods and other dangerous places. The single threat of a mountain cat (lynx) is also to prevent children from going into the woods.

The domestic animals may be divided into two sub-sets: those kept primarily as pets, usually with access to the house (dog, cat) and those kept outdoors for work, food, milk etc. (goat, bull, horse, cow). The dog has an ambivalent status, being at once the friend of man and also commonly used in threats. Significantly the ferocious bulldog and the large (though benevolent) Newfoundland dog account for 3 out of 9 citations. Of the five general references, two describe the animal as big and black, and a third refers to a 'big dog'. Dogs are mainly used in threats against general misbehaviour (7 citations), once to keep the child away from forbidden places, and once to get the child to sleep. The single report of a cat as a threatening figure is in the context of general misbehaviour.

Among the farmyard animals the goat rather than the bull is most frequently reported, perhaps as bulls are comparatively rare. Both the bull and the goat are used for general misbehaviour, but the goat is given strong supernatural characteristics in two threats aimed to keep children away from the Orange Lodge and to keep them quiet during church services and Sunday School. The horse is said to bite children who go near it and is also used to discourage misbehaviour, while the single reference to a cow is to prevent children from interfering with animals. Significantly, sheep are not regarded as threatening figures in the Newfoundland corpus, no doubt because of our benevolent attitude towards them as harmless creatures.[15] Although sheep are not reported in the English study either, there is a single reference to a black pig in threats, this animal being absent from the Newfoundland reports.

Reptiles such as frogs (used here to prevent children from going to undesirable places) are natural choices for threatening figures, as are also worms (used to discourage thumb-sucking). Spiders, along with insects such as bugs, lice and wasps, also arouse strong feelings of dislike and are used to discourage children from going to forbidden places, to get them to sleep, to keep themselves clean and not to suck their thumbs, respectively.

Among the fish, marine and freshwater animals, the voracious shark holds pride of place in the Newfoundland threats, only one (freshwater) fish, the pike, being reported in the English study. The pattern of coastal settlement and proximity to the sea accounts for the relatively high number of 18 citations in this sub-set. All of them, including the tansy—a long, thin fish common in harbours, —are used to warn children away from wharves and other dangerous places near the sea, or from ponds.

Birds of prey predominate in the 7 references to birds as threatening figures. The owl is said to carry away bad children and is used to get them in before dark. The greep (eagle) is also used for this latter purpose, while it is said that the hawk will pick out the eyes of children who go near water or onto a frozen pond when the ice is unsafe. The jay would 'have you' if you went out with holes in your clothing, and the mother sparrow would peck out the eyes of a child who killed its young ones in the nest.

From this brief survey it is clear that many animals are used in the traditional verbal social controls employed by adults in their interaction with young children. Of the 32 individual threatening figures, 23 have unpleasant connotations in varying degrees. Attitudes towards the remaining 9 may be regarded as more or less benevolent (cow, horse, mole, moose), ambivalent (cat, dog), or neutral (jay, sparrow, conger eel), and each of these 9 has attributes which could be utilized in threats to arouse fear or dislike.

Animals are used as threatening figures to control a wide range of children's behaviour, and these functional aspects of traditional threats in turn reflect not only the range of animals found in a given geographical area but also some of our traditional attitudes towards animals, both wild and domesticated. It remains to be seen whether this particular sub-group of threatening figures retains a place in the verbal control systems employed by adults in English-speaking areas in their interaction with children, especially in view of rapidly increasing urbanization in Britain and North America. In the meantime the range, structure and function of threats and other forms of social control call for systematic and detailed investigation as an important aspect of the ethnography of communication.

REGIONAL STUDIES

The Black Dog in English Folklore

THEO BROWN

A number of people have been working on this phenomenon for some forty years, among them Mr. Harold Coote Lake, Miss Bonham Carter, Dr. M. A. Murray and Mrs. E. H. Rudkin, besides many others. My first paper on the subject was published in 1958,[1] so this should be seen as a continuation of that one. The quantity of material which has accumulated since has amplified but hardly modified the picture of the problem as it then stood, but a few further points have emerged which must be summarized briefly.

It should be explained that the term 'Black Dog' is now accepted generally to cover ghostly dogs of all colours, but still excludes those of known pets which are often reported to appear for a short while after death.

The objection may be raised that this study, like the previous one, pays scant attention to the authenticity—or otherwise—of these apparitions and makes use of them as though all are of equal value. Of course their evidential value varies enormously, from recent first-hand accounts to the flimsiest local rumour, worn thin by mythologized oral transmission. However, there are two reasons which justify this sketchy method. One is that few ghostly encounters can be proved with total certitude, and in any case it is seldom possible to ascertain all the intimate personal and social factors involved, or even desirable without giving great offence. We must accept, as a court of law has to, that most people do tell the truth as far as they are able. Secondly, as folklorists we are not concerned with proving the actuality of supernatural phenomena. We are in business to study beliefs, particularly patterns of belief.

One outstanding characteristic of the Black Dog is that it appears to have its roots both with locality and with persons. At once we are faced with an apparently insoluble problem but it may prove to be not so incongruous as it seems.

By far the majority of Black Dogs are associated with a definite locality, which is implied by its name 'The Black Dog of Newgate', 'The Black Dog of Bungay', and so on. In the local traditions of hundreds of villages it is 'known' that a certain place is haunted by this creature, or a whole area by something that appears in numerous shapes, the commonest of which is probably a dog. It would be expected, naturally, that some of the inhabitants will from time to time most obligingly see just that, but, in fact, this does not often happen. What does happen sometimes is that a total stranger, knowing nothing of the local superstition, will see something at that place, quite spontaneously. Obviously this is a most difficult point to establish, but it is worth intensive investigation. The most remarkable instance of this was carefully reported by a member of the Society for Psychical Research from Hoe Benham, a scattered village near Newbury in Berkshire, where, early in this century, an entity manifested itself to various people in a very limited area mostly confined to one lane, under no less than eight different guises.[2]

Assuming a genuine haunt, it might be suggested that some ghosts can only contact a percipient at a subliminal level where of course normally it would pass un-noticed. If this were the case, then, in theory, if it was sufficiently powerful it could seldom arrive at conscious level except by a kind of projection. This involves a crossing of the *limen* of consciousness by a process of 'un-scrambling' which would convert a shapeless impression into a sensory image, the nature of the latter being dependent on the mental 'wardrobe' supplied by the percipient's store of traditions and symbols. If something like this happens, it would explain why the entity appears differently to various people. The experience while being totally subjective actually originates from without. Thus the question remains: Who or What is trying to communicate What to Whom? The rationalist if he is prepared to consider any world beyond his own must conclude it is a mad one, gabbling to us in an outmoded and meaningless jargon, but to the folklorist it may prove to be a code that has once held significance of an archetypal nature which may with patience be recovered. Indeed it may be in the complex realm of mythology that some hopeful clues may be found.

If a count be made of the kind of places favoured by these apparitions one thing becomes plain. Quite half the localities are places associated with movement from one locality to another: roads, lanes, footpaths, ancient trackways, bridges, crossroads, gateways, doorways, corridors and staircases. These examples tempt us to include hollow trees, graves and prehistoric burials whose attendant hounds proliferate densely in Wiltshire[3] and West Somerset[4] on the grounds that they can be seen as passages downwards to the World of the Dead, and so also suicide graves and scenes of execution; but if these must be omitted, since they are barely passages in the literal sense, it does not drastically alter the picture.

The mention of roads raises an obvious doubt. A traveller in the night time is on the road himself and is unlikely to see anything far to left or right. Many reports suggest merely a stray dog returning from an evening's hunting or courting. But the event looks less than normal if a hand passes through it or the dog sinks into the road. Besides, many sightings occur in broad daylight; four Black Dogs have been described by modern motorists, three having been run into without bump, scream or mishap—or body.

In Lincolnshire,[5] North Devon[6] and down into Cornwall[7] there are networks of ancient trackways and roads patrolled by Black Dogs reported at various sectors. It is possible that some of these are ghosts of the guard dogs that accompanied the pack-horses and wheeled carriers. One well-known dog that runs from Liskeard to Launceston is actually called 'Carrier'.

But such traditions can only account for some of them. For the rest we have no clue to the origin. It seems reasonable then to consider folklore and mythology for pointers. There seems little help to be found in Celtic or Saxon mythology simply because so very little is known for certain that it would be dangerous to speculate and the little we do know seems to have no bearing on our problem. Thus it is necessary to look further afield in search of what must necessarily be oblique clues, remembering that if a myth or belief is sufficiently basic to a human need then eventually a parallel may be found nearer home.

The best-known dogs of passage are to be found associated with Rivers of Death and Entrances to the Otherworld, of which the classic examples are to be found in Greek and Near Eastern myths[8] and also in the New World.[9]

An early reference to the Black Dog comes in a papyrus: κυρία Ἑκάτη εἰνοδία κύων μέλαινα.[10] This creature is seen to be the dog of the road, and in some way identified with the kaleidoscopic nature of Hekate.

Its frequent association with death and its occurrence in the vicinity of burials can hardly be due to chance and so one must conclude that the ghost if regarded purely as a symbol must represent some universal guardian of the threshold personified in various cultures as, for example, Anubis, Cerberus or Hekate. This takes us far into prehistory, perhaps even to a period centred approximately round 3000 BC when the character of Artemis, the Bear-Mother, also the Terrible Mother—both nurturing and destroying—appears gradually to have split into numerous beings named, at one extreme, Artemis, the positive, virgin-mother and cruelly immaculate huntress, and at the other, Hekate, the sombre death-goddess and protectress of child-birth, both accompanied and appeased by dogs. The one overwhelming and terrifying Bear gradually receded and was seen no more except in nightmares.[11]

Much of this is of course highly speculative, and so also were my attempts to relate the triplicity of Cerberus and Hekate with the questions surrounding the *trivium*, the Roman 'place-where-three-roads-meet' which we know as the crossroads.[12] This appears to express in diagrammatic form the inward pulling gravity of the universe, the dynamic drawing together of the dimensions of time and space into a comprehensible, bearable 'here and now', which also marks a critically controlled fracture in the earth's surface through which the dead may pass by a kind of funnel visualized as a feminine entrance to the underworld of death—and possibly of rebirth—employing the symbol of the inverted triangle, the female pubis. This is actually depicted, vastly exaggerated, on numerous Near Eastern statuettes of the Great Mother from 6000 BC onwards.[13] Even at that period one suspects it was no innovation, for the inverted triangle as an abstract sign can be seen in two Aurinacian cave drawings at La Pasiega, where they appear far more likely to be apotropaic, protecting the entrance to the cattle corrals, than, as G. R. Levy believed, fertility symbols.[14]

However, if the morbid, dark side of the *trivium* be considered, here at once is the popular association of Hekate with witch-meetings, with gallows and gibbet sites, and with the burial of suicides, all accompanied by dog visions of many kinds, guided by three or four roads converging on a point where there is a break in the earth's surface down which evil spirits are sped, but from which other beings may erupt if summoned.

In a happier mood, it may be recalled that dogs in ancient Rome were sacrificed to propitiate the goddess of births, *Genita Mana.*[15] Diana also presided over births—one of her titles was 'Opener of the Womb'[16]—and chthonic Hekate too. So, in the Sixth Book of the *Aeneid*, it was appropriate that when Hekate and her pack of hounds arrived at the mouth of the Cumaean cave it was not merely the sign to Aeneas that he could now descend into the World of the Dead, but perhaps also a half promise of rebirth.

Modern scholars are fascinated and puzzled by the mysterious iconography of the Gundestrup Cauldron. Numerous dogs flit in and out of the human figures and griffons and round the great bull. A variety of guesses are being made as to their significance, so perhaps one more may be allowed in respect of the so-called sacrificial scene. Crested 'knights' on foot approach a sanctuary, beneath a leafy tunnel, while others seem to ride away from it on horseback. Between comes the focal point: a priest is dunking a man, head downwards, in a curiously shaped vessel. On the side of this is a long shape which has no apparent meaning beyond an odd decoration, but it could possibly be a stylised female vulva. Dr. H. R. Ellis Davidson in discussion remarked that the priest is holding his victim exactly as a midwife does in delivering a baby.[17] If this interpretation is acceptable, then the scene shows an initiation ceremony, and this would explain the presence of a huge dog raging, either in anger or in welcome, at the oncoming neophytes on foot.

How then does Anubis fit into this complex? He is the supervisor of the psychostasis, and later he is the psychopomp. He escorts the well-weighed soul into the Judgment Hall of the Gods. One of his numerous titles was 'the Opener of the Paths'. Above all, mythologically he is essentially a Black Dog in his character. Until recently he was supposed to be a jackal on account of his association with death. Jackals, like dogs, are notorious scavengers and in the desert they were said to dig up and chew the corpses of the common people buried in shallow graves. But this theory is now obsolete. There are indeed jackals in Egypt, but they are grey in colour and have short pointed noses and bushy tails besides other points of difference from the well-known appearance of

Anubis. I am greatly indebted here to Mme. Christiane Desroches-Noblecourt, the eminent Egyptologist, for a long and most generous letter answering my many questions.[18] She informs me further that black in ancient Egypt was not a funerary colour but it indicated transformation. More of her comments will be cited later.

Although most phantom Black Dogs have no known history or cause, yet a number of them are believed to accompany a human owner or, more typically, to represent one. The absence of an etiological tradition does not mean that these things are the echo of absolutely nothing at all: possibly the historical cause lies far beyond the reach of folk-memory. Indeed many existing legends bear all the marks of superimposition. In the absence therefore of anything like an adequate cause we have only the probabilities to go on and we must get down to the most obvious factors. A start may be made with a description of the canine character based on human observation and persistent superstition. The dog has five particular characteristics:

1. It associates itself freely with man.
2. It protects man and his property.
3. It is believed to see spirits, and even, it is said, the Angel of Death.
4. It scavenges.
5. It howls at the moon.

No other animal shares all these characteristics, especially the first two, and nearly all the mythology and superstition about dogs stem from this.

The historical perspective is even more remarkable. The domesticated dog is far older than was thought until recently. Horses were hardly thought of as anything more than a wild source of protein until nearly 2000 BC, yet dogs, which are known to have existed as far back as 18,000 BC, may already have been herding reindeer by then in Northern climes according to Zeuner, since by 13,700 BC they were rounding up ruminants further south. In the Natufian (Mesolithic) Culture of Palestine horse and cattle bones were those of wild animals, but the dog was probably domesticated—that is, c.10,000 years ago.[19] There are marked skeletal changes when an animal becomes domesticated, but obviously these alterations do not come about overnight. The quite definite Neolithic Maglemose and Starr Carr examples imply a very long history indeed, and Bökönyi[20] admits that domestication of the day may well have commenced in the Pleistocene age and was certainly present by Mesolithic times.

Bökönyi considers that the earliest men ate any animal that came to hand, dogs included. Later, when conditions permitted, they ate the older animals they caught and began to preserve the young as a future food-source. But they do not appear to have followed this plan with dogs though plainly it could have been done. Either they did not taste as good as mutton or perhaps they were beginning to be positively helpful. Otherwise there seems no immediate economic reason why men should have bothered to tame them at all. How and when did the friendly hunting compact develop? Bökönyi says it is thought by some authorities that man made no conscious effort to train the dog: the dog adapted itself to man voluntarily[21] rather in the manner envisaged by Rudyard Kipling in the *Just So Stories* (1902).

Dog, then, has kept us company for an incredibly long time. He and the caprovines (especially the sheep) seem to have been the earliest domesticated animals, but sheep are hardly friends in quite the same sense. If, as has been proposed, every man contains within himself the history of not only his own personal development but also that of his race, then dog has been in at the very beginning either way. The creature has hardly been noticed because he is so homely a part of the household. He goes back to the earliest memories of childhood when he tumbles around with babies on the doorstep, their earliest friend and confidant and guardian. Yet babies are heartless people, regarding their playmate with no veneration whatsoever: something to play with, sharing food and bed, to envy for its speed and its privileged uninhibitedness—and then often to ignore when the baby is grown to man's stature—or not, according to the prevailing culture.

Until recently, some of the most 'backward' races on earth were to be found in the forests of the Andaman Islands, living at what was assessed to be a Palaeolithic level of culture (though it must be remembered there was no proof that they were living fossils: equally they may have regressed). They had no tools, agriculture, cooking, crafts, rituals or speculations about the hereafter. Their main (and, one would think, monotonous) diet was shell fish gathered from the sea-shore. In living memory some pariah dogs were introduced from India as an experiment to keep down the wild pigs in the forest as the natives did not know how to catch them. The result was remarkable. The dogs flourished on the pigs, and to everyone's surprise became tame, attached themselves to the villagers and started to help them hunt the pigs. The Onges treated them as members of the family, allowing them to sleep on the communal beds, and the women even suckled their pups on occasion. But as they died their carcasses were thrown out into the forest and were no more thought of. Lidio Cipriani has left us a brilliant description,[22] but he does not draw the possible inference: that something like this may have occurred among prehistoric people.

The point is that if this did happen, then, as a tribe began to develop sophisticated notions, the image of the dog might well become an unacceptable reminder of a frighteningly recent infantile past with the ensuing terror of regression, the more so if a dawning monotheism presented an ever increasingly stern challenge to the first feeble steps towards cultural maturity. I suspect that the very widespread superstitious fear of the Black Dog is as likely to spring from such a conflict of levels as from the horror of scavenging and corpse-eating. In a more sensitive and less idealistic culture, more in sympathy with the realities of human nature, this fear is not found among mature adults. In the last hundred years anecdotes seem to be on the increase in which dog ghosts appear as protectors of the innocent and vulnerable, escorting lonely men and women through dark paths at night, past robbers and unpleasant tramps, and fade out as home is reached. There is nothing sinister or diabolic about these kindly creatures: indeed, one grateful person called it his Guardian Angel, and we recollect that St. John Bosco had a strange dog that came and went.

What are these things? Real animals turning up at a critical moment?[23] Or are they, as a Jungian would put it, mere projections from the unconscious, a part of oneself?—though, as been mooted above, these may sometimes be sparked off by an actual haunting in some localities. Or should we entertain certain primitive beliefs that some people are born with a personal totem assigned to him, often in animal form, the identity of which is hidden from him until the rites of puberty reveal it clearly, when it will henceforward guide and protect its owner?

Such notions are foreign to Western thought, and we go to great lengths to avoid acknowledging anything so embarrassingly infantile and apparently un-christian. Yet even in the most severely monotheistic society people did not always ignore the insights offered by animals. Balaam listened to his ass, however reluctantly, and Tobias took with him on his adventures not only an Archangel but a dog as well. This went with him and it returned with him, plus Angel, plus the new wife and all the servants and herds he had won. This is all that is said of the dog—it went with him, and it returned with him. Apparently it seems to have no significance whatsoever, but, then, why was it mentioned at all? Was it more important in some earlier version? As it stands the arrangement seems to be that the Angel comprises the higher aspect of Tobias' spirituality, the masculine hero with the drive and cunning to attempt the impossible task, but this would be to no purpose if he devalued his instinctual side which was needed to deal with Sarah's unusual problem.[24] The two companions complete the man.

I am, of course, aware of the probable Magian origin of Tobias' dog.[25] It is believed that the tale has come through many variations from Persia via Egypt. In Persia, among the Zoroastrians it was held to be impious to expose a body on a *dokhma* ('Tower of Silence') until death had been confirmed by the approach of a dog to the corpse. The rite of *sag-did* ('the glance of the dog') is still observed among the Parsees of India. As obviously no such ritual would have been understood or approved by Jewish readers, Tobit buries the corpse of the stranger as an act of piety and the dog who can have no part in this is transferred to Tobias in the role of companion. The author of that remarkable novelette seems to have had a sure intuition that prevented him from deleting this item and led him instead to transform it into quite a different character. But of course its role is not stressed for that too would have been unacceptable to a Jewish reader. Its mention is so casual that it seems almost to have slipped in by accident.

If the Black Dog be studied as an aspect of a person at every stage of life, appearing as the protector which only manifests itself visually at times of crisis—death, danger, illness, and also the ghost that is said to be the spirit of a dead person—the thing begins to look like a kind of 'double' in disguise, a friendly *doppelgänger*, perhaps of a nature that can still be visible after the death of its companion. A *fetch* is in some ways comparable to the Norse *fylgja* which was seen as a ghost or in a dream in animal form, but which did not survive death. Vaguely the *fylgja* was believed to be the spirit of the afterbirth which was thought of as a dead twin. The species of animal corresponded to the status of the man: a white bear meant a man of noble parentage.[26]

At this point there seem to be further ideas from the Egypt of Tutankhamen which may offer hopeful parallels. Mme. Desroches-Noblecourt writes that an ancient name for Anpu-Anubis was *Imy-ut*, that is, 'he who is in the skin (or placenta)', meaning the unborn child.[27] Again, another name (also very old) was *Impou*. This has two meanings: (1) a young dog, and (2) a young child. In the New Empire in which Tutankhamen reigned, it was common to find young princes and princesses addressed as *Impou*, as, 'When Your Majesty was still an *Impou*'. Philologically Mme. Desroches-Noblecourt considers the word to apply to a being still in its mother's womb, but just ready to emerge, like the instant before the dawn. She pictures the lovely statue of Anubis from Tutankhamen's tomb as lying head erect at the door, facing outward, towards the rising sun. Thus it appears to represent not only Anubis escorting the young king towards his reawakening, but the Black Dog also represents Tutankhamen, either the king himself, or the canine image is invested with his *fetch* to harmonize with the death god and so to assist in his transformation.[28]

Supposing that such a personal *fetch* does exist, even though it plays a very minor part in the human cosmos—and it must indeed be relatively unimportant for both society in general and the Christian Church to have so totally ignored it, it may perhaps be equated with the 'shadow', some small fragment of the personality that separates at death but should be reintegrated immediately in some way we know nothing about. If the manner of dying be not satisfactory—by murder, suicide or execution, for example, or even by an earth-binding obsession—may its detachment be unduly prolonged and survive for an indefinite period? Suppose, in theory, that such a shadow, or memory, could become absorbed into the genetic stream of its descendants as do its traditions. In Britain it is commonly believed that this happens. Many families claim such spirits. Of these there are at least nine in England and Scotland alone who possess Black Dogs who come to warn their relatives of impending disaster.

An attractive but over-hasty attempt was made by F. B. Jevons to draw an exact parallel between our Black Dogs and the Roman *lar*, which he supposed to have been the ghost of the first man buried in a house. In early Roman times he assumed that when the family saw a Black Dog about the house or a man dressed in dog skins this was only their *lar* keeping a friendly eye on their affairs.[29] However, there is no evidence that the *lar domesticus* did take the form of a dog but it was typical of the city protector, the *lar praestites*. And further Professor A. B. Cook observed that there is much confusion about the exact relation of the *lar domesticus* and the *genius* of the family which anyway usually manifested itself as a snake. Prof. Cook thought it possible that the *genius* might be related to the first ancestor buried in a house, as funerary urns have been found under the floors of some dwelling houses. Sometimes, when depicted on Greek sculptures, these are shown in pairs and so are ascribed to the Dioscuri, though he quotes Rendel Harris's idea that 'they were a Greek parallel to the pots used throughout Africa etc., for the burial of a twin or of a twin's placenta'.[30]

Warde Fowler disagreed with Jevon's idea that the Roman *genius* was a relic of totemism, though in another passage he admitted that 'the doctrine of Genius may certainly have had its roots in a totemistic age; but by the time it reached us in Roman literature it has passed through so many stages that its origin is not to be dogmatized about.' In any case he was sceptical also about the burial within existing walls in historical times.[31]

In general the family *fetches* cling rather to families than to places. They appear to members of the family wherever they are and probably emigrate with them. When the Wykham-Martins left Leeds Castle in Kent in 1918, the dog went with them.[32] On the other hand, long after Arisaig had been abandoned, their Black Dog was seen snuffling sadly round the ruins as one of the Macdonalds was dying in South Africa.[33]

Banshees are sometimes known by the name of the family seat, but more often by their patronymic: the Black Dog of the Haynes, of the Baskervilles and so on. But it is remarkable that when Professor Sidgwick, in his famous Report on the Census of Hallucinations, commented that some of the hallucinations under discussion were hereditary he actually numbered two in which the descent appeared to be matrilineal:

(1) A lady constantly saw yellow cats and black dogs, and this commonly happened in her mother's family. Some saw a white dog before a death in the family. No first hand accounts.

(2) Mrs. E. L. Kearney, 1892: her step-father was ill, and a cat appeared to her. The patient died the next day. And she remembered that her mother saw a cat wandering round her father's bed the day before he died.[34]

Two cases prove nothing and the evidence is all too slight. The statements were not followed up at the time, no doubt partly because they were given by women and were therefore perhaps put down to hysteria or imagination. It would be extremely interesting to follow up any future cases like these, but it is a difficult task. Very few people can follow the female line further back than the maternal grandmother, some not even that far. While writing this (October 1976) I have spoken to a woman who gets premonitions of a ghostly kind which she tells me she shares with her mother. Yet they have never discussed this openly and she has no idea whether the gift extends further back in time, e.g. to her maternal grandmother, and her mother is now too senile to consult.

Hitherto the only area in which the female inheritance of ghostly beings has been accepted without serious question has been that of witches. In the seventeenth century witch trials some women said that their 'familiars'—whatever was meant by that—had been passed on to them by their mothers or a friendly older witch.[35] Whether these familiars were inherited ghosts or real animals is as remarkably ambiguous as the mysterious foxes maintained in certain shunned Japanese families, as Dr. Carmen Blacker has told us.[36]

To forestall an obvious question: it might be supposed that family crests might be linked to these creatures, but, up to the present, this does not appear to be the case, with the possible exception of the Baskervilles who adopted the head of a wolf-hound with an arrow in its throat. There are quantities of greyhound and talbot crests but none of these correspond to families maintaining ghost dogs. Moreover, Black Dogs are usually nude, though occasionally the sound of a clanking chain announces its presence aurally, but all crests showing whole dogs have them collared and tied with a rope, never a chain.

We have to remember that although crests have been used from very early times (e.g. the Gundestrup Bowl), in medieval England they were highly personal and erratic until the beginning of the thirteenth century when they began to be inherited.[37] Therefore the reasons governing the initial choice have seldom been recorded and there is no certitude one way or another. The fox crest of the Preston family of Gormanston is ancient and coincides both with a very early tradition and phenomena witnessed in this century, but we can only say at this stage that no comparable antiquity can be proved about Black Dog crests.

There is a peculiar relation to time which needs careful investigation. First, there is the odd clinging to normal time, the time of day and the season of the year, though the latter may possibly depend as much on the changing conditions of light, weather and atmospheric pressure as on the actual calendar.

Secondly, the Black Dog frequently seems to live in a time outside our own. Many students of psychic research are inclined to pursue the etiological aspect unduly and ask only 'How does it originate?' Generally this is a most fruitless quest. We do not know and we rarely have any hope of knowing the answer. Oral tradition sometimes gives us a legend, but this has probably been invented to explain the ghost and in some cases it is quite obvious that a later tradition, even involving a historical event or personage, has been superimposed on an entity of far greater antiquity.

The commonest superstition about Black Dogs is that they are ominous: that is, they point, not to the past, but to the future. Just a few proclaim good news, but in the main they are believed to herald disaster of some kind, communal or personal, usually the latter. If all those dogs with a reputed past are counted, and also that are ominous, the numbers will be found to be nearly equal. In some cases there is an overlap.

We are left with many questions to be asked and few solved. When a site which appears to illustrate a 'gateway' has attached to it a legend recalling a deed of horrible violence, and a Black Dog is alleged to be seen there whenever something grim is about to occur, we have to attempt to balance the probabilities of these three elements. We cannot establish any of the factors with scientific certainty, but in order to discuss the matter at all we must accept that superstition is a real enough factor in itself and also that folk-memory does seem to refer to an emotional first cause, or two causes, or it may be many causes overlying one another and relayed only by folk-tale, and even theoretically by another factor lying yet in the future. Does then such a haunting relate essentially to the archetypal notion of otherworldness, or to the distressed mind of the past victim of violence? Does the forecasting of future doom emanate from some timeless observation-point of the victim, long dead but earth-bound, or from the subconscious awareness of the here-and-now percipient?

*Animal Lore and the Evil-eye in Shepherd Sardinia**

ALEXANDER LOPASIC

The Sardinians of *Barbagia*, being largely shepherds, have a close relationship with the animal world, some sections of which played, or continue to play, a particular role in their folklore. The widely spread belief in the evil-eye is also related to the animal world, and as the material on that belief is considerable it will be discussed at some length. One should also add that the evil-eye is related to some basic principles of the Sard shepherd society, and therefore it is worth a more thorough investigation.

The shepherds, of course, became Christians a long time ago, but a number of pre-Christian beliefs have survived in one way or another until the present day. They include the belief in the evil-eye and evil spirits, including some of the representatives of the animal world. It should not be surprising that the *fox* plays a particular role in shepherd folklore. It is an animal with many attributes, such as being particularly cunning and inventive. Also it symbolizes a free shepherd who, with open ears and eyes, moves across the machia and mountains always ready to attack and then disappear covering his traces. The fox is well described in one of many Barbagian stories.

'Una borta margianne ait fattu unu votu, de faere unu cunigliu e a fattu su villu e nasciu margianne e tottu' (Once a fox made a promise to mate with a rabbit; a rabbit was born but it was

* The author wishes to acknowledge the financial help of the Social Science Research Council, London (SSRC) for the support of the field-work undertaken in Sardinia between September 1972 and October 1973. Further support during the Summer of 1974 was received from the University of Reading.

a fox as well) or 'Su marianne perde su pille e sa strassa mai' (The fox may lose his hide but never his cunning).

A fox symbolizes not only that cunning, sly, independent and crafty shepherd, but also a successful cattle-thief. He will be described as 'Su marianne de sa zona', the fox of the area, the most dangerous and the most daring cattle-thief of the area, carefully and regularly watched by his neighbours. There are some supernatural qualities attributed to the fox which have found expression in Sard poetry, as in the poem by Diego Mele (second half of the 19th century) describing how.

'In Olzai (village in the Nuoro-Province) the fox does not live any more because he was deprived of his "pasture". People, making one's mouth water, invented the mustard of Arbutus (a Mediterranean plant, the fruits of which are used for making fruit-juice and marmalade) which satisfied even the most violent appetite. They (people) have taken the fox's food away but this he replaced with kids. Neither the pursuit nor the most powerful exorcists from Dualchi could stop him (Dualchi is a village in the Nuoro-Province feared for its magicians). Offences are increasing and neither sucking-pigs nor lambs are spared.

If stealing, he is (the fox) excused because hunger deprives him of sight, putting him in the position of cutting a poor and ugly figure. He obtains his provisions in complete and full liberty and defies the best of the moralists who want to deny him an acquittal'.[1] The fox is sometimes treated as a 'Compare' (godfather) and offered the first lamb as a propitiatory sacrifice. According to this custom, a shepherd would leave some food of which he has eaten half in a place frequented by the fox, the remaining half being reserved for the fox-godfather. After this ritual the shepherd would be obliged never to shoot his 'godfather' to whom he is supposed to be particularly close. All this is related to the fox's supernatural qualities, which have survived in Sard folklore.

Another animal enjoying certain supernatural qualities is the *ox*. If the fox symbolizes cunning and resourcefulness, the ox stands for strength, endurance, energy and power. His importance is already mentioned in the Sard institution of feud, in which stealing of an ox or, even worse, slaughtering one, demanded a most severe retaliation. It is an extremely severe offence intended to deprive a man of 'the seed of his flock' and ultimately of his existence. The seed symbolizes manliness and male power, and stealing or slaughtering of an ox damages and challenges the manliness of the owner, which he must vindicate. This explains why such an offence would easily provoke the most severe retaliation and even a blood-feud.

It is not surprising that the ox has a place in Sardinian folklore, and it is even represented among the masks of the Barbagian Carnival (particularly the masquerade called 'Boes' [oxen] with its wooden masks representing oxen with large horns called 'Merdules' in Ottana).

Such Carnival masks have large horns, as already indicated, and the dancers wear heavy cow-bells and a shepherd 'Mastruca' (a coat made of sheep hide usually black in colour). They march through a village shouting and mooing and singing funeral praise-songs, the 'Atittos', around a puppet representing a dead person who is lamented. The well-known '*Mamuthones*' from Mamojada wear human masks but also heavy cow-bells, small and large in size, mostly produced in the nearby village of Tonara. Like their fellow-masqueraders from Ottana, they dance, sing and frighten people who watch them.

According to some Sardinian folklorists such masquerades with cow-bells and masks represent a 'survival' of some 'pre-Christian' orgiastic ritual. Marchi[2] expresses the opinion that Mamuthones originally represented oxen and were personified by local dancers. Whether Mamuthones were representations of oxen or demons as postulated by Moretti[3] remains in the field of speculation.

The meaning of the word 'Mamuthone' is given by Wagner[4] in his etymological dictionary as: 'scarecrow or puppet for scaring birds'. The same meaning was given to me both in Mamojada and other Nuoro villages.

According to Alziator[5] Sardinian masks are to be divided into two groups: (a) silent masks and (b) talking masks, the former referring to individual, the latter to collective, expressions of the face. Mamuthones belong to the first group, indicating formal features only. Another representative of that powerful and strong animal is the so-called '*Mooing ox*' (Boe muliache), a mythical ox which is possessed by the spirits of those who have committed suicide. This creature announces with his night-mooing some public disaster or misfortune. If such mooing is heard during the night people ask anxiously what is going to happen next. It is also believed that the spirits of the 'mooing ox' can possess a human being. Such people usually behave during the day in a normal way and in the night become possessed and take the form of a mythical ox, starting to moo in a most horrible way, thus announcing some forthcoming disaster. This is supposed to have been ordered by destiny or some high power. Should people encounter such an ox in the night they would die from terror.

According to Marchi,[6] who wrote on those mythical animals, a woman described her brother, being possessed by such evil spirits, as leaving his body during the night and taking the form of an ox with horns and chains. He would then place himself in front of the gates of one of the village houses and moo three times, but in such a terrible way that the whole village would tremble. This is supposed to announce forthcoming death and disaster. Before dawn he returned to his bed, not being aware of what had happened to him.

It seems that this belief and similar beliefs in monster or mooing oxen are widespread in Barbagia and neighbouring Baronia (East and Central Sardinia).

The religious '*Festa*' *of St. Isidoro* used to be the occasion for a village procession of cows and oxen nicely decorated and eventually blessed by the local parish-priest. St. Isidoro represents a remnant of pre-Christian beliefs related to cattle, which became absorbed into the Christian agricultural calendar. Such 'festas' are nowadays rare, for the simple reason that the number of cattle in the village is diminishing.

A completely mythical animal, however, is *Musca Macedda* or *Müska Maggedda*, a gigantic fly, which brings destruction or creates havoc; it is sometimes described as 'Musca Macedda da Mancu' (a fly belonging to the left hand side, namely, to the devil. The right hand side belongs to God, according to Sard beliefs).

Such enormous creatures are often imagined to have the form of a fly but to be as big as a sheep, with huge and powerful wings. Musca Macedda is also provided with a large sting whose puncture is considered deadly.

These 'Muscas Maceddas' are supposed to hide in boxes and barrels found in the cellars of dilapidated houses or behind the altars of some old churches, usually guarding hidden treasures.

Sardinian folklore is particularly rich in such tales. It is also believed that such gigantic flies have been responsible for the destruction of many ancient villages. The belief in such mythical flies must be very old; certainly older than the time of Spanish rule, as some Sardinian writers have suggested. It is possible that the different pestilences or plagues which have destroyed some Sardinian villages in the past, and malaria, endemic for many centuries, were carried by flies and mosquitoes; these are somehow connected with that mythical animal becoming in the end a symbol of plague and death in the old days.

A comparison is to be found in Rumania, in the flies which are known by the name '*Musca Columbaca*', which originated, according to legend, from a disintegrated dragon's head killed by the hero Jovan Jorgovan and found in the caves of the ruins of the old fortress of Golubovac near Belgrade. It was a name given to real flies, *Simularia columbacensis*, which used to attack cattle and sometimes even human beings every spring in large swarms. Such swarms were particularly seen in the ancient fortress of Golubovac which gave them their name. In Brittany the flies were believed to have led cattle to disaster, and were supposed to be the size of a horse's head.[7]

Vidossi[8] also points out the diabolic nature of these flies which is also present in Sardinian legends, as shown by Bottiglioni.[9]

Vidossi found similarities in other parts of the Mediterranean and the Middle East. Belzebub, for instance, was the ancient Syrian god of flies and insects, and the Greek deity of dirt, Eurynomos, was depicted in the form of a fly. The Persian god of death, Drukhs Naçus, was also described as having the appearance of a fly.

Before discussing the evil-eye, another custom should be mentioned, namely *Tarantism*, which has played a prominent role in Sardinia. Tarantism is known in Sardinia under the name of *Àrgia* or *Àrza*, coming from the latin adjective Varius, meaning of 'different colours'. The reference is to Àrza, a large spider measuring up to even 20 cm in length, of many different, often bright colours covering the body and the legs as well. Particularly during the summer months, Àrza can easily sting a person working in a field, producing strong pains, even a high fever, but hardly ever death. As the sting was very painful people were particularly afraid of it and consequently some traditional remedies were introduced. This spider did not achieve the same fame as the Tarantism in Puglia, which gave its name to the phenomenon of the tarantella dance. Tarantola was a local name for the spider already described.

But the same name was also applied to the much less dangerous *Mutilla calva*, a kind of a simple ant, whose bite produces much less discomfort. It seems that a similar confusion between the two animals is also to be found in some ancient Roman writing.

The local cure consisted of putting the unfortunate victim into a refuse-heap up to his neck. He was then surrounded by seven widows and seven widowers dancing around the dung heap. If the patient laughed that was a sign that he would recover; if not, he would die. The second remedy was similar to the first, except that the dancers were widows only, who sang a little song called 'Don, don, don'. The dance was known as 'Su Ballu de sa pia Àrgia'.

The reason why only widows used to dance was related to the sex of the animals, which was always assumed to be female, and therefore either married, widowed or single. I know only of dancing widows, but in some cases unmarried and married dancers participated as well. The widows also wept and sang 'Attitos', as if to a dying person. The dance was repeated by all three categories of women, depending on the reaction of the patient. It usually lasted as long as the patient's health did not improve, in general three days. The third remedy consisted of putting the patient into a suitably warmed oven which produced considerable sweating, similar to the sweating resulting from being placed in a dung-heap on a warm summer day. Such sweating was supposed to remove the effect of the poison entering the body of the patient. It was certainly not a very hygienic cure, but basically sound scientifically, since it was an attempt to remove the unpleasant effect of the sting, even if in a somewhat drastic way.

It seems that the therapeutic immersion or laying of bodies known in Sardinia was unique.

It is rather interesting that Tarantism in Sardinia was already described and compared with that of Naples by an English traveller in the early 19th century, J. W. Tyndale.[10]

He describes the already mentioned dance of widows, maids and married women, adding that the patient buried in a dung-heap was entertained by small bells called 'Tintinnos' tied around the necks of sheep and goats, and supposed to frighten away the evil spirits in the poor patient.

Rather interesting is a comparison between the two *tarantisms*, one in *Puglia* and the other in *Sardinia*.

In Sardinia it is a cure for a real bite, in Puglia it seems people re-experience the effects of the original bite, the following year and for years after, making it an institution rather than an ad-hoc remedy as in Sardinia. In Puglia, it can even be 'inherited'. Also it is related to St. Paul, who is supposed to be responsible for curing people of tarantism and shrines are even dedicated to him. Every year people experiencing such bites besiege the shrines of St. Paul. Once bitten such people seem to remain related to the saint for the rest of their lives.

In Puglia women are often patients, who are supposed to be cured by dances on the shrines of St. Paul. In Sardinia the women are the curers, the exorcists, dancing around the man immersed in a dung-heap and behaving very differently than in their normal life. Perhaps in both cases the emphasis is on the position of women, dissatisfied with their social position or position within a family, or emphasizing the otherwise unknown abilities of their own sex. If they are able to cure a man, they are showing that in some particular sphere they are not only equal but even superior to him. It is a cathartic ritual, giving the women the possibility of relief and freedom in a very specific situation.

A pre-Christian belief very widespread in Sardinia and indeed throughout Southern Italy, is that of the *Evil-Eye* (Ocru Male, Orcu Male [Sardinia] or Mallochio [Italian mainland]).

If a shepherd loses his animals on a large scale, either as a result of illness, or because of unusual circumstances, it is believed that somebody has cast a spell on the flock. In order to protect oneself from the evil-eye special medicines or amulets called *Sas Rezzettas* are made. They are made of leather, into which a small relic or crucifix or other objects like blessed bread are placed, then sown-up, and put into the bell of one of the animals. They were supposed to protect the flock from the evil-eye. The animals chosen for carrying a Rezzetta were often strong animals or animals which gave much milk etc.; in other words, particularly valuable animals. It was also a custom to take some holy water from a church and sprinkle the animals kept in a pen. Another way was to put a Rezzetta under a stone across which the flock would have to pass, and this was supposed to protect them or even heal them. A particularly powerful medicine was to dig out a skull from a cemetery and make a hole into which the skull was placed. The hole was covered over and the animals made to pass over the buried skull three times, after which the flock started to recover. The skull was afterwards returned. During the sheep-shearing, holy water was sprinkled on the animals. An important protection against the evil-eye was a greeting used when seeing a shepherd milking or working in his pen. The greeting 'Deus Las Varvete' (God protect them [his animals or his action]) served as protective magic against the dangers of the evil-eye. If the passer-by did not say it, it was considered offensive or done intentionally to harm, in which case the shepherd would return to his hut. The shepherd would answer the greetings with the words: 'Deus Nos Benedicat' (God bless us). It is interesting that the same formula was used by a magician (*Su Piddinu,-os*) from one of the villages which enjoyed a reputation for powerful magicians, in order to protect other people from his own powers of 'casting an eye'. On similar occasions he would also touch a person. Such Piddinos were men who had the ability to cast a spell and also remove it. The people would go and ask them for advice when in trouble but otherwise avoid their company as they feared them. Such Piddinos could take revenge if they felt hurt, and they could harm people if asked to do so.

Once a shepherd had thirty of his cows and eight horses slaughtered on account of 'Vendetta' and he, out of desperation, approached the local 'Piddinu' who, so it was claimed, made the man's opponent infirm for life. Another man was made impotent for a period. Another story, one of many, tells about a 'Piddinu' who wanted to travel by bus but could not find a seat for himself. Out of revenge he prevented the engine starting, and until he was offered a seat the bus could not move. On another occasion two oxen were fighting when a 'Piddinu' passed by. Later one of the oxen was found dead with its heart split into two. 'The evil-eye has killed them', was the answer.

To offer praise is to tempt the power of the evil-eye. Praising cattle, sheep, horses or even children was considered dangerous. Animals might collapse or even die, and the children become ill. The evil-eye attacks all pretty and attractive things, objects, animals or human beings, particularly children.

Except the 'Piddinos' (local magicians) already described, whose name refers to the evil-eye ('Oju (Ocru) de Peddi'—leather-eye), a person who looks peculiar, a squint-eyed or strange looking person, other people may possess such qualities even if they are not always aware of them. In any case they are believed to inherit such qualities and such people may be either men or women.

A popular remedy in such cases was to take a glass of holy water and say prayers, after which either corn seeds, or some embers or olive-oil were put into the glass. When the oil or corn appeared on the surface it was a sign that the evil-eye had been removed. The embers would cool down, giving the same results.

One of the protections against 'Piddinos' when they passed by was either to clench the fists with a finger between or spread two fingers, either in the pocket or behind the back of the 'Piddinu'. One of the practical aids given by 'Piddinos' was a medicine against worms pestering domestic animals or mice. 'Piddinos' who possessed special abilities were sometimes priests, or even unfrocked priests. They made '*Sas Pungas*', amulets worn by men to protect them against the evil-eye and the bullets of their enemies.

An interesting type of 'Pungas', called 'Arghentu vivu', were known in some villages of the Nuoro-Province, where a small quantity of mercury was mixed with some flour and placed into a shell of an almond, thus replacing the nut.

'*Pungas foltizzas*' (Personal 'Pungas') were supposed to protect famous bandits like Tolu or Derosas. In the Nuoro-Province they were known as 'Guramentu' because they were used when swearing to speak the truth when somebody was suspected of theft.[11]

A *priest* with abilities to cast a spell or 'Throw an evil-eye' (Ponnere Ocru [Sardinia] or jettare di mallochio [Italian mainland]) on somebody combined the abilities of a traditional 'Piddinu' and a priest of the Catholic Church. Particularly dangerous were such 'priest-Piddinos', because they could use special formulae from secret books, literally employing 'the magical power of words'. One of these unfrocked priests, even forty years after his death, is still remembered and feared for his exploits.

Learned men in general were suspected of possessing the ability of 'casting an evil-eye'. This is possibly related to the suspicion to which learned people were exposed in peasant societies.

Different types of *amulets*, used as protection against the evil-eye, took different forms (e.g. horns of mufflons in Campidano or talismans painted in green and yellow [protective colours against the evil-eye], or black stones called Kokko[-s] worn around the neck by children). Other stones called 'S'ogu de St. Lužia' were thrown into a glass of water and were supposed to cure headaches or sore eyes.[12]

The evil-eye, in a more general sense, is an expression and interpretation of the uncertain, the unexpected or even uncontrollable in life, for which there must be some explanation as to how and why it happened. It is closely related to the whole idea of uncertainty in a shepherd society, where a flock might be doing well to-day and dying from some pestilence tomorrow, or where somebody might be a wealthy owner of 300 sheep and find half of them slaughtered in his pen next day. The evil-eye explains the family with healthy and prosperous children who suddenly became ill or encounter an accident. It is a magical interpretation of the ups and downs in human life, of the unpredictability found in a society where nothing, or almost nothing, comes as of right. The evil-eye is also a recognition of the existence of evil forces, which when applied, can trouble or even destroy something valuable. Therefore praise or compliments may have a result similar to a curse. Praise is therefore particularly feared, and has to be protected by special magic and formulae.

One admires something because one desires it, and, if one desires, one can also envy. Therefore *admiration, desire and envy* are closely related, and the power of envy exists in practically all human societies. There is a well-known Sard proverb saying that 'Envy never dies' (S'invidia non morit mai).

As one cannot have the desired object oneself, one may, through 'casting an evil-eye', deprive somebody else from having it (e.g. a large and prosperous flock, healthy children, an attractive wife, the ability to create wealth).

The evil-eye could be interpreted as a protective mechanism of equal distribution. It is a way of interpreting in magical terms a competition which is rather severe and socially very important in Barbagia. If one cannot fight by other means, then the forces of evil are used to help either to strike down a competitor or to settle an old rancour. In some parts of mainland Italy the evil-eye is called envy (Invidia), summarizing the most important drive behind such a happening.[13]

Envy was often described as a powerful motive for killing or poisoning of the sheep or cattle of rich or successful proprietors in Sardinia. Envy was also considered to be one of the reasons for development of enmities and the feuds which followed. Wagner gives us an interesting example from the village of Fonni in the Nuoro-Province where the words Vendza, Endza meant both envy and Vendetta, relating feud and envy in linguistic terms as well.[14]

How widely known a phenomenon the evil-eye is appears, for instance, from an example from South America described by G. Reichel-Dolmatoff. Among the Aritama (a Mestizzo community in N. Columbia) were people who were able to 'cast the evil eye' (Mal Oyo), which was supposed to be caused by 'electric force', destroying everything. Such people are looked at with envy and curiosity.

Economic assets such as crops, houses, domestic animals or fruit-trees were particularly exposed to the evil-eye and the main reason given was envy.

Among people particularly exposed to the evil-eye were children, but adults could become victims as well. Cases of children exposed to the evil-eye usually ended fatally and patients died in terrible pains accompanied by high fever.[15]

Helmut Schoeck even writes about an 'institutionalized envy' manifesting itself in malicious gossip, envious sorcery and the evil-eye. A number of examples from peasant and 'primitive societies' describe a close relationship between the evil-eye and envy.[16] All those and other examples form a part of that social phenomenon known as '*envy*', which is the main subject of Schoeck's well-known book *Envy*, the last edition of which was published under the title: *Der Neid und die Gesellschaft* (*Envy and Society*).[17] But the evil-eye is more than that; it regulates antagonisms between parties (individuals or groups),[18] or protects the identity of a village against the dangerous and treacherous outside world.

A society which depends on the environment to a great extent is vulnerable (e.g. pestilences, illnesses, droughts), and this element of vulnerability is interpreted as Evil, which, being personified (e.g. evil-eye, the forces of evil) can be checked, isolated and combated. The evil-eye, in effect, symbolizes the ideology of the fortune and misfortune of human life.

Witchcraft and Magic in the Old Testament, and their Relation to Animals

J. R. PORTER

In considering our topic, there are a number of problems which arise in attempting to assess the evidence at our disposal. The first is the question of definition, or perhaps rather lack of definition, a difficulty which always crops up when dealing with witchcraft and magic. Perhaps the point can be illustrated by two examples. If one looks up one of the standard modern Biblical reference books, *The Interpreter's Dictionary of the Bible* and refers to the word 'Witch', it only says '*See* Sorcery'. If one looks that word up, it merely says '*See* Magic' and there finally the relevant information is to be found. On the other hand, Professor Parrinder in his very interesting book *Witchcraft: European and African*, after surveying Hebrew words for witches, concludes: 'These and other types of activity, loosely translated "witchcraft" or "wizardry", are in reality magic, good or bad, and sorcery. They are conscious and deliberate practices, that may be intended for useful or for harmful ends. They are not the unconscious or nocturnal witchcraft in which Europeans and Africans have believed'.[1] Again, speaking of the Old Testament he writes: 'Certainly there is not the abundance of belief in witchcraft that might have been expected. The evidence is extremely meagre',[2] while by contrast the late Professor Guillame in his book *Prophecy and Divination* says: 'Evidence for a belief in the evil powers of demons and sorcerers covers the whole period of Hebrew history from Genesis to the present day. I would go so far as to say that no belief is so well documented.'[3]

Obviously the wide discrepancies in the judgements of these various authorities, all basing themselves on the same corpus of material, spring from different definitions of the topic under review and therefore it is necessary to give some indication, however tentative, of one's own standpoint on the matter: and here two points, perhaps, may be made.

First, it seems safest to opt for the widest and most inclusive, though no doubt also the vaguest, definition available, if only for the reason that the material at our disposal does not itself draw the clear distinctions which modern scholarship inevitably has to try to make. Indeed Parrinder himself recognizes this when, speaking of the European situation, he points out that the distinction of witchcraft from magic 'was often far from clear in the olden days'[4] and the same point is frequently made by Old Testament specialists, for example, by T. Witton Davies in *Magic, Divination and Demonology among the Hebrews and their Neighbours*, which, though published as long ago as 1898, is still in many ways the best work on the subject. 'It is almost certain', he writes, 'that at first magic and divination were not dissociated: words used for one were used for the other'[5] and he has other statements to similar effect. Parrinder in fact gets into an impossible situation with regard to the Old Testament precisely because of the narrowness of his definition. He accepts Evans-Pritchard's famous description of witchcraft: 'A witch performs no rite, utters no spell, and possesses no medicine. An act of witchcraft is a psychic act'.[6] But when in his chapter on 'Witchcraft in the Bible and the Near East' we come to the subsection headed 'True Witchcraft',[7] we find that Parrinder's primary and clearest example is Ezek. xiii, 18–21, a passage to which we shall return, where the women described by the prophet certainly perform rites, utter spells and perhaps even possess a kind of medicine. Further, such difficulties largely arise because the Old Testament has no *terms* corresponding to such generalized concepts as 'witchcraft', 'magic' or 'sorcery'. All it provides us with are a number of words which designate particular persons according to the activities in which they are supposed to indulge. We always have to be very cautious in subsuming these under classifications of our own, which are not found in the Bible and which we cannot therefore necessarily assume to have formed part of the thought-world of the ancient Hebrews.

Secondly, what has just been said must not, however, be taken to mean that the Old Testament does not have its own kind of classification and its own kind of rationale in this area that we call that of witchcraft, magic and sorcery. That it indeed does so is shown by the fact that the famous key passage in Deut. xviii, 10–11 groups together various practitioners of certain arts under a common viewpoint, and this viewpoint is that the activities of the people in question are forbidden within the society of Israel, they are disapproved of and ought not to be practised. But we must be clear about what this viewpoint implies for the Old Testament. We shall probably be inclined to say that in ancient Israel, as in most if not all societies, there was 'white' and 'black' magic and sorcery, that is, that rites and spells of essentially the same character were sometimes considered to operate for the good of society and thus meet with official religious and social approval but in other contexts were regarded as hostile to the social order and therefore were visited with official disapprobation. We may consider the means by which Elisha in 2 Kings iv, 31–41 revives a dead boy or purges a poisonous pot of broth to be magical acts but acts of white magic, whereas the operations of the women in the verses from Ezekiel already referred to are equally magical but are acts of black magic. But we have no warrant for importing this attitude into the Old Testament because for it the two sets of actions are not variants of one and the same way of looking at the world and seeking to manipulate it. They are essentially different, simply because one is good and the other bad. Or to put it another way, if we want to use the terms witchcraft or magic or sorcery for activities of which the Old Testament writers disapprove, then, *for them*, activities of which they approve would not have been magic or sorcery at all, however generically similar they might seem to us.

This paper, then, will not be concerned with defining, much less differentiating between, witchcraft and magic in the Old Testament. Rather it will try to give an inevitably very brief description and evaluation of the practices commonly included under those terms which are condemned in its pages. Both description and evaluation, however, run into further problems, in addition to those already mentioned, about which a word or two must be said because they are not always apparent to the non-specialist. On the one hand, the real meaning of the Hebrew words used for the people and the practices we have to consider is not always easy to establish and is often very much disputed. Even when we may feel fairly sure that we have correctly traced the etymology of a particular word, we cannot always be sure that it retained its original significance in the context of the Hebrew language and society, for words have a history as well as a derivation. So whether, in any particular passage, we find a reference to magic or witchcraft will often depend on the judgement of individual scholars. Take, for example, Isa. ii, 6 and compare its rendering in two modern translations, the Revised Standard Version and the New English Bible. The former has:

> 'For thou hast rejected thy people, the house of Jacob,
> because they are full of diviners from the east
> and of soothsayers like the Philistines,
> and they strike hands with foreigners.'

The latter has:

> 'Thou hast abandoned thy people the house of Jacob;
> for they are crowded with traders
> and barbarians like the Philistines,
> and with the children of foreigners everywhere',

which of course cuts out any reference to magical practices altogether.

On the other hand, even when we may feel fairly sure that we know what a passage really means, how do we evaluate it? In the verse just quoted, does 'they strike hands with foreigners' mean a sign of fraternisation or a magical rite? When David cut off a piece of Saul's cloak as he lay asleep was he performing a hostile magical act, such as we know to have been practised by Mesopotamian wizards, or was he merely seeking to provide proof that he had had Saul in his power? When we read Ezek. xiii, 4, 'Your prophets, Israel, have been like jackals among ruins' is the comparison with demons who were thought to inhabit waste places, as again some Mesopotamian evidence might suggest, or is it with natural animals and their observable characteristics? Such questions are especially important when we come, as in due course we shall, to consider the very important evidence in the Psalms. Are the 'enemies' of the righteous man there foreign foes, legal opponents, wealthy oppressors—or sorcerers?—or, perhaps, sometimes one and sometimes another? All this, which could be developed much further, is just to warn that the interpretation of the Old Testament is very much of a minefield and he who walks through it too confidently, as the demands of brevity will compel us to do, must expect to get blown up.

It was said earlier that the really important dividing line in Israel in this area of witchcraft and magic was between activities which were disapproved of and those which were not. That does, in general, stand, but the matter becomes a little more complicated when we look at the reasons for which certain practices and persons were disapproved of. Basically there are two main grounds. First, there are a number of activities which appear to have been always condemned either because they were viewed as being characteristic of non-Israelite peoples and their cults, in contrast to Israel's own Yahwism, or because they implied involvement with supernatural agencies other than Yahweh, although we cannot draw too sharp a distinction between these two positions. So, to take one instance from many, in what we have called the key-passage in Deut. xviii, the ground for the proscription of the various classes of persons in verses 10 and 11 is given in the preceding verse: 'When you come into the land which Yahweh your God is giving you, do not learn to imitate the abominable customs of those other nations' and the whole section is followed by the statement 'These nations whose place you are taking listen to soothsayers and augurs, but Yahweh your God does not permit you to do this' and by the description of the prophet of Yahweh who is to take the place of the soothsayers and augurs in Israel. Perhaps, in view of Margaret Murray's theories about witchcraft, it should be said that there is no evidence that the Old Testament views these persons it condemns as devotees of pagan cults: what they do, it is claimed, is to introduce into Israel certain practices which properly belong to those cults but not to Yahwism. Perhaps the clearest example of a practice which is universally condemned because it was thought to involve supernatural agencies other than Yahweh is necromancy: and the reason for this is that necromancy meant recognizing the dead, or some of them, as divine beings rivalling Yahweh, and hence the numerous passages in the Old Testament which stress that the departed cannot be sources of power and knowledge for men—'in the grave, for which you are bound, there is neither doing nor thinking, neither understanding nor wisdom' (Eccles. ix, 10).

The second ground of condemnation of sorcerers and enchanters was that they were anti-social—'enemies to public safety and to private peace'. They were those whose actions brought sickness and death on individuals and caused dissension in family and social relationships. So, in the book of Malachi, they can be classed with a wide range of social undesirables, where Yahweh says: 'I will appear before you in court, prompt to testify against sorcerers, adulterers, and perjurers, against those who wrong the hired labourer, the widow and the orphan and who thrust the alien aside' (Mal. iii, 5). But it is important to realize that the kind of people we should describe as witches and sorcerers are by no means always condemned in this way because of their deliberately willing to do evil and harmful acts. They may be attacked when they are attempting to procure a good result if what they intend is in fact against the will of Yahweh in a particular situation. In other words, once again our distinction between 'black' and 'white' magic is of only limited application to the Old Testament. Take, for example, Jer. xxvii, 9: 'Do not listen to your prophets, your diviners, your wise women, your soothsayers and your sorcerers when they tell you not to serve the king of Babylon'. Now certainly at least two of the categories mentioned here, the prophets and the wise women, were normally respected and valued elements in Israelite religion and society, as we know from other evidence.[8] Also, in the present instance, they were all aiming to do something which they would have considered beneficial: they were all trying, by their different techniques, to bring about the overthrow of the king of Babylon, the foreign ruler of Israel, and so to achieve the nation's independence, and of course they would have assumed that this was what Yahweh, the national god, wanted. But Jeremiah, claiming to have a deeper awareness of Yahweh's purpose, opposes them, not because of the activities and purposes themselves, but for the misdirection of these which could only lead to the opposite of what was intended.

Bearing in mind these various considerations and cautions, let us now look at least at some of the practices and persons that are condemned in the Old Testament, with the object of trying to see, on the one hand, how they operated and, on the other, what they were aiming to bring about. The special emphasis of this essay is on the relationship of witchcraft and magic to the animal world, but it is doubtful whether the Bible is very informative here. There are some indications of such a relationship in ancient Israel but they are scanty and, as we shall see, not easy to interpret precisely, although it may well be that, were our evidence fuller, we might find that animals played a larger role in Hebrew witchcraft and magic than our existing texts would suggest. It should also be emphasized that, in what follows, we are concerned with the place of animals solely in relation to the practice of magic and witchcraft, and not with their place in Old Testament folklore generally.[9] But I think it would be true to say that in the Old Testament, witchcraft and magic are viewed primarily as trafficking with supernatural beings and particularly with the departed: this latter practice is more frequently condemned than any other. It has commonly been supposed, particularly on the basis of the famous so-called 'witch of Endor', that this was done by means of a familiar spirit and modern writers have suggested that there were people in Israel akin to the modern medium, who similarly had a control by whom they could summon the departed. The difficulty is that the Hebrew word *'ôb*, usually translated 'familiar spirit', is sometimes used as the object of verbs which make it difficult to recognize it as meaning a ghost or a spirit. Thus the *'ôb* is said to be 'made', or 'destroyed' or 'removed and burned down'. Hence it has been frequently suggested that it was some material object in the possession of the witch or sorcerer, used to make contact with the departed, although there is no agreement as to exactly what it was. One proposal is that it corresponded to the 'bull-roarer', which made a noise like the squeaking and muttering of the dead as they came out of the ground. Another proposal is that it was a pit dug to give the deceased access to the upper world for a brief period of time: we know that one of the activities of what are probably sorcerers in the Psalms, and certainly so in related Mesopotamian material, was the digging of pits to ensnare their victims and send them down to the underworld. Or again, the word *'ôb* may be linked with the very similar word meaning 'father' or 'ancestor' and be an image or representation of such a person: it would then be similar to the *teraphim*, i.e. statues of the ancestral household gods, with which in fact it is associated in some Biblical passages. But whatever its precise meaning, the *'ôb* was a means of conjuring the dead, to make use of the power and wisdom they were supposed to possess, and this is the reason for its condemnation, as we have already seen. We may note also that the practice we are considering has at least some of the characteristics of what Parrinder would call 'true' witchcraft. It is particularly, though not of course exclusively, the preserve of women and it is something hidden and secret, that takes place at night, as is shown by the episode at Endor or by what is said, referring probably to necromancy, in Is. lxv, 4, about those who 'crouch among graves, keeping vigil all night long'.

When we turn to most of the other Hebrew expressions which often accompany the prohibition of necromancy, particularly in Deut. xviii, we are on much less firm ground. There are only two things that can really be said about them. First, originally no doubt they were quite precise in meaning, denoting distinct and specific magical rites. Secondly, however, it is now extremely difficult to say just what these were: the Old Testament itself gives no explanation of them and scholars differ widely in the etymologies they give for them, which is the only clue we have as to their exact sense. So when one comes to translate such expressions, it is really not much more than a question of finding different English words to translate different Hebrew ones, although one will always be able to adduce some justification for one's rendering in any given case. In doing so, the modern translator is probably not too far from the intention of the ancient Hebrew writer. His aim was not to describe the practices he mentions—indeed, he would have thought it undesirable and harmful to do so—but to lump them altogether under a blanket condemnation as elements alien to the religion of Yahweh, for that was all the consideration they merited. Hence the terms easily become interchangeable and acquire a general sense, such as 'magic' or 'divination' or 'sorcery', considerably wider than what was no doubt originally the case.

Similar problems of interpretation arise in connection with possible references to demonic animal beings in the Old Testament. For example, there are three references, Ex. xxiii, 28; Deut. vii, 20; Jos. xxiv, 12, to Yahweh's sending 'the hornet' to drive out Israel's enemies on the occasion of the invasion of the Promised Land. It should be noted that the expression has the definite article and that the word used for 'hornet', *ṣirâh*, only occurs in these three passages. The definite article is usually taken as indicating a collective noun, 'hornets', and the word is understood as a vivid metaphor for the terrifying power of Israel's God: or a different meaning is proposed for it and hence the rendering 'panic' in the New English Bible. Alternatively, a popular suggestion has been that it originally referred to Egyptian campaigns in Palestine which decimated the native inhabitants and so paved the way for Israelite successes, since on Egyptian monuments the hornet sometimes appears as a symbol of the Pharaoh's rule.[10] Again it might refer to an otherwise unknown marauding desert clan, perhaps allied with Israel, which had this insect as a kind of tutelary deity.[11]

But this last suggestion may enable us to go a little further and, in view of the widespread belief in flies and similar insects as demonic agents of death and destruction, to speculate whether we may not have here the mythical concept of a gigantic insect, similar to the one believed in in Sardinia,[12] which could be employed in a magical way against enemies.[13] How far this concept, if it in fact once existed, was still alive in the thought of the Biblical writers is of course another, and not easily solvable, question.

Perhaps the point can best be illustrated by taking one particular expression, which may be of special interest for the concern of this paper. This is the word *menakēsh*, translated by the Revised Version as 'enchanter' and by the New English Bible as 'diviner'. Now this latter translation at least can be justified from Gen. xliv, 5, where the same root is used to describe Joseph's cup 'which he uses for divination'. Hence we might be led to conclude that the term we are considering has a precise technical sense: it refers to someone who practises hydromancy, and from this it comes to acquire the more general sense of taking an omen by any means, as for example at 1 Kings xx, 33. But was this its original sense or is the Genesis passage rather a case of a word that has already acquired a wider connotation being applied to a particular instance? The root of the word is exactly the same as the Hebrew word for snake, *naḥash*, and there is another Hebrew word, *laḥash*, which is merely a dialectical variation of *naḥash*, and clearly means 'serpent-charming'. Now there were certainly professional snake-charmers known in ancient Israel whose operations were regarded as beneficial because they neutralized the harmful biting power of a poisonous snake—they were a kind of rodent operator in fact—as we see from Eccles. x, 11: 'if a snake bites before it is charmed, the snake-charmer loses his fee'. But if the original sense of the word translated 'diviner' is really snake-charmer, why is he condemned in a number of passages? Surely because we are presented with two different practitioners, whose operations, however much alike they may seem to us, were regarded quite differently by the Hebrews. The one who was condemned sought, by means of some spell, to acquire for his own purposes the great power and the great wisdom which the serpent was supposed to possess in the world of the Ancient Near East.[14] But in the Old Testament, as we see in Gen. iii, the snake is essentially a being with a supernatural dimension, who is Yahweh's rival and so any attempt to avail oneself of the serpent's mighty powers was to place oneself over against Yahweh. Once again, it is the object of the magical act, not the magic itself, which requires its condemnation. Indeed, so powerful was the snake considered to be that, for a time, the magic associated with him could only be neutralized by being taken up into the official national cultus. So we find the bronze serpent in the Jerusalem Temple, which was supposed to have been made by Moses and which healed sufferers by what might be called 'sympathetic magic': and the same kind of motive seems to lie behind the story of Aaron's rod that turned into a snake and finally ate up the snakes similarly created by the Egyptian wonder-workers —the serpent magic really belongs to Yahweh alone. So we can distinguish three attitudes to the serpent and the rites accompanying him in the Old Testament:

(i) The snake is a being of supernatural power, belonging to another world of being than Yahweh, and therefore not to be trafficked with:
(ii) the snake has supernatural power but this can be absorbed into the religion of Yahweh and can operate beneficially in that setting:
(iii) the snake is just an animal, although a nasty and dangerous one, and spells may legitimately be used against it to render it harmless.

And what we may suppose to have happened is that a term which originally referred to serpent magic, because of the wide-spread nature of this practice, has gradually been extended to cover other kinds of magic and divination as well.

Having touched upon what is perhaps the most striking case in the Old Testament of the connection of an animal with magic, something should perhaps be said at this point about Hebrew demons, since a number of these are depicted in animal form. It is just this fact which again raises our by now familiar difficulties of translation and evaluation. Are, for example, the creatures mentioned in Is. xxxiv, 14, the names of animals, as the Authorized Version and the New English Bible would suggest, or those of the fabulous demons of Hebrew folk-lore, as the Revised Standard Version would indicate? Again, even if they exist, such demons may not provide clear evidence of witchcraft belief: we have no absolutely certain evidence that they were viewed as human beings whose souls wander about in the dark to devour their fellows or even that witches and sorcerers were thought to make use of them for magical purposes. It is however suggestive that there are close parallels between what the demons are said to do and what, as we shall see, magicians are said to do in some of the Psalms—both groups work in darkness and secrecy, send disease, devour human beings, shoot arrows and, not least important, some assume animal forms. There would seem to be one very clear case of belief in animal demons, known as the *sairim*, because in Lev. xvii the Israelites are forbidden to continue offering sacrifices to them. The word means 'hairy ones' and the rendering 'satyrs' has often been proposed, but since in Is. xxxiv, 14 the same word is used of the wild he-goat, found in waste places such as demons were also believed to inhabit, we should probably think of a supernatural being who was held to take the form of a goat and so perhaps translate the Hebrew as 'goat-spirits'. It is in this same verse of Isaiah that we meet with the famous Lilith.[15] Whatever may have been the original significance of the word there, certainly in later Jewish folk-lore it is taken as the name of a female demon and identified with the Mesopotamian *lilitu*. The name is not connected with the similar sounding Hebrew word for 'night' but with the Sumerian word for 'wind', doubtless because of the power of magical flight which Lilith so strikingly possessed: on a Canaanite magical plaque of the 8th century BC she is called the 'flying-one', in Jewish folk-lore she becomes identified with the nightjar, and significantly in the Isaiah passage she haunts desolate places and is accompanied by birds considered by the Law as unclean, such as owls, ravens and kites. It is easy to see how she could become linked with witch-craft, for, in the Mesopotamian tradition, she is at once the *succuba* who tempts men in sexual dreams and the hag who steals children from their mothers. Another animal demon may be referred to in the cryptic verse of Prov. xxx, 15:

> 'The leech has two daughters;
> "Give" says one, and "Give", says the other.'

Now, of course, this might be no more than a male chauvinist comment on the insatiable demands of wives or mistresses, pictured as having the characteristics of the blood-sucking leech, and so it is generally understood by commentators. But the mysterious, gnomic form of the saying may point to the leech being also the vampire—

an Arabic word very similar to the Hebrew term has this meaning. If this is so, are the daughters witches claiming their fee from those who employ them on nefarious purposes or even perhaps vampires themselves, demanding blood?

There are, of course, other references to specific demonic beings in the Old Testament, some of which we shall meet when we turn to the Psalms, but we are confining our attention only to demons that are clearly associated with animals. There is just one final point to be mentioned in this connection. Some of the Old Testament demons are plainly originally deities in other religions and one explanation of the distinction between clean and unclean animals in Lev. xi is that the latter were once creatures sacred to various gods in the religions surrounding Israel, which came to be viewed as having demonic powers because of this association and were therefore highly dangerous and to be strictly avoided. This theory could well account for the inclusion of at least some of the animals listed in Lev. xi in the unclean category: for example, Is. lxv, 4 and lxvi, 3, 17 show that the eating of swine and other unclean animals was an element in secret, magical rites—to quote the last reference,

> 'Those who hallow and purify themselves in garden-rites,
> one after another in a magic ring,
> those who eat the flesh of pigs and rats and all vile vermin'.

Thus the range of demonic animals recognized in Israel may have been much wider than our existing Old Testament would at first sight suggest.

Finally, we come to the second part of our enquiry, what the practitioners of magical rites and spells were aiming to bring about. I must confine myself to two key areas of evidence, the first of which is the famous passage in Ezek. xiii, 18–21, which has already been briefly mentioned. Once more, both its text and its interpretation are very debatable but the following seems perhaps to be the likeliest rendering:

> (18) 'I loathe you, you women who hunt men's lives by sewing magic bands upon the wrists and putting veils over the heads of persons of every stature. Will you hunt the lives of my people and keep their lives in being for your own profit? (19) You have profaned me before my people with handfuls of barley and scraps of bread, bringing death to those who should not die and life to those

> who should not live . . . (20) I am against your magic bands with which you hunt men's lives like birds. I will tear them from your arms and those lives that you hunt I will let go free like birds. (21) I will tear up your long veils and save my people from you.'

On this very interesting passage, six comments may be briefly made:

(i) The aim of the witches is to catch men's lives, that is the psycho-somatic unity which was what the Hebrew understood by a person and for which he used the term *nephesh*, the word translated 'life' here, verse 18. We may compare the way in which African witches claim really to dismember and eat their victims but equally claim that this is done spiritually or psychically.

(ii) This catching of lives can be done either for evil or for good, verse 19, although no doubt the idea of the former is more prominent. But both are usurping the power of life and death which properly belong to Yahweh and so are condemned.

(iii) It is, however, taken for granted that the witches really have this power. They are rendered powerless not by scepticism but by superior divine strength.

(iv) The witches' power is gained by sewing magic bands on people's wrists and by covering them all over with long veils, verse 18. The first of these practices is probably a piece of symbolic magic by which the client's wrists were bound to effect the snaring of the life of the person against whom he was employing the witch. The veiling may have had a similar purpose, but, in view of our second consideration, it may represent a beneficent action. The magic veil was perhaps to protect the wearer from harm: we may compare the way in which Elijah covered himself with his cloak in the face of the dangerous divine presence.

(v) The *nephesh* or life is represented as a bird which can be trapped or released, verse 20. This is a common concept and a common procedure of magic among many peoples and we shall see it recurring in what are probably magical concepts in some of the psalms.

(vi) The witches profane Yahweh's holiness 'with handfuls of barley and scraps of bread', verse 19. This may be a slighting reference to the pitiful fee they received for their witchcraft, but it is difficult to see why this should produce so serious a result as the profanation of Yahweh. So perhaps it is another magical practice: since the *nephesh* is conceived as a bird, it can be symbolically caught as a bird would be by a baited trap.

The other area of evidence to be considered, again all too briefly, is that of the psalms. A large number of these have the form of a lament by an individual, who is in a condition of distress, sickness and mortal danger, and this condition is brought about by enemies who are described as plotting and scheming against the sufferer. Clearly the situation is a very real one: it is not a question of metaphorical or figurative language. Now, as mentioned earlier, there has been a good deal of discussion as to the identity of the enemies, largely provoked by the theory of the famous Norwegian scholar Sigmund Mowinckel that the common expression for them, usually translated as 'workers of iniquity', actually means 'sorcerers'.[16] From the standpoint of our particular concern, however, this debate is largely irrelevant: the question is not so much whether the psalmist's enemies were themselves professional sorcerers or wizards but whether they were employing magic against him, and what we learn of the activities of the enemies is very suggestive.

They are generally represented as plotting together in groups and in secret. Not only do their machinations bring various kinds of disease, very vividly depicted, on the object of their hostility, but they are even accused of cannibalism—Ps. lvii, 4 describes them as 'man-eaters'. They make a circle round their victim, they bind him with knots and cords, and they spread nets and snares to catch him. They also dig pits for him and the significance of this is made clear by references to the sufferer going down to the realm of the dead or sinking into the waters of the underworld. Very significantly, they are often said to shoot arrows and that the object of this was to kill by magic a life in the form of a bird is strongly suggested by Ps. xi, 2:

> 'Why do you say to me,
> "Flee to the mountains like a bird;
> see how the wicked string their bows
> and fit the arrow to the string,
> to shoot down honest men out of the darkness" '?,

for no *real* marksman, of course, would shoot at anybody in the dark. The same consideration seems to apply to what is said about nets and traps, as is shown for instance by Ps. cxxiv, 7: 'we have escaped like a bird from the fowler's trap.' Further, the enemies appear as hostile wild beasts which, as we shall see, probably mean that they are thought of as demons in animal guise, most commonly as lions, but also as bulls and dogs. There is also a certain amount of evidence that the enemies are considered to be working through demonic agents. For instance, in Ps. lxxvi, 4, the expression usually translated as 'fiery arrows', is literally 'the Reshephs of the bow': Resheph is the name of a demon[17] and even if the language here is only figurative and literary, it indicates that the concept of a magical arrow was once well known in Israel. But the clearest evidence is provided by Ps. xci, which T. H. Gaster entitles 'a coven of demons'.[18] Here the traps and spells of evil men are accompanied by what are probably a number of demonic assaults such as 'the terror by night' and 'the destruction that wasteth at noonday' and at the end the psalmist is assured: 'you shall tread upon lion and adder, the young lion and serpent you shall tread under foot' which surely is not to be taken literally but refers to the repelling of the sorcerers' demonic attacks.

To all these descriptions we have already seen that there are parallels in the Old Testament itself to suggest that they imply magic and witchcraft and many of them are also parallel to what we learn of activities of witches in other societies. But the strongest support for this view comes from a comparison of the psalms in question with similar Babylonian psalms of lamentation.[19] These have the same form as the Hebrew psalms: both are descriptions of distress and pleas for help from the attacks of enemies, but in the Babylonian material the enemies are unambiguously sorcerers and their activities are virtually identical with what is said about the psalmist's enemies—both form secret conspiratorial groups, spread nets, bind with cords, dig pits, are compared with lions and so on.[20] We also find in both literatures that the prayer element in the psalms often has the form of a kind of counter-spell designed to turn the magic of the sorcerer against himself as, for example, in Ps. vii, 15–16:

> 'If he dig a pit, let it deceive him,
> And may he fall into the ditch he makes.
> Let his mischief return upon his head,
> And may his violence come down upon his own pate.'

In view of all this, it seems at least a possible conclusion that there were groups of people in ancient Israel who practised witchcraft and magic against individuals to harm them in various ways and even to kill them, that there was a phenomenon that can fairly be compared to witchcraft as we know it in other societies. This paper has necessarily had to be very selective and there is, of course, much other evidence in the Old Testament that ought properly to be considered. But one should again emphasize a couple of cautions already made. First, all the suggestions in this essay must be very tentative: the interpretation of almost every passage to which reference has been made admits of more than one alternative and it would need a lengthy technical discussion to justify the understanding proposed for each particular case—and, even then, not all other scholars would be convinced. And, secondly, arising from this, we have always to exercise great caution in the application of our own terminology to the Hebrew phenomenon and not to read into the Old Testament distinctions, definitions and analogies which may do violence to the real nature of the material with which alone we have to deal.

Animals and Witchcraft in Danish Peasant Culture

JOAN ROCKWELL

It is not surprising that a country in which the major economic activity was small-scale farming for several thousand years, and in which the majority of the population have been peasants engaged in it, should have a considerable body of magical beliefs and rituals in which animals are prominent. These span a great difference, both in content and in the requirements of the ritual, from simple acts such as rubbing the cows' teeth with soot on Christmas Eve in the hope of a lucky year, which anyone can do, to more drastic remedies such as one said to be 'unfailing': to bury a new-born calf alive under the barn-floor, to cure contagious abortion in the herd. Such a cure would be recommended by a cunning-man or woman, and not everyone would follow it.[1]

These cunning-men and cunning-women are to be distinguished from witches; their function is to cure, both people and animals, and they are practising everywhere in Denmark to this day, including the capital city of Copenhagen, although the advent of scientific agriculture has deprived them of their veterinary practice.

Witches are very different beings. No one will admit to being a witch, while there is no secret about being a cunning-woman. Witches were said to harm people by making them sick, blind or otherwise damaged, and they could not only spread sickness on another farm, but also 'milk other folk's cows' by driving a knitting-needle or spike into their own wall or a beam in the house, when milk from the bewitched cows would drip from it.[2] By this means they always had milk, and could drain a cow for milk and then for blood until it died. These attacks on animals by witches were one of the great grievances against them, but they also had two particular relationships with animals.

One was the animal as familiar: in Denmark usually a great black dog, but sometimes a cat, toad, bird or other animal. Marcel Mauss, in *A General Theory of Magic*,[3] tells us that the power of a magician who has a familiar 'is derived from his dealings with animals'; and these are of course not ordinary animals, but demons or perhaps the Evil One himself, taking the form of an animal. The presence of an animal familiar is proof of an alliance or pact with the Devil.

The other is the matter of shape-changing, in which the witch is able at will to assume the shape of an animal such as a hare, cat, raven or the like. Werewolves and vampire-bats notoriously change their shapes as well, always with evil consequences for human beings but not always voluntarily. These beings generally appear in folklore as lost souls, excluded from human society and Christian communion. Perhaps they are driven to devour human flesh and blood because they cannot partake in the communion of the Mass with its *symbolic* sharing of the same. It is interesting that in the 'vampire areas' of Europe they appear as landed aristocrats who of course are outside the peasant society.

There is one matter which I think I must describe, at least in outline, when we are considering beliefs about animals in Denmark, and that is the animal-tabus, particularly with respect to the *horse*, and a special class of untouchables called the Rakker-folk, who had the function of dealing with the horse in its *tabu* aspects.

The *rakkerfolk* were literally untouchable: not only could they not intermarry with the peasant population, but neither could they use the same eating or drinking vessels or sleep in the same rooms when they visited the farms to do their special jobs. These jobs were the unclean functions of untouchables everywhere: cleaning latrines and chimneys, formerly they helped the hangman in the towns, they were called upon to cut down suicides. Their duties in connection with animals were also 'unclean': flaying dead horses or any cattle which had died of disease, killing and skinning cats and dogs, castrating them, slaughtering horses (often in a very cruel way). The point about horses is that although they were the most important work animals on the farm, their flesh was absolutely tabu as food, and no peasant would have anything to do with a dead horse, or even help a mare to foal if she was in difficulties; since they wanted the hides to use and sell, and the foals to raise as work-animals, the *rakker* was called in on these occasions. Their fee for skinning animals was the carcase, and what made them particularly unclean was that they ate (and also made sausages, candles etc.) of unclean meat: horsemeat, dog- and cat-meat, and the flesh of calves which was also tabu, strange though it seems to us. (They had a diet far richer in protein than that of the peasant, which was based on grain and milk: bread, porridge, milk and cheese, some fish, and some simple greens such as kale as well as a few hardy fruits: apples and pears, gooseberries, currants and wild soft fruits.)

The tabu on horsemeat is said by Danish scholars to date from the establishment of Christianity, which was late in Scandinavia: 1000 in Iceland, the twelfth century in Denmark and Norway (although St. Ansgar and other missionaries went to Denmark in the ninth century they had little effect on the religious practice of the majority of the population), the thirteenth century in Sweden. The previously-dominant horse-cult, which at one time stretched from England (or Ireland?) right across North Europe to Mongolia, was put down with some severity, and the ritual feasts of horse-meat were made ritually unclean by the new religion. Horse is still not a popular meat in Scandinavia, in marked contrast to the south of Europe, and neither is it in England for that matter. The *rakker-folk* who continued to act as if they were unaffected by this religious proscription are perhaps a segment of the population which was 'left behind' in the change of religion in the North, excluded in many ways from a peasant culture which nevertheless made use of their special services for a long time. Their occupations include almost everything but agriculture: besides the unclean ones mentioned, they were horse-copers, smiths and metal workers, glaziers, tinkers and such small trades. They are to be distinguished from gipsies however, as although they travelled round in families or bands, they belonged to towns or at least to areas in Denmark and were legally bound to carry out their particular jobs, at least until the nineteenth century. *Rakkers* who petitioned for release from their duties as hangman's helpers in the eighteenth century were refused.[4]

Despite this close and special association with animals from the 'wrong' or 'unclean' side, they seem to have surprisingly little to do with actual witchcraft.* Some of their wives did a bit of fortune-

*Although the skills of the 'cunning-man' are often attributed to them. Thus in St. St. Blicher's well-known (but untranslated, except from Jutland dialect to Danish) master-

telling, but the folk who were witches or *troldmen* in peasant society, although they had made themselves 'outsiders' in one sense, as secret enemies, had not the permanent social and occupational rôle of outsiders, like the *rakkerfolk*—on the contrary, they are to be found at the very centre of village life.[5]

The people most often accused of witchcraft or pacts with the Devil or working magic were of two sorts: the locally prominent, particularly the village pastor, the blacksmith, anyone who seems unreasonably prosperous, as a rich farmer or trader who may be supposed to have made a pact with the devil—and of course the gentry and nobility, who are frequently described as carried off or torn to pieces when the Devil comes to collect his own; and on the other hand, the ordinary wives of the village, who might perhaps all turn into witch-hares to persecute an old man they were angry with for some reason by invading his house in the evenings, or the housewives or servant-girls who milk the neighbours' cows by witchcraft; or they are merely well-respected housewives like the mother of the boy who wanted to see the witches ride on Midsummer Eve. She advised him to go to the smithy, get a new harrow which had never been used, place it at the crossroads as one ordinarily sets up a harrow but with the teeth outward, creep under it and he would see the witches ride: he does so, and the first witch he sees is his mother riding on a broomstick: and he says, 'Mother, if you are in that pack, I needn't have gone to all this trouble, for I see a witch every day at home'.[6] This story is certainly intended as a humorous one, and there is a decided tendency to levity and scepticism in much of the Danish material. But it does emphasize the point that a witch can be *anyone*, even anyone's respectable mother, concealed behind an ordinary village persona.

What may be thought more surprising is the frequency with which the Pastor is a witch, a cunning-man, or at least has some ambiguous relationship with the forces of evil which he is supposed to combat. Tang Kristensen when he published numerous accounts

---

piece, *E Bindstow*, the young peasant reflects: 'Bad luck to these *Rakkerfolk*, they are not such fools! They can both foretell the future and "show again" [that is, "see" stolen or otherwise lost articles], and they can do both good and ill, just as it chances'. However, in this story the *Rakker* who owes him a service gets him his sweetheart 'whose parents say I have too little, and that's true enough' by hinting that otherwise 'the red cock may crow over the farm'—i.e. it may burn down; and this very practical offer which could hardly be refused indicates a scepticism at least from Blicher's side as to their magic powers.

of priests as witches or *troldmen* was savagely attacked for it, and defended himself on the grounds that it certainly was a widespread belief among the Danish peasantry. Marcel Mauss tells us that 'It is also true that priests in a number of societies have a remarkable disposition towards magical practices';[7] and Danish peasant society certainly seems to have been one of them.

This seems surprising, as 'witchcraft must be learned before a child is confirmed, as when it has once been to the communion-table it is too late'.[8] On the other hand, 'All priests have to study in the Black School'[9] (of witchcraft); this is necessary for them to be able to *combat* witchcraft, but also the occasion of some of them being captured by the Enemy.

Priests are well-known *dobbeltgængers*, seen in two places at the same time (Mauss mentions a priest named Johannes Teutonicus of Halberstadt, who in 1221 'is said to have performed three masses, concurrently, at Halberstadt, Mainz and Cologne'[10]). But many others besides priests—farm-labourers, girls, farmers, smiths, anyone in fact may become one: 'If anyone wants to see his *dobbeltgænger*, he has only to go to a lonesome place where no one can hear him, and call three times to himself, each time answering "Who is calling me?". Then he will see his own double'. To conjure up one's own double is not identical with changing shape to an animal or having an animal 'familiar', but it may be thought a related phenomenon.

Priests are more particularly known to be magicians by their familiar, usually a Black Dog: there are numerous examples in Tang Kristensen's material of a farm-labourer who for some reason looks into the priest's study window late at night: the priest cannot see him as his back is to the window, but a great black dog, shaggy and with piercing eyes, which he has never seen before, glares at him. The next day the priest reproaches him for 'being where he should not have been, and seeing what he should not have seen'; the dog had told him all about it, of course.

These village priests are not, on the whole, accused of maliciously harming people, milking their cows or striking down their farm animals, but of excessive learning, including the reading late at night which makes Jews look in the window, and particularly of the possession of certain magic books, particularly *Cyprianus* and *Henrik Smidth*. These are books of magic formulæ, couched in Christian terms:

> In Jesus Christ's name I require you, all evil spirits and *trollfolk*, in the name of the living God which is without beginning and end, the Lord of the clouds up to Heaven and in Heaven, and on earth here below, who will and can help you out of the trolldoms-desperation you are come in ...
>
> (*Cyprianus*, Den første Bog No.1 (copy in DFS; publ. in Malmøe, 1561 'by "R G", written by "H G"')

and dedicated in the preface to 'all Christian, honest and learned readers, to be used only for good, and against the forces of evil'. While it contains formulæ for exorcism like the one whose beginning is quoted above, it also has many magic recipes for healing, for finding lost or stolen articles (sometimes by magically striking out the eye of the thief), for 'binding' a gun so that it won't shoot, or horses so they can't move. But in the collected folklore material the most significant thing about *Cyprianus* is that by reading in it, one 'reads the Devil to one', in the first instance in the form of various animals: usually big black flies which begin to fill the room, sometimes a cock or chickens or other birds such as ravens. There are numerous stories, the pattern of which is:

> My mother's sister served as a maid in a vicarage near Silkeborg. The Pastor was a very nice man, and he had a lot of books. Since my aunt cleaned in all the rooms, she was permitted to be everywhere in the house and was also often in the Pastor's study. But he had strictly forbidden her to touch his books or read any of them. One day he was away on a visit, and she went into his study and took a book. It was a lovely book to read, and she kept on for a while, but then she noticed that the room seemed very strange, and it was full of flies. Suddenly the door flew open, the Pastor rushed in all in a sweat: he tore the book out of her hands, boxed her ears and said, 'What would you have answered, if he had come?'. He then quickly read back in the book, and soon everything was as before in the room. Afterwards my aunt left the Pastor's books alone.

This story was collected in 1911, and the respondent notes:

> My mother told this story about her sister 30 years ago. It must have happened about 1825.[12]

There are several interesting points about *Cyprianus*. One is that the reading is compulsive: once started, it is impossible to stop, especially when one gets to the *red letters*, when it is too late; another is the gathering of animals preceding the Evil One and as his representatives (a device effectively used by Kingsley Amis in a modern novel, *The Green Man* (1971) with small green flies); another is that in these stories the book's owner, who can tell at a distance that it is being read, always arrives in time and 'reads the evil back again'; another is that these stories are based on the principle that *all peasants can read*: it is always a child, an ordinary servant-girl or farm-labourer who reads them—which might mean that the belief is quite a late one: regular schooling was established in every village only in 1814 in Denmark. However, the deacon's duties included teaching village children to read from the sixteenth century in order to read the Catechism at least. This was one of the achievements of the Protestant Reformation. *Cyprianus* was in fact first printed in Denmark in 1797; the early examples such as the one quoted are from Sweden (although Skaane belonged to Denmark in 1561, and it is in Danish) or Germany (or handwritten copies). One would like to know more about its distribution in Europe, as Norman Lewis mentions it in the present time as '*The Book of St. Cyprian*, a country handbook of magic always to be found in such out-of-the-way places' (in Sicily where Mafia oaths are sworn on it).[13]

By the middle of the eighteenth century, according to the Danish historian Axel Steensberg,[14] educated people had ceased to believe in witchcraft, and in the 1720s Holberg had already made belief in it the theme of one of his comedies; however, this belief certainly remained anchored solidly in the common people. The most troublesome and persistent form of witchcraft seems to have been the witch's interference with butter-making: she charmed her neighbour's butter into her own churn, and according to Steensberg this was believed right down to the modern establishment of the cooperative dairies from about 1890. Efforts were made to destroy this belief: a book on farming, *Den nyeste Bondepractica*, published in 1798, begged the housewife not to believe her butter wouldn't come because of witchcraft if the weather was thundery, if the milk was too hot or too cold, or if the churn was not absolutely clean; but this rational advice is rather mitigated by another hint—not to suppose that it is impossible for a young handsome woman to be a witch as well as an old ugly one.

Witchcraft in Denmark had a decidedly practical motivation: the witch could charm away her neighbour's butter, milk her neighbour's cows, as well as doing acts of revenge on being refused some small favour or charity, as elucidated for England by Alan MacFarlane in *Witchcraft in Tudor and Stuart England*. Pacts with the Devil were made by ordinary people—not witches themselves but wanting some special advantage, and they were always for gain: to become a 'free-shot' who could never miss what he aimed at—frequent among huntsmen and gamekeepers on estates; to draw a 'free-lot' for conscription, so as not to have to go; to have a coin which can never be spent, no matter how often it is given out; to have a 'spiritus', a white worm with a red head, which lives in a bottle and gives advice on trading, or a homunculus in a box which does the same: these obviously desirable objects are hard to get rid of, though attempts are made when the time to be fetched by the Evil One approaches—thrown in ponds, they are found in the window when you get home; though one of Kristensen's respondents, describing how his neighbour tried to get rid of his 'vekseldaler' said: 'I would have liked to have it'. Sometimes it is the tenth owner who belongs to the Devil.

The priest, with his ambivalent relationship to the forces of evil, is called to break these pacts with the Devil himself; for the minor mischief of witches, the cunning-man or cunning-woman is called in, and sometimes fetched from long distances to the farms. A cunning-man called *Hals-Præst*,[15] for example, is called to a farm where the horses are dying. He was said to be 'so wise that he could see by looking at a mare, whether the foal would be male or female, and what colour', and he had been known to tell girls who laughed at him for his grotesquely ragged appearance that they were pregnant, or that they had already buried two infants secretly born to them. The point of these accusations was that they were true, but known only to the girls. The folklore material assumes that his information is magically acquired, but telepathy is far more likely. He was a marvel at curing animals: at one place, Elkjær,[16]

> the horses were sick and couldn't be cured, and they died one after another. So *Hals-Præst* was called and said they were bewitched. To get rid of the sickness they should bury a horse alive under the port to the stable, and the witch would come. When the horse was buried, sure enough an old woman appeared, who was 'said to "know more than Our Father"'; and she came in through the port. It is not known if she was charged with witchcraft, but Hals Præst always stayed at Elkjær after that, and the owner thought a lot of him.

Witches are seldom seen directly in the Danish material: they appear as 'the other', as in this story which, like most of them, is about the cure rather than the witch's practice. What the cunning-man or woman does is often described: to salve the axe with which the patient cut himself, for instance, which is then hung on the wall for further treatment. They usually have a whole series of such tools hanging for treatment; but of the witch's actual activities very little is said, and that often with scepticism, about peculiar neighbours, at least by the time Tang Kristensen was collecting at the end of the last century. Thus a hare, tamed by children who had caught it, got loose in the autumn and hopped around the neighbouring village,

> and often went to the beach between Svinning and Alum in the evening and folk were all afraid of it—mostly in Svinning, because they were more superstitious there, and they thought one or another of their wives was a witch ... it hopped over the half-door into a couple of houses, and some people were very angry as they felt they were almost accused of witchcraft.... But someone shot the hare and gave it to the Deacon, who said he would eat the witch with pleasure.[17]

There is a whole series of such de-mystifying stories, but also some fragments of beliefs: 'Old Per Overlade put eggs in ant-hills, and Lavst Smith believed that Per was a witch ... ' (and bewitched his plough so the horses couldn't pull it). The same Per Overlade is said to have suddenly flung himself down and rolled over and over on a toad which crossed the road. 'I asked him why, but "That's my business", he said, and I was no wiser'. Some people are afraid of moles, because they cross the road zigzag, 'Especially one big one, I know him all right, it's old Kristen Johansen, don't you think it's strange every Sunday when he goes home from church he zigzags across the road in just that way? Sörren didn't think it so strange, as the man was drunk every time he was in church'. And a man called Kragh-Niels said there were 90 witches on his farm, and when there were 100, the world would come to an end.[18]

I think we may conclude, about Danish witchcraft and witches, that by the time most of the material was gathered it was not a very serious affair either in the practice or the punishment, and was subject in the accounts to the typical Danish mockery; but certainly the stories and perhaps the legends particularly point back to a time when witchcraft was really a dangerous practice, with deadly consequences in every sense. The witchcraft said to exist is easily contained within village life—at the worst, the Pastor or alternatively the cunning-man or cunning-woman can be called in to combat it. There is no great astonishment at any reversal of the natural order, as indeed why should there be for people who make the sign of the cross in front of the horses when they plough the first furrow in the Spring? Witches are seen as secret enemies, 'the other' in the village, but unlike the *rakkerfolk* they are essentially part of the village community. The casual tolerance of this mild form of witchcraft, and the positive acceptance of the curative powers of the cunning-man or cunning-woman, are doubtless the social background against which we should see the well-known Danish saying: 'Every village has its witch, and every parish has its cunning-man'.

The Role of Animals in Witchcraft and Popular Magic

With special reference to Yorkshire

KATHRYN C. SMITH

Animals have played a part in witchcraft and magic within many cultures over a long period of time. The relationship between animals and early man was necessarily more crucial than it is now in many parts of the world. Animals, then, were a natural component of a total world view which, from evidence derived from archaeology and anthropology, was a magical world view, as it still remains for much of the world's population.

Humans have been believed to be able to metamorphose into animal form for many centuries; certain people have had attributed to them the power to summon creatures, at will, to obey them. Others have used animals, dead or alive, in various magical rites or they have been believed to do so by their own communities, or by those in authority. In other instances, animal characteristics perceived in men or women have been attributed to witchcraft powers. Thus, there is a direct relationship between the animal and the human world within the sphere of magical activity. This paper explores the nature of this relationship, especially as perceived in one particular area of study—the county of Yorkshire.

Most folklorists are familiar with many of the standard folk motifs which concern animals as connected with witchcraft and magic. However, in the early period of collecting this kind of material, any distinction that existed between folk belief and folk fiction has often been lost. It is not now always possible to discover such a distinction, but it is certainly worthwhile examining all available material which reflects these folk themes. There are three main areas in which animals play a key role;

(i) Metamorphosis; shapeshifting, in which the human being is transformed into animal form, either willingly or unwillingly.[1]

(ii) Animal as agent; in which the human uses an animal in order to practise magic, healing or harming etc. The animal may be dead or alive, whole or not, it might be in the nature of a 'familiar'.[2]

(iii) Animal as receiver; where magic is practised, or thought to be, in order to affect an animal, either adversely or propitiously. For example, some witches were believed to be able to milk cows at a distance, or to make them produce bloody milk.[3]

Metamorphosis

Stories of shapeshifting have existed for centuries. Apuleius wrote of such transformations when the theme was doubtless already old. Gervase of Tilbury wrote that 'women have been seen and wounded in the shape of cats by persons who were secretly on watch.'[4] Krämer and Sprenger told of it in the *Malleus Maleficarum*, and it found many mentions in the English witch trials of the 16th and 17th centuries. For example, John Webster, the Yorkshire cleric, wrote in 1677 of those who say 'they are transubstantiated into dogs, cats and the like'.[5] Witch metamorphosis was mentioned by Edward Fairfax of Fewston, West Yorkshire, in his *Daemonologia*. On April 4th, 1622, William Fairfax started a hare out of a bush and set a dog on it. The vicar, Smithson, saw it, his dogs also gave chase but lost sight of the hare. That day, the 'strange woman' appeared to Helen Fairfax, and told her that she had been the hare. Fairfax writes

> the changing of witches into hares, cats and the like shapes, is so common as late testimonies and confessions approve unto us, that none but the stupidly incredulous can wrong the credit of the reporters or doubt of the certainty.[6]

In the post-trials period fictional motifs were attached to local people thought to be witches in their own community. In 19th century Yorkshire, especially in the North Riding, the witch-as-hare is a frequent and much told tale, containing almost always the same elements: the witch, transformed into a hare, is pursued by the local hunt, generally, and is wounded in some way, escaping into the cottage of the witch through a crack in the door, or key-hole. The huntsmen enter the cottage soon after, and recognize the witch as hare by the wound on the corresponding part of her body, or broken limb, which remains after the resumption of her normal form. Another tale, often told about the same witch, is that of the seemingly invincible hare seen in the fields or causing damage to new plantations, and which has survived all attempts to shoot it. Recourse is then had to a silver bullet, a method reminiscent of the folkway of dealing with werewolves. Interestingly, however, the silver bullet appears not to be used for witch cats. The principle of recognition found in the witch hare motif plays an important part in the various other metamorphosis themes. For instance in the witch-as-cat motif, the witch is generally recognized in her resumed human form by a missing hand, where a paw was severed. This particular theme is used dramatically by Algernon Blackwood in *The Empty Sleeve*.[7] Nevertheless, despite the ubiquity of most of the shapeshifting themes, there seems to be as yet no satisfactory way of accounting for such universality of motif. The witch hare is found frequently in 19th century Yorkshire, yet not apparently in Essex, a county notorious for the number of witches tried and executed in earlier periods, in comparison with other English counties. It also occurs in North Wales: for instance at Bedd Gelert, the local witch, Beti Ifan was supposed to transform into a hare, much to the annoyance of an unsuccessful local poacher there, who was unable to shoot the hare. A wise man advised him to place mountain ash (rowan wood) and vervain under his gunstock and gave him a written charm to read out backwards whenever he saw the witch hare, whereupon he would see her in her true form and shoot her in the leg. The poacher later entered Beti's cottage to find her sitting by the fire, with blood streaming from her leg. However, there is another side to this tale, which may well be of greater significance within the total context of witch making: both the poacher and the village cobbler used to tease Beti unmercifully, promising her food when in fact they had no intention of giving it to her.[8] This relationship of oppressor and oppressed is not uncommon in the sociology of witchcraft cases. It is likely that the tale had originated with a factual relationship, which was invested with a largely fictional and pejorative (to the witch) motif, allowing a reasonable justification for any subsequent actions on the part of the poacher. If Beti were to be believed a witch hare, his counteractions could be considered legitimate. This will be seen to be a recurring theme throughout many of the following tales.

Yorkshire material from the 19th century reveals many stories recorded concerning metamorphosis, told in direct relation to an identified person. However, Yorkshire has largely been ignored by modern historians and social anthropologists with an interest in witchcraft: there is a large corpus of material which reflects folk fiction, and folk belief in witchcraft and magic. In order to illustrate the prevalence of 19th century witches and their relationship with the animal world, some figures may help to provide the background. In the North Riding, of twenty-eight named and located witches, only eight were specified as being capable of shape-shifting. Of fifteen, named and located, in the West Riding, only one, and of nine in the East Riding, none. It must be stressed that there were many other tales in which the witch is not identified. In 1961 a tale was collected in the East Riding, that told of a witch who transformed herself into a fox, was chased by the hunt and was later recognized by a broken leg.[9]

It would appear that the ability to metamorphose was not automatically attributed to a witch. Indeed examination of other, primary sources confirms this.

The Calvert MS., a substantial collection of folklore from the North Riding, was completed in 1823 by a Kirkbymoorside man. It provides a list of witches, and even a key by which to identify their individual specialities. Different symbols were provided for a witch who changed into a hare, or into a cat. Of this additional number of twenty-one witches, six could change into a hare, four into a cat, while only one could perform both transformations.[10]

The belief in such shapeshifting is well illustrated by a case study of a village on the North Yorkshire moors.[11] In the 19th century belief in witchcraft was common in Goathland, as in other similar villages. Stories persisted about Nanny Peirson, and have continued to do so. There is some confusion about how many generations of Nanny Peirson were considered to have been witches. Peirson is a very common Goathland name, and research in parish registers reveals large and complex families. Not surprisingly there is reluctance to claim relationship with any of the Nanny Peirsons, although there is evidence of belief in the witch and her powers up to the present day. The Calvert MS mentions Nanny Peirson but does not attribute to her the ability to metamorphose. One account concerns Nanny Peirson as witch hare.[12] The local squire of Goathland at the beginning of last century was also called Peirson. He had a daughter who wished to marry a young farmer, but the squire favoured an older, richer man whom the daughter disliked. This older man, fearing that the two young people might elope, sought the help of Nanny Peirson, who bewitched the girl so that she was unable to walk. The young farmer then went to the wise man of Scarborough, some distance away, who showed him a mirror in which he saw Nanny Peirson. The wise man told him he must massage the girl's legs with some drops of the witch's blood, a seemingly impossible task. He returned to Goathland, and armed himself with a gun and some silver shot. He lay in wait and when he saw a hare he shot it with the silver bullet, and obtained some drops of the witch's blood in this manner, since the hare was the witch transformed. Nanny Peirson herself did recover. This story may well be based upon real events, but departs into folk fiction with the witch-hare motif. Another tale of the witch in hare form was related by a Goathland woman in 1926 and concerned a man called Stanforth. He was working on the railway at Beckhole, just outside the village, when he saw a hare on the line. He immediately threw his spanner at it, striking it on the leg, and when he later returned to Goathland, Nanny Peirson was in bed with a broken leg. Stanforth himself lived from 1815–99, according to parish registers, and the tale was related by the daughter of his friend.[13]

From recent fieldwork in the village, there is evidence that belief in the witch hare and the witch cat still survives.[11] Many people can identify the house where the witch had lived and knew tales about her. For example, a white hare used to sit in the pinfold, watching, and was considered to be the witch. One day this animal was injured, and the witch was discovered to be ill at home. The taleteller then asked this researcher what would have happened to Nanny Peirson had the hare died. Another informant told of a lame black cat, seen regularly in the churchyard and the house. This cat was believed to be Nanny Peirson, and thought to influence the electric lights in the house. She was also seen as a tortoise-shell cat, in which form she had acted as a good omen, and had eventually disappeared without trace. All this had occurred within the last twenty-five years.

Perhaps the nature of hares and cats might throw some light on the reasons for their role in popular myth making. It is unlikely, however, that one will ever account for the relationship of witches and particular animals. Certain features of the hare provoke interest: for instance, unusual gynaecological aspects, double pregnancies, males giving birth; its shriek is disturbing in its resemblance to the cry of a child, it displays odd behaviour at certain times. These may all be contributory to its part in folklore. Nevertheless one cannot ignore some other, more prosaic reasons for some of the tales: in some parts of the country stuffed hares were used as scare-crows in cornfields. Such an animal would thus be impervious to shot.[14] However, this can never account for the proliferation of similar motifs throughout the centuries and in many different areas. It is known that the hare was considered an unlucky animal to meet in mediaeval times. A middle-English poem reflects this fear:

The one it's ill luck to meet
The one that makes people flee
The one that makes people shudder
The creature it's taboo to name.[15]

A similar pejorative and interesting remark was made about the nature of haremeat by Robert Burton:

> Hare is a black meat, melancholy and hard of digestion, it breeds incubus often eaten and causeth fearful dreams.[16]

One other note of interest is that 'pussy' is a nickname given to both cats and hares, as is the less familiar malkin, or mawkin. The familiar of one of the witches in Macbeth was called Gray-malkin.

In accounts of shapeshifting by witches after the witch trials period, there appears to have been no wish to take further action against the witch, once she had been exposed as such. Obviously there was no longer any legal action permissible, thus the folk methods of counteraction had to be sufficient. The principle of recognition was cathartic in itself. In other recorded cases of witch-craft at this later date, specific measures were often taken against a suspected witch. This may well indicate a distinction between folk fiction and folk belief. Indeed, during the trials themselves, there appears to be no case of a witch being brought to trial on the sole accusation of metamorphosis. It is often a major point of the prosecution, but there is generally some other reason for the original presentment. In later instances, there may well be an element of fear of possible retaliation by the witch. For example, in the latter half of the last century, the hunt chased a witch hare, Peg Humphrey, in the Bilsdale area. She was bitten by a dog, and recognition came about through the wound. However, the witch cursed the owner of the dog, and soon after this man fell from his horse and died.[17]

Animal as agent

Animals have often been used as magical symbols, totems or catalytic agents, and continue to be so used in many parts of the world. Animal sacrifice, recorded from biblical times, is an act of magic designed to secure the favour of the god, or other all-powerful-being, worshipped. In later centuries, when witchcraft beliefs were legitimized by law, witches were believed (on the Continent mainly) to meet in covens and worship the devil in the form of a large black cat or goat. In such instances human form is subsumed by that of an animal. The animal sacrifice in many cases is a direct substitute for that of a human. But when the Devil is symbolized by an animal, such as a cat, then his characteristics, his persona, are transferred to this animal form. The difficulty is to decide whether the notion of evil was already associated with certain animals, hence the symbolism; or whether the personification of evil by an animal ensured the subsequent association of the idea. Cats, for instance, still retain an aura of mystery and unholiness.

On another level, animals have played a part in magical activity by carrying the element of magic. In this way animals act as a catalyst, or as an agent bearing the wishes of the magician, such as the witch or wise man. Examples of this are 'familiars' believed to obey their owner, generally a witch. Edward Fairfax noted in detail the nature of the familiars of some of the Fewston witches. For instance, that of the widow, Margaret Waite:

> Her familiar spirit is a deformed thing with many feet, black of colour, rough with hair, the bigness of a cat, the name of it unknown . . .

(He later spoke of it as a cat); that of the very old widow, Jennet Dibble, a black cat called Gibbe which had attended her for forty years or more; and that of her daughter Margaret Thorpe, which was a familiar in 'the shape of a bird, yellow of colour, the bigness of a crow' and named Tewhit.[18] These were supposed to obey their mistresses at all times and be the purveyors of omens, foreknowledge and other aspects of bewitchment of the Fairfax children. Some three hundred years later a similar belief was recorded in Essex. In 1928, a Horseheath resident told how a dark stranger had called on a woman nearby called Redcap, (who died in 1926) and asked her to sign her name in a book, whereupon he promised her she would have five creatures to obey her. Shortly afterwards she was seen with a rat, cat, toad, ferret and mouse, which were assumed to have been her familiars.[19]

In 19th-century Yorkshire the incidence of recorded material concerning familiars is not high. In the 1820s a woman who ran a small shop in Skipton, and who was called Kilnsey Nan, claimed that her guinea pig was her familiar.[20] This may well have been a ploy to increase her custom. In only one other recorded tale does a familiar appear, and it is an atypical tale, allied to the witch-hare tale type. A new plantation in Cleveland was suffering damage from hares, and although most of them had been dealt with, one hare was persistent. Recourse was had to the wise man of Stokesley, John Wrightson, who advised on the use of silver shot. As the hare was shot, an old woman carding wool some distance away flung up her hands crying out that they had shot her familiar spirit, and died. Both sources for this tale stress that the woman had not been out of her cottage, in an attempt to show the distinction between animal metamorphosis and belief in familiars.[21]

In Yorkshire it seems that animals or parts thereof were important in the counteraction to witchcraft. These measures were often variations on a central theme: an object such as an animal heart was stuck with needles and pins, and burnt in a fire, often at midnight and often accompanied by verbal formulae or biblical verses. There were different methods, such as burying an animal, or part of it, in a bewitched farm. Some examples may illustrate the activity which took place, or was believed to, in Yorkshire and other areas, in order to counteract the effects of witchcraft. A farm was bewitched at Appleton Wiske in the North Riding, or so the farmer believed, and he consulted a wise man who showed him a mirror in which he would see the witch responsible. The countermeasure taken against her was a pigeon's heart stuck with pins and thrown onto a fire at midnight, with all house doors and windows firmly barred.[22] The methodology here was believed to destroy the power of the witch and stop any further harm issuing from such power. On another occasion a black cat and a black cock were roasted on a rowanwood fire, similarly an oxheart was stuck with pins and roasted, as was a heifer's heart, stuck with 9 rows of new pins and new needles. A sick woman recovered after the destruction of a sheep's heart stuck with pins which was found underneath her window.[23] The origin of such methods remains obscure, but it is certainly linked to the idea of sticking pins into an effigy of a selected person to cause them harm. The use of an effigy is a logical substitution for the real object of the wish to injure or kill. An animal heart is closer in many ways to that of a human being than an inanimate replica created by man. The use of animal heart also embodies an element of sacrifice. One may question the origins of such features as the number of pins and needles required, or why they had to be new, but it is unlikely that any explanations, or attempts at such, could throw any further light on the real nature of witchcraft counteractions. Burning an object in order to make the witch reveal herself is a standard folk theme (Stith-Thompson, G 257.1).

In other instances the animal formed an essential part of the magical countermeasure. For example, a North Riding farm was suffering considerable losses of livestock. The farmer thought it must be bewitched and went to the wise man of Scarborough for advice. To end the misfortune a sheep was cut up and buried in the four corners of the farm.[24] Similarly a farm near Barmby Moor in the East Riding was losing cattle, and so the farmer consulted the local wise man George Wales, known to be a religious man. Wales ordered all the farm hands out of sight, and with the farmer's help he dug a pit in the gateway of the farm and buried a young foal. This was followed by some kind of incantation, and the nailing up of horseshoes.[25] About 1840 another East Riding wise man from Haisthorpe diagnosed a case of witchcraft at Kirkburn. He held a ceremony at midnight at which he said verses from the Bible, offered to call forth the devil and buried a black hen in the garden of the house concerned.[26]

This element of sacrifice may or may not have been recognized as such by the participants. It is noticeable that, in most of the recorded cases of such counteractions in the last century, the advice of a wise man was first sought. It is impossible to know if the same methods would have been used without such counsel, that is, whether such knowledge was general or whether it was restricted to certain members of a community. If such remedies involving the use of animals were commonly known this would have different implications from a situation of restricted knowledge. If most people in the community were familiar with the possible methods of counteracting magic and witchcraft using animals, the conclusion might be drawn that a certain common heritage based on agricultural and other occupational history caused such common knowledge. It would seem also that this had persisted to a much later date than the current orthodoxy generally assumes. Such a common body of knowledge derived from a shared, essentially rural background. The industrial experiences was not so overwhelming that it destroyed the heritage of those brought up with animals and whose livelihoods were inextricably tied to the seasons and to the health of their animals. Furthermore, if such knowledge were commonplace, then those who practised witchcraft, or were believed to do so, would also know of the countermeasures. In which case the counteraction itself was essentially a ritual part of the then current pattern of social behaviour, as well as a method to negate witchcraft. Thus an enactment of some kind of ritual counteraction was an expected act. This is not always the case in other societies which accept with fatality the power of a witch curse. The position of wise men is interesting in this respect. By consulting a wise man and acting upon his advice, the client was justified in his subsequent actions however anti-social these might be. If he had acted independently, one questions whether such actions would have been considered legitimate even by his contemporaries. Basic mob retaliation against alleged witches, such as ducking, which occurred several times in 19th-century England, may have been the result of lack of consultation with a wise man, and a limitation in perceived counteraction. It is interesting that no recorded instance of ducking exists for Yorkshire in the last century.

The role of the animal which itself has been harmed, in destroying the power of the ill-doer, is interesting. As late as 1890 at Sible Hedingham in Essex, an old labourer was accused of bewitching a cartload of hay. His words were to the effect that the carter would not get far with his load. Further along the road the horse fell down and had to be destroyed, but not until the carter had cut a piece of horseflesh and burned it in order to harm the supposed witch.[27] Thus the animal itself formed the countermeasure. In another way, a goose on a farm in Goathland, North Riding, which had suffered from the powers of the witch Nanny Peirson finally caused the witch's supposed downfall. The farmer's wife regularly gave Nanny Peirson a jug of milk, and was beginning to resent this act of charity. She was advised to put some holy water in the bottom of the jug in order to curtail the witch's powers. Peirson took the jug whereupon the goose flew at her, knocking the jug from her hand, and spilling the holy water over the witch, thus allegedly stopping her activities.[28] Both tales illustrate the notion that the harm can be reversed to the detriment of the wrong-doer. Animals were seen as a powerful agent in sympathetic magic.

Animal as receiver

In the witch trials of the 16th and 17th centuries one of the most common charges levied at English witches was that of bewitching farm livestock, or, even more anti-socially, the one cow or other animal on which a family depended. In Yorkshire several women were brought to trial accused of bewitching horses, cattle, and other livestock. Sometimes the animals were sick, but on some occasions they died. However many other people, both men and women, were taken to court for healing animals through allegedly arcane means. For instance, James Sykes of Guiseley, was presented in 1590; he admitted curing horses by writing prayers on paper and hanging the paper in their manes.[29] Wise men could give advice about a lost cow but it was often the client of the wise man who was taken to court.[30]

Animals were central to the livelihood of most working people at this period. Family life was bound up with animals to a greater degree than can perhaps be imagined now. Thus, the sickness and death of an animal was a catastrophe to a family and household. Bewitchment of stock, then, was a direct attack on the well-being of that family. Little wonder that countermeasures were taken, and the wish to have revenge on the supposed witch was taken to the furthest possible limits. Veterinary science at this period is hard to assess, but it is likely that amateur cow doctors were as effective as any others. However, it is also likely that many people would have had just as much faith in magical methods. The close domestic relationship between animals and humans made such close magical links inevitable.

Belief that animals could be bewitched survived until very late. In about 1887 a farmer at Wrenthorpe in Yorkshire suffered losses of pigs and cows. His friend told him that someone had put the evil eye on them and advised him to make a straw effigy of the suspected woman and burn it on the kitchen fire, so that the smoke went up the chimney. As the effigy burnt so would the troubles disappear. This tale was told in 1965.[31] An earlier tale from Goathland concerned John Wrightson again, the well-known wise man of Stokesley. A farmer named Collinson had been brought to the verge of ruin by what he considered to be witchcraft. He had lost all his animals except one calf when he went to consult Wrightson, who sent him back to Goathland with instructions to make secure all the doors and windows of his house, by which time the wise man himself would come to Goathland. (It is interesting to note that, over the moorland roads, the distance between these two would be about 58 miles, quite a way to travel.) At midnight Wrightson read out extracts from various books, and told Collinson to kill any animals which appeared in his field. A toad appeared, Collinson killed it and asked the wise man to make sure that the witch was henceforth unable to bear sun or wind on her skin. The implication is that the toad was the witch in transformation; yet she was not killed by the killing of the toad. It is possible that the tale-teller did not consider this important. The significant point was that the toad was the carrier of the witch's evil-doing, be it a familiar or a witch-toad. Henceforth, Nanny Peirson was always seen to cover herself up, to be beyond the reach of wind or sun,[32] but it seems that her activities continued; about 1890 a Goathland man believed that she had bewitched his pigs, and he refused to go and look at them. When he did go to see in the morning, they were all dead.[33]

John Wrightson, wise man of Stokesley, called himself a cow doctor. There is substantial evidence for this, evidence which establishes him as a real person, not just a legendary and convenient figure in folklore. In 1807 he voted in the Poll at York.

He also appears in the Stokesley Churchwarden's Account Book. In addition to both these sources in which he is called 'cow doctor' he also had a trade card printed which read as follows:

> J. Wrightson, Cow Doctor, A Seventh Son, Stokesley, begs leave to acquaint the public that those who are afflicted with any kind of inward disorders, white swellings, scurvy, Evil, Itch, Jaundice, shortness of breath or any kinds of soreness, may be relieved by sending their water. Likewise any cattle that do not thrive he can be of service to them. Apply to his own house or at....

He was much involved then with animal healing of any kind. From the recorded tales about him it seems that he was very successful. An envelope still in existence is inscribed with a cow cure on one side, and 'john Wrightson, to the care of Mr Richard Wilson, innkeeper, Stokesley' on the reverse. The cure is this

> ky meal cake made with hor own water, 3 small needles stuck in it an then burnt. in thee fire at 12 o'clock nig(ht) a horse show read Hot[34]

This is not, then, a medical cure, but a charm designed perhaps to rid a cow of witchcraft. The same elements of needles, the time of night, and burning the object again occur. Atkinson also quotes from a similarly incomplete cow cure, in similar style, which may also have been from Wrightson.[35]

It is probable that John Wrightson, and many others of his sort, combined genuine veterinary ability with certain other features, such as traditional magical lore, and strong business acumen. This does not in any way detract from the very valuable role he fulfilled in his own community. He was probably astute enough to know when to use the magical and when not, or when to employ both. There are few recorded cases of suspected witchcraft which resolved themselves without recourse to a wise man. This reinforces the possibility that such people provided a method of legitimizing actions which might otherwise be considered socially hostile. If they also possessed real veterinary knowledge, curing whenever possible, they increased their own prestige in the community.

The psychology underlying charms for human sickness is explicable to some extent, but not so for animal sickness. Men could naturally understand what was said or written in most cases, especially biblical phraseology. Anything which appeared to add a certain complexity to the cure could perhaps help in their recovery. If they had faith in the powers of the wise man, and if they had faith in magical cures, then such charms were indispensable. In the case of animals, however, there is greater difficulty in accounting for such charms. The animal's owner could appreciate the nature of the charm and perhaps be impressed by the wise man's methodology. There are three possible justifications. Firstly, the wise man might be astute enough to employ magical charms only when he was certain that the animal would recover, and thus increase his reputation. Secondly, he might use such charms only in cases which he could not cure, and could thus claim that the witchcraft was too strong and was the reason for the death of the animal. There is little evidence to support this view, it is inconsistent with the extant material, but it is a view held by some authorities.[36] Thirdly, one cannot discount the fact that the wise man may well have had a strong belief in the efficacy of magical charms and methods. The fact that so many methods of counteracting witchcraft, curing animals etc., share similar essential elements may suggest genuine faith in them. Such faith might well be the result of the repetition of a behaviour pattern, constructed over a considerable period of time.

Animals then fulfil significant functions in the sphere of witchcraft and other magical activity. They have done so for many centuries, as the earliest archaeological finds indicate. Such close association between man and the animal world existed until very recent times in many western, technologically-based societies. In these societies industrial experience began to be that of the majority of the population, but not all. It seems, from recent field studies, that, for those people whose lives are still closely linked with the animal world, some of the beliefs and themes recorded here are not so remote from their own experiences as might generally be assumed. Yet the more that such societies remove themselves from a dependency on the health and well-being of animals and the facts of agricultural life, the more will such folk themes become isolated and total fictions. It is likely that this will indeed happen. The knowledge of animal life is already limited to a small minority; it remains to be seen whether industrial societies will reduce or increase this minority. In either case it is probable that the assumptions about animal behaviour and the nature of the relationship between men and animals will change. In a society which holds a magical world view the functions of animals within that view is clear. It will be interesting to note how a technological society deals with those aspects of the animal world which may not fit in with an industrial philosophy. Sufficient material survives to show how, in previous periods, men saw the role of animals within their own belief system.

SHAPE CHANGING

The Snake Woman in Japanese Myth and Legend

CARMEN BLACKER

In Genesis Chapter 3, verses 14 and 15, it is written, 'And the Lord said unto the serpent, because thou hast done this.... I will put enmity between thee and the woman, and between thy seed and her seed. It shall bruise thy head and thou shall bruise his heel.' This last enigmatic sentence is rendered in the New English Bible, 'They shall strike at your head, and you shall strike at their heel.'

My intention in this paper is to explore the manner in which, in many parts of the world and particularly in the Far East, this commandment of God has been ignored. We find on the contrary a close and mysterious identification between serpents and women. The snake who appears in shape-changed form as a woman, and who lives for years in the human community with her true nature unrecognized, or the woman who finds herself possessed by a snake lover, are figures appearing in the mythology of much of Europe and Asia, but very prominently in China and Japan.

In its various appearances throughout the world, however, the figure of the snake-woman is seen to refract in a curious manner into extremes of good and evil. In some parts of the world she appears as the Enemy, the monstrous antagonist whom the god has to overcome before order can be established in the world, a figure representing chaos and death. The *drakaina* or she-dragon in Greece, variously called Python or Lamia or Echidna, whom Apollo had to slay before he could open the sacred place of Delphi, the serpent antagonists of Zeus and Perseus and Heracles, all carry the evil, monstrous face of this complex image, and the waters whence the creature emerges represent chaos and death.[1]

In the Far East, on the other hand, we see its contrary face.

Here the dragon is not the monstrous destroyer found in our own tradition, but a majestic and benevolent beast, whose close association with the element of water turns him into a dispenser of fertility in a wet rice growing community. He becomes a potential source of disaster, through flood and storm, only when wrongly treated. So also with the snake woman. She too is found connected with water, with the sea, lakes or pools, and her appearances in myth and legend are those of a bringer of enhanced life rather than of death.

The tradition of a miraculous world of bliss and wealth and power beneath the water is an ancient one in Japan, deriving only in part from China. At the bottom of the sea, or beneath the waters of the lake, there stands a magical palace, shimmering with walls of coral and jade, doors of crystal, and with carpets of silk and sealskin laid on the floors. This is Ryūgū or the Palace of the Dragon. The Dragon King Ryūjin, however, whose domain it is said to be, is seldom to be found there. The only inhabitant of the underwater paradise is a mysteriously beautiful lady, sometimes described as the daughter of the sea god. This lady welcomes the guest, fisherman or woodcutter, from the human world, marries him, treats him to a blissful interval of time in the submarine Venusberg, and when the time comes for him to return to his own world bestows on him a magical gift of power and wealth.

This lady is at the same time a snake. Most of the legends make her *shōtai* or true form to be that of a snake, her appearance as a woman being a transformation only. The numerous legends concerning this figure can be distinguished to advantage in Hiroko Ikeda's excellent *Type and Motif Index of Japanese Folk Literature*.[2] Here I propose to concentrate on one particular group of tales: those which describe a marriage between the supernatural shape-changed snake and a human being. These stories, which are known in general as *shinkontan* or divine marriage tales, I believe to be the residue of a ritual of a once flourishing cult of shamanistic kind which has long been lost and fragmented.

Stories in which a human being marries a supernatural animal in human disguise are frequent in Japanese folklore. A human girl may become the bride of a horse, a monkey, a frog, a dog or a snake. Likewise a man may take to wife, in all innocence of her true identity, a bird, a fish, a fox, and again a snake. In both cases the animal prototype is in all probability the snake, the other creatures occurring later as substitutes. The precise relationship between the snake-wife and the snake-bridegroom tales has not yet been satisfactorily investigated, but I hope to suggest that they represent different stages of the residue of the lost religious cult.[3]

Let us look first at the snake-wife tales. These can be conveniently divided into two broad categories. First, there are the stories in which a human man visits the magical snake-lady in her palace at the bottom of the sea, and returns bearing a gift of power from the submarine elysium. Second, we have those stories in which a snake-woman emerges from her water world to marry a human man, but returns to the water when he breaks a taboo.

The tales which describe the visit of a man to the water palace have a wide distribution all over Japan. The oldest recorded version comes in the 8th-century *Tango Fūdoki*, a gazetteer of local history and legends of the province of Tango. Known as *Urashima Tarō*, the story is well known to every Japanese schoolchild, and to anyone who has read a book of Japanese fairytales. It describes how the handsome fisher boy Urashima was fishing one night in his boat when he caught a large five-coloured turtle. By morning the turtle had vanished, and in its place sat a beautiful woman who invited him to visit her home at the bottom of the sea. There Urashima found a marvellous palace of coral and crystal, and every delight that the mind could conceive. He married the lady and lived with her for three blissful years. Then he began to feel homesick and begged the lady to let him go back to see his family. The lady gave him a box to take with him, telling him that if he wished to return to her he must never open it. The turtle guided him back to his native village, where he found to his horror that he recognized no one, and that the place was utterly changed. He realized that a supernatural lapse of time had occurred, as with our own rash visitors to fairyland inside hollow hills, and that in fact not three years but three centuries had passed. In his despair he opened the box. At once his hair turned snow white, his skin fell into wrinkles and he withered away to dust.[4]

In this 8th-century version the snake nature of the lady is not stressed, but in later versions it is made more explicit and the magical gift more prominent. The tales often begin with the man throwing into the sea a bundle of wood he had gathered on the mountain. In the polar tension which exists between mountain and water, an ordinary bundle of wood from the mountain becomes a precious rarity at the bottom of the sea. The lady therefore rises to the surface of the water to thank the man for his kind gift. She takes him back to her palace, where he sees the wood neatly stacked at the gate, marries him, and when the time comes for him to go home presents him with a magical gift. This treasure, provided he follows the simple rules she explains to him, will bring him everything his heart could desire. Always human frailty proves unequal to the supernatural blessing. The man forgets to carry out the simple rules, and his riches and the magic gift vanish at once.[5]

A good example is the tale known as *Hanatare-kozō*, or Boy Snotty-nose, included by Yanagita Kunio in his collection *Nihon Mukashibanashi*. Here, as in several other versions, the magic gift is an ugly small boy.

Once upon a time there was an old woodcutter who every day went to cut wood on the mountain and bring it down to the town to sell. One day he couldn't sell any of it. He tramped all over the town, but no one wanted to buy a single bundle. At last he was so tired that he sat down on the bridge over the river and dropped the wood, handful by handful, into the river. Soon the most beautiful lady he had ever seen rose to the surface, holding in her arms an ugly little boy with a snotty dribbling nose. She said she was the daughter of the dragon god, who was so pleased with the kind present of wood that he had sent in return a present of the ugly boy. All the old man had to do was to give the boy some shrimp salad every day, and he would give the old man anything he wanted. The old man took the child home and fed him on shrimps as instructed, and soon found that he only had to ask for something—rice, vegetables, fish—for the boy to make a sound as though he were blowing his nose and there stood the thing the man wanted. Soon he had a wonderful house and servants and delicious food every day, and at last could think of nothing more that he wanted. Then he found it a nuisance to get the shrimps every day, and told the boy that he had no further need of him. The boy ran out of the house, and at once the splendid mansion and servants vanished, and the old man found himself back in his hovel.[6]

So much then for our first group of snake-wife tales. Let us now turn to the stories where the snake-woman leaves her water world to marry a man. These frequently begin with a man saving a snake from being killed, or buying it back from some boys who are teasing it and setting it free. That night a mysteriously beautiful woman comes to his house, begging a night's lodging as she has lost her way. He takes her in, falls passionately in love with her and marries her. She becomes his wife on one condition: that he does not look into the room when she is giving birth to their child. For several months they are blissfully happy, and the wife brings luck and prosperity to the house. When the time for her confinement arrives, she retires to a parturition hut. The man cannot resist peeping through the cracks of the wall to watch, and sees to his horror that she has become a snake, and is slithering and sliding about the hut. When she realizes that she has been seen and the taboo broken, the woman returns to her water world and the luck of the house ceases from that day.[7]

Some of these tales, which again have a wide distribution throughout Japan, have an extra episode in which the snake gives one of her eyeballs for the child she leaves behind to lick as nourishment. In some versions both eyes are required for this purpose. The snake therefore asks for a bell to be cast in the nearby Buddhist temple whose tolling will tell her the time of sunset which in her blindness she would not otherwise know. But this ending seems to be excrescence added to the main tale to account for the making of certain famous bells, such as that of the Buddhist temple of Miidera.[8]

This story has a remarkable number of parallels all over the world. The Chinese have numerous examples, one of the best of which is Arthur Waley's translation of the T'ang story *Mrs. White*. In Europe we have it in the tale told by Gervase of Tilbury of Raymond, the lord of a castle in Provence, who was riding by the banks of a river when he met a lady of rare beauty who addressed him by name. He then, in Hartland's words, made improper overtures to her. These she declined, but consented to marry him on one condition: that he should never look upon her naked. Should he ever do so, all the blessings and prosperity which she would bring him would vanish. They married, and every earthly felicity followed, wealth, strength, devoted friends, children of great beauty. But one day Raymond came back from hunting and determined to see his wife in her bath. He tore aside the curtain, and saw that she was a snake. Instantly she vanished, and the family was thereafter ruined.[9]

In later versions of the tale the lady is known as Melusina, Countess of Lusignan, and the taboo imposed is that she should not be seen on Saturdays. When Raymond violates this taboo and bursts into her room on a Saturday, he finds her, as in the earlier version, in her bath, with her lower half turned into a serpent's tail.

Hartland in his *Science of Fairy Tales* makes this theme a sub-type of his Swan Maiden stories. Here the main type describes how a man comes upon a group of ladies bathing in a pool, their clothes left on the bank. The man steals one of the robes and finds it to be made of the finest feathers. The lady begs him to give it back to her, as without it she cannot return to her proper home. When he refuses, she consents to become his wife, to leave him some time later when she succeeds in recovering her feather robe from the chest in which it is hidden. At once she becomes a bird—the different versions tell of a swan, a crane or a dove—and flies away.

There is an excellent example of the Swan Maiden story in the Japanese tradition. Its most celebrated version is probably the Nō play *Hagoromo*, the Feather Robe, though the oldest recorded version again goes back to the 8th century.

A fisherman discovers a beautiful robe of feathers on the sea shore. A distraught lady appears and tells him that unless he gives it back to her she cannot return to her celestial realm. He agrees to give the robe back to her on condition that she dances for him. There on the seashore under a line of pine trees, she performs for him a marvellous magical dance, and on receiving the robe of feathers flies away into the sky.

Hiroko Ikeda, in classifying the *Hagoromo* legend under the type *Tennin-nyōbo*, celestial wives, makes the interesting observation that the legend often attaches itself to lakes and ponds. Likewise in Hartland's fascinatingly numerous examples, from the Arabian Nights, from Sweden, Russia, Hungary and the aboriginal tribes of Guiana, the hero always finds the girls bathing in a pool or lake, the feather robe which give them their bird transformation having been left on the bank while they swim. Here again therefore, the element of water appears prominently in the story, suggesting that despite the feathers, we are not so far removed from the snake woman of the water world.[10]

Before we leave the snake woman in her lake and pass to the

snake lover, a brief consideration would be relevant of the curious group of legends known as *wankashi-densetsu*, bowl-lending legends.

Certain lakes, pools and caves were believed, according to these legends, to lead downwards to the miraculous world of Ryūgū. They were guarded by a benevolent Warden or Guardian (*nushi*) who was usually the snake woman. This Warden would obligingly lend bowls, cups or trays of superior red lacquer to anyone who wished to borrow them for a party or celebration. In Hyōgo prefecture for example there used to be a celebrated bowl-lending pool. All one had to do was to go there the previous night, state the number of bowls required, and the next morning one would find them neatly set out on a rock in the middle of the pool. In the mountains near Toyama there was a bowl-lending lake in which the service was even quicker. One stood on the shore and stated the number of bowls required, and immediately there would float to the surface of the water, and presently be washed ashore at one's feet, bowls of superior lacquer exactly to the number ordered. In Yamanashi prefecture there was another such pool where the guardian required the order in writing. One wrote him a letter stating the number of bowls required, and the next day they would be found neatly ranged on the edge of the pool.

But always it was necessary to return the borrowed vessels as soon as one had finished with them, in perfect condition and exactly to the number lent. One bowl returned damaged or short, and the Warden would never again lend a single vessel. At the sites of these legends human frailty has once more proved unequal to the gifts from the water world. Always, sometime in the past, someone broke a cup or refused to return a bowl, so that the lending as always ceased. Yanagita Kunio tells us, indeed, that several times he came across a family who proudly preserved a bowl of costly red lacquer as a chalice from Ryūgū. It was a bowl which their ancestors had on one occasion borrowed and refused to return to its rightful owner.[11]

In these legends it seems that the communication between the human world and the world of water is a step less direct. The two realms are gradually drawing apart. No one is invited to visit the palace at the bottom of the lake, and the former magical gift—the inexhaustible bag of rice or the magic wishing child—has become a mere empty vessel. Power was perhaps originally contained in this vessel, but it now stands for no more than a useful receptacle. The gift, moreover, is no longer given, but lent for a short season only.

Let us not forget, however, that the motif of a cup or bowl borrowed from the Other World is remarkably widespread throughout the world. In England we have an example in the huge cauldron which used to be in the vestry of Frensham church, and which Aubrey in his *Natural History of Surrey* tells us was originally lent by the fairies of Borough Hill nearby. Hartland too in his *Science of Fairy Tales* has an interesting chapter on the cups which are not merely borrowed and kept from their supernatural owners, but deliberately snatched away. Of all the articles stolen from fairyland in European legend, he writes, by far the most frequent is the cup or drinking horn. Many such vessels are still preserved, or were at the time when Hartland wrote, of which the Luck of Edenhall and the Oldenburg Horn are the most celebrated.[12]

We now pass to the second category of divine marriage tales, the *hebi-muko* or snake-bridegroom stories. These have been the subject of considerable investigation by Japanese folklorists, whose attention was first arrested by the extraordinarily wide distribution of the tale. Examples have been found all over the main island, where as many as 130 different versions have been collected, from all over Shikoku and Kyushu, and even in many of the Ryūkyū Islands.[13]

The tale is first found associated with the Miwa Shrine, purporting to account for the semi-divine ancestry of the priestly family in whose charge the shrine lay. Its oldest version is recorded in the 8th-century chronicle *Kojiki*, Chapter 66, which recounts how the girl Ikutamayorihime was visited mysteriously night after night by an unknown lover who got her with child. Her parents, anxious to discover his identity, instructed the girl to sew a thread of hemp to the hem of his garment, and to follow it the next morning to wherever it might lead. The girl did as she was instructed, to find that the thread passed through the keyhole of the door, and led straight to the shrine of the deity of Mt. Miwa. They accordingly knew that the girl's lover had been the Miwa deity Omononushi in snake form. The girl later bore a child, who became the ancestor of the family serving the shrine.

Another version of this snake lover tale appears in the 13th century work *Heike Monogatari*. Here the figure of the snake appears much more powerfully than in the bald *Kojiki* legend. The girl follows the thread for miles over the entire province until she sees it disappear inside a cave. She calls into the depths of the cave that she wishes to behold her lover's face. A voice from within answers that were she to do so her heart would burst with fright. But the girl still begs to see him, so that at last there crawls out of the cave a monstrous serpent, quivering all over, with a needle stuck in its throat which is slowly killing it. So horrific is its appearance that the girl faints at the sight. But the child which she eventually bore the creature grew to be an enormous boy called Daida who in due course became the greatest warrior in Kyushu.[14]

Another version, which Seki Keigo labels Type C, describes how the girl and her parents follow the thread to a cave, and overhear the snake say to its mother, 'She may have killed me with that iron needle of hers, but at least I've got her with child.' 'Rubbish', its mother replies, 'human beings are quite clever enough to know that all they have to do in a case like this is to have a bath of sweet flags.' The girl without more ado goes home and gets into a bath of sweet flags, whereupon several small snakes come streaming out of her body.

So much for the *hebi-muko* or snake bridegroom stories. One more type of legend remains to be mentioned however before we pass on to the possible connection of these stories with a shamanistic ritual. These are the *hitobashira* or human pillar tales, again found scattered over a large area of the country and in many places still believed to be true. Here the woman is not the mistress of the serpent but its victim. She is buried alive as a propitiatory offering to the serpent presiding over a river or lake.

A dam or dyke has been broken so many times by raging floodwater that the villagers realise that a sacrifice is necessary if it is ever to be successfully repaired. Sometimes a passing traveller was seized for this dreadful purpose, each shrine having its own rules for determining what kind of person should be captured. Some specified a man, some a woman. Some required the first person to pass through the village to be seized, some the second or third. The hapless victim was always drowned or buried alive under the dyke, which needless to say from that moment remained intact. The victim was afterwards worshipped as a divinity.

A celebrated example of this legend concerned the woman Tsuru and her thirteen year old son Ichitarō. A dyke controlling the water of the ricefields belonging to the Usa Hachiman shrine in Kyushu was constantly collapsing. A man named Yuya Danjō Motonobu was chosen to be the victim, but at the last moment Tsuru and Ichitarō offered themselves as human pillars in exchange. They were buried alive in the river and afterwards worshipped as guardian deities of the place.[15]

Now in each of these last groups of tales, in which a woman is either sexually possessed by a snake or drowned as a sacrificial offering to a snake, there are interesting links to be found with the figure of the *miko*.

The *miko* was the female shaman who before the introduction of Buddhism into Japan was one of the principal sacral figures of the old Shinto religion. It is thought that by a special ritual, which we can roughly reconstruct, and by special music and dancing, she could summon into her body the deities known as *kami*, and enable them to deliver oracular pronouncements through her mouth. Through her mouth the tutelary deity of the village could be cajoled into answering questions relating to the welfare of the village and its families. We have some idea of what she looked like from the clay pottery figures called *haniwa* recovered from the tumuli of the 4th and 5th centuries AD. But since the introduction of Buddhism and Chinese learning from the continent, she was driven gradually further downwards into the folk tradition, and is now to be found only in a few remote places in Japan.

The links between this ancient sacral woman and the woman who is both loved and killed by the snake are first verbal. Yanagita Kunio was the first to point out that the name of the girl seduced by the supernatural snake was Tamayorihime. This name, he argued, was a generic one for a *miko*, denoting a girl, *hime*, possessed, *yoru*, by the spirit of a god. The story therefore points to a cult in which a *miko* was specially chosen to serve a deity connected with water and serpents.[16] Likewise in the human pillar legends, the woman sacrificed is very often stated to be a *miko*. In a village in Rikuzen where the dam kept collapsing, for example, they seized a travelling *miko* who happened to be passing through the village, and buried her alive under the dam. The dam was at once successfully repaired, and they built a shrine to the *miko*'s spirit on the very spot. Many similar tales exist which relate how, for one reason or another, a *miko* is sacrificed to the snake guardian of the water supply. Here too there are verbal connections. In the case of the celebrated victims Tsuru and her son Ichitarō, worshipped at the Aibara shrine in Kyushu, Yanagita again pointed out that the boy's name Ichitarō may be connected with one of the words for a shaman, *ichi*. Here too therefore lurks the suggestion of an ancient association with a *miko*.[17]

Matsumura Takeo however, in his important work on the myths of Japan *Nihon Shinwa no Kenkyū*, interprets these tales rather differently. He believes them not to be based on fact, but to reflect an ancient and lost cult in which a woman was offered as a 'living sacrifice' to a water snake deity. Not however in the sense that she was murdered in the horrible manner described, but in that she thereby died to her ordinary human life. She was snatched from her familiar world and pressed into a sacred calling which represented death to her old manner of living. By becoming his bride she was indeed sacrificed to the deity.[18]

No one has yet satisfactorily established the relationship between the tales in which a woman is possessed, sexually and spiritually, by a supernatural snake, and those in which the snake-woman appears as a single being. I am inclined to think the snake paramour tales to be of later date; to belong to a time when the two realms were beginning to draw apart, and the shamanistic woman to feel herself not so much one with the snake as possessed by it, often against her will.

One more piece of evidence may be relevant here in support of the theory that these stories are the residue of an ancient shamanistic cult. During my investigations into the disappearing shamanistic practices of Japan, I sought out a number of women who are still able, through trance, to act as mouthpieces for gods. They would tell me how they were first impelled into the sacred life, often by a dream or by a sudden unpremeditated possession by a god. They would tell me the names of the deities who appeared to them in dreams, and thereafter acted as a guardian spirit, supervising their ascetic practice and speaking through their mouth when an oracular pronouncement was required.

I always asked them, what did your deity look like? With remarkable frequency, irrespective of what the recognized appearance of the deity might be, they answered, 'A snake.' One woman, a Mrs. Sasanuma, told me that at a critical moment of her life, when she was at the point of utter despair, the Buddhist goddess Kishibojin appeared to her. This goddess is usually represented in iconography as clad in orthodox Buddhist floating draperies and glittering crown. To Mrs. Sasanuma, however, she appeared as a snake. Indeed, she would appear in snake form with such overwhelming vividness that Mrs. Sasanuma often felt that she too had become a snake.[19]

Another Buddhist goddess, Benten or Bezaiten, has likewise been accorded the attributes of a snake. Usually Benten is associated with music. A lute in her hands, her shrines are to be found on islands in the sea or in lakes, or on islands specially constructed in the ornamental pools of private gardens. In these shrines are frequently to be found offerings of eggs, clear proof that her worshippers associate her with a snake, since snakes are believed to be passionately fond of sucking eggs. Benten too has thus been assimilated to the ancient snake-woman, who has persisted with such tenacity in the folk tradition, and on the level of the Japanese mind which issues in visions and dreams.

By way of epilogue, here is another passage from the *Heike Monogatari*, the long epic saga describing the rise of the Heike family to power and wealth, and its eventual downfall at the battle of Dan-no-ura in 1183. In the 7th book of this work there is a chapter entitled *Chikubushima*, the name of an island in the middle of Lake Biwa. It describes how the celebrated warrior and musician Taira no Tsunemasa, exhausted with fighting, found himself one morning on the shores of the lake. Far out over the waters he saw a green island. 'What is that island?' he asked his companions. They answered, 'That is the famous island of Chikubushima.' At once Tsunemasa determined to go there, found a boat and pushed out from the shore.

It was just the month of May, and the trees were bursting into green and the air was full of the song of birds. To Tsunemasa when he landed on the shore, the place seemed so beautiful as to resemble the paradisal island of Hōrai. Making his way to the shrine of the goddess Benten, he made a prayer for victory in battle. Presently the sun set and moon rose over the lake, so that the shrine was bathed in bright silver. The priest of the shrine, knowing Tsunemasa's talent for music, brought him a lute, and overcome by the beauty of the scene, he played the secret tunes called Jōgen and Sekijō.

Thereupon the whole shrine was flooded with light, and as though the goddess could not restrain herself from responding to so exquisite a performance, the apparition of a white dragon was seen hovering over Tsunemasa as he played. Overcome with numinous awe, Tsunemasa stopped playing for a while and composed the poem:

Chihayaburu
Kami no inori no
Kanaeba ya
Shiruku mo iro no
Arawarenikeri

'Surely my prayer must have been heard, so vivid and manifest is the sign that has appeared.'

Then, convinced that after so auspicious an appearance as that of the dragon goddess herself, he must certainly vanquish the enemy, Tsunemasa got into his boat and rowed away from the island.[20]

Shape-changing in the Old Norse Sagas

H. R. ELLIS DAVIDSON

It is impossible to get very far in the study of Old Norse literature without meeting the phenomenon of the change from human to animal shape. In the myths, stories and poems, men and women appear in animal form, and gods and goddesses manifest themselves in the shape of animals, birds and fishes, while the art of the pre-Christian period is full of animal symbolism, and gives some evidence for the use of animal masks and of men in animal disguises. Faced with so much and such varied material, the problem is where to begin.

It might be as well to start with words. In Old Icelandic the word *hamr*, 'shape', can be used for an animal skin, the wings and feathers of a bird, and also for a non-human shape assumed by someone with special powers. A man with supernatural gifts may be called *hamrammr*, 'shapestrong', while the verb *hamask* means to fall into a state of wild fury, an animal rage, and one in such a state may be called *hamslauss*, 'out of his shape'. We find also the word *hamhleypa*, 'shape-leaper', 'leaper out of his skin', used of someone with powers of magic, and in later times for a man with unusual powers of energy and strength. It is said in *Eyrbyggja Saga* 61 that a certain individual was *eigi einhamr*, 'not of one shape', until he was converted to Christianity. Particularly interesting is the term *hamfarir* (in the plural), 'shape-journeys', used in the sagas to denote the sending out of the spirit in animal form while the man's body rests in a state of sleep or trance. The use of these terms indicates that magic powers and powers beyond the ordinary were associated in some way with a change of form and possibly with the taking on of animal shape, but it is not easy to know how far this is metaphorical use of language and how far belief in an actual change of appearance is involved.

These terms come from Icelandic literature, since nearly all early

Norse material from about the eleventh century onwards comes from Iceland. The sources of this may be native oral tradition, or tales brought in from abroad and retold in Iceland, or written sources in Latin or other languages introduced after the conversion. The Icelanders accepted Christianity in the year AD 1000, and their written literature must therefore be later than this, since it is derived from manuscripts produced in monasteries; nevertheless it may include material current before the conversion, since the Icelanders were immensely proud of the early traditions from what they regarded as an heroic period and a golden age, and they were anxious to preserve them. All this has to be borne in mind in attempting to assess ideas about magic in the Icelandic sagas. Moreover the Icelandic storytellers were so skilful in welding together their diverse material that it is no easy task to detect the source of inspiration behind any particular episode. There is a rich background of mixed tradition behind the tales of shape-changers which seem so spontaneous and naive, and I want to suggest what some of the main influences behind them may be.

Animals which play a part in shape-changing stories are bears, wolves, walrus and pigs, and occasionally cattle, goats, dogs and fishes. An example of how vigorous and yet how elusive such accounts may be is a story from the saga of Hrolf kraki, an early king of Denmark. This belongs to a group known as sagas of old-time, or 'lying sagas', and is a tale based on old heroic traditions skilfully retold, popular folklore, and strange happenings set in the pagan past. The central figure is not so much King Hrolf—who like King Arthur collected many celebrated champions around him—but one of his loyal followers, Bodvar Biarki. Bodvar's father Biorn had been changed into a bear by a wicked stepmother when he rejected her advances, and he was finally hunted to his death by men and dogs. During his time as a bear, he was able to resume his human form at night, and a girl called Bera joined him in his cave. Before he was killed he warned her never to eat bear's flesh, but the wicked queen forced her to swallow a mouthful. Bera bore three sons at a birth after Biorn's death; the first was half man and half elk; the second had dog's feet; and the third was Bodvar Biarki, who at first appeared wholly human. But when the time came for King Hrolf to fight his final battle against overwhelming odds, since he was being attacked by evil supernatural powers, Bodvar showed that he too had characteristics beyond the ordinary.

He was unaccountably missing from the forefront of the battle, but a wonderful event took place there:[1]

> Men saw that a great bear went before King Hrolf's men, keeping always near the king. He slew more men with his forepaw than any five of the king's champions. Blades and weapons glanced off him, and he brought down both men and horses in King Hjorvard's forces, and everything which came in his path he crushed to death with his teeth, so that panic and terror swept through King Hjorvard's army....

Meanwhile Bodvar's friend Hjalti had gone to look for him, and when he found the champion sitting motionless in his tent, he railed on him for his desertion of the king in time of need. At last Bodvar rose and went out, saying that now he could help the king far less than he could have done had he been left where he was. When he reached the battlefield, the bear had gone, and from this point the tide of battle turned against Hrolf and his followers, and they went down fighting round their king. This powerful image of a mighty bear wreaking terror and destruction upon an army has recently been used again with great effect in Richard Adam's novel *Shardik*.

The implication here is clear: Bodvar fights in bear form while his body remains motionless in his tent. The battle in which he fought was one famous in Danish heroic tradition, and we have an account of it by Saxo Grammaticus in Latin, written at the beginning of the thirteenth century, based apparently on an old poem *Biarkamál*, of which some Icelandic fragments survive. It seems that Biarki (the name used by Saxo) was the original one borne by the hero, and Bodvar (*bǫð*, a poetic word for battle) was really a nickname: he was the Biarki of battle, that is, a warrior.[2] There is however no indication that Saxo knew the story of the bear, or that this came into the original poem. Biarki means Little Bear, while Biorn, his father's name, means Bear, and Bera, his mother's name, She-Bear. The story of his birth in the saga indeed follows a well-established folktale pattern, that of the Bear Mother.[3]

The story is that of a human girl who becomes the wife of a bear, and whose children are half bear and half human, and are thus able to form a link between man and the animal world. The Lapp Turi, whose account of his own people and their beliefs was written down in 1910, clearly knew of such a tale, at least in an incomplete form:[4]

> I have heard that there was once a girl who spent a whole winter in a bear's house ... and she slept very well through the winter ... and the bear was a he-bear and he got the girl with child. And the child was a boy, and its one hand was a bear's paw, and the other a human hand, and the one hand he never left uncovered. And once a man wanted him to show it to him, although he said that he could not show it because it was dangerous. But the man didn't believe him and insisted ... And when he had uncovered it for the man, then he couldn't control himself, but tore the man's face to pieces. And then folk saw that it was true, what he said about his hand.

In the seventeenth century Edward Topsell, in his delighful *Historie of Fourefooted Beastes*[5] refers to a tale which a man from Constance 'did most confidently tell' to him, of a bear in the mountains of Savoy which carried off a young girl to his den. He brought apples each day for her to eat, and treated her very lovingly; in the end she was rescued by her parents, but there is no mention of children born of the union, or of whether the bear was killed. The tale is indeed found as far away as Mongolia, and is also illustrated on totem poles and carvings made at the end of the last century by American Indian artists, some of whose names are known, among tribes on the north Pacific coast and in the northern Rockies.[6] In this region the tale is a myth, told to account for the origin of the bear-hunting ritual. It was said that after the father bear had been killed, the children of the bear mother taught the hunters of the tribe how to catch bears, and how to sing the correct dirges over those which they killed. Barbeau published a number of these carvings, which show great skill and powerful imaginative treatment; some had spread to areas like Queen Charlotte Island, where there were no bears. He claimed that the tradition must have reached North America from eastern Asia. His examples remind us of the complex relationship between myth, magic ritual and folktales, and how the existence of all three could keep alive the sense of a close relationship between man and animal. When the hunting magic no longer retains its power, and the bear becomes a creature remote from the life of the community, the traditions finally degenerate into tales for children.

The bear was the most powerful and dangerous animal in the Scandinavian north, likely to leave a vivid impression on those who hunted him for food. Bear skins were evidently used as something on which the dead could be laid, or perhaps wrapped round them in the grave, as is shown by traces of the claws surviving in graves in Norway and Sweden in the period before the Viking Age.[7] Snorri Sturluson in the introduction to the *Prose Edda* has a reference to the youthful Thor proving his strength by lifting 12 bearskins from the ground at once; this may be no more than a simple trial of physical prowess, but it is unlikely to have arisen in a purely Icelandic context, and the association with the young god is interesting. In a search for traces of initiation ceremonial in the Icelandic sagas, Mary Danielli[8] quotes a number of tales where the hero has to encounter a bear as proof of his manhood; in one of these a youth wears a bearskin cloak until he comes back with the bear's snout to prove that he has overcome it; in another the fur cloak is thrown at the bear by the leader of a band of men 'testing' the young hero, and he has to recover it and to cut off the bear's paw. Moreover in several of the stories the company of men (sometimes specified as berserks) is twelve in number, and the leader is called Biorn; it is therefore possible that the twelve bearskins lifted by Thor have some special significance, and that behind such confused traditions lies the memory of testing young warriors entering a company of berserks by arranging an encounter with a bear, real or simulated, and that the warriors put on bearskins for such ceremonies.

Among the Lapps in later times we know that the bear was honoured by special names and elaborate ceremonies, which have been well recorded in a number of different regions.[9] The word *saivo* used of a slain bear is the same as that used for the spirits of men who have died, and at the bear-feast it may be noted that the hunter who had killed the bear put on the head and skin of the dead animal.[10] There was a well-established custom also of drinking the blood of the bear, in order to obtain something of its strength and courage.[11] Such practices form a promising basis for tales of shape-changing between men and bears. Those who have studied the bear cult among the Lapps and other northern peoples emphasize that it was the enormous strength of the animal and its strange habits which distinguished it from other wild beasts, above all the ability to survive the winter without food, which caused wonder, and made the bear specially revered by those who hunted it. Although highly dangerous and a formidable adversary, the bear was not thought to be an evil beast, like the wolf. Its flesh was of great benefit to men, and many parts of the body, especially the fat, were believed to possess special powers of healing. It was felt to have a close link with men, partly because of its tendency to rear itself on its hind legs, and to strike a victim with its forepaw, or to hug him to death; its footprints resembled those of men, and it was thought to look like a human being when skinned.[12] It was also felt that the bear had no natural antagonism towards human beings. To quote again from Turi:[13]

> The bear is a wonderful animal who lives through the winter without eating. And he is not angry with a person who comes up to him and does not do anything to him. . . .
>
> The bear's law is this, if he kills a human being then he may not sleep in peace through the winter. And the oldtime Lapps thought that the bear had a conscience; and for another thing, if the Uldas (spirits) are his providers during the winter, then they wouldn't bother any more with a bear who had besmirched himself with human blood.

It was also believed by the Lapps that a bear would not willingly attack a woman, and one meeting a bear had only to hold up her skirt to show that she was one for him to leave her alone.[14]

Since there were no bears in Iceland and the largest land animal was the Arctic fox, it seems probable that the detailed story of Biarki's birth and appearance in bear form came in from Norway. A more homely story of a man who fought in the form of a bear comes from *Landnámabók*, the thirteenth-century account of the settlement of Iceland at the end of the ninth century, based on what was remembered of the early settlers. Among these were two men called Dufthak and Storolf, who were neighbours. Dufthak was a slave who had gained his freedom and bought land, while Storolf came from a distinguished family in northern Norway. It was said of Dufthak:[15]

> He was very shapestrong (*hamrammr*), and so also was Storolf Hœngsson, who lived at Hval at that time; they quarrelled over grazing rights. One evening about sunset a man with the gift of second sight saw a great bear go out from Hval and a bull from Dufthak's farm, and they met at Storolfvellir and fought furiously, and the bear had the best of it. In the morning a hollow could be seen in the place where they had met, as though the earth had been turned over, and this is now called Oldugrof. Both were wearied out.

The man who took bear shape was a son of the famous Ketil Hœng, who came from a region where the Lapps dwelt and where there must have been abundance of bear lore. Another piece of bear tradition is linked with one of Ketil's descendants, Ǫrvar-Odd.[16] When marooned with his crew on an island off the Baltic coast, he was threatened by hostile people from the mainland, and he set up the head and skin of a bear, supported across a stick. When a giantess was sent to attack them, he put embers into the beast's mouth, and then drove her back with his magic arrows. The setting up of a bear skin in this way is found among the rites associated with bear-slaying among the Lapps and other peoples.[17]

A practice which may have helped to keep up the tradition of a close link between man and bear in Scandinavia was the use of animal names for men of distinguished families. There has been much argument as to the origin of this custom, and how far it was based on pre-Christian beliefs in the Germanic world.[18] It is clear that the two most popular names of this type were those based on the bear and the wolf, either in a simple form (Biorn, Ulf) or with an additional syllable (Arnbiorn, Kveldulf). In Germanic usage both names are used together with words for battle, as in the names Hildewolf and Guthbeorn, or for weapons and armour. There seems little doubt that both bear and wolf were associated with an important form of magic, that concerned with battle, the ritual which sought to establish good luck and victory for warriors. This was current among both German and Scandinavian fighting men, and was linked closely with the God Wodan or Odin. The northern sagas have many allusions to the men called berserks who were among Odin's followers. As described by Snorri Sturluson in the thirteenth century in *Ynglinga Saga* 6:

> His (Odin's) men went without their mailcoats and were mad as hounds or wolves, bit their shields and were as strong as bears or bulls. They slew men, but neither fire nor iron had effect upon them. This is called 'going berserk' (*berserkgangr*).

The term *berserkr* may have been based on the wearing of a bearskin (*serkr* = shirt), and this is suggested by the alternate name given to them: *úlfheðnar*, 'wolf-coats'. Alternately, the first part of the word might come from *berr*, meaning 'bare', 'naked', and Snorri appears to take it in this way, since he stresses their practice of fighting without mailcoats; they may well have been accustomed to fling off protective armour when the berserk fury came upon them. The latter interpretation was that given in the early dictionaries, but since about 1860 the link with the bear has been the accepted derivation as in the *Old Icelandic Dictionary* by Vigfusson and Cleasby. Noreen defends the earlier theory in an article published in 1932,[19] but I do not find his arguments altogether convincing. We are told in *Vatnsdœla Saga* 9 that

> . . . those berserks who were called *ûlfheðnar* had
> wolf shirts (*vargstakkar*) for mailcoats

The term wolf-coats is used again as an alternate name for berserks in an early poem, *Hrafnsmál*, composed about AD 900,[20] and here the noise made by the warriors is also emphasized: 'the berserks bayed ... the wolf-coats howled'. In the same poem there is a description of such warriors at the court of King Harald Fairhair, who ruled in the second half of the ninth century:

> Wolf-coats they are called, those who carry
> bloodstained swords to battle;
> they redden spears when they come to the slaughter,
> acting together as one.

We do not have any detailed descriptions of these savage fighters wearing bearskins or wolfskins, but on the other hand we find what appear to be human figures with heads of bears or wolves, dressed in the skin but with human feet; they are depicted on helmet plates or scabbards, mainly from the pre-Viking period in Sweden.[21] It is perhaps worth noting that in a paper on werewolves by Nils Lid stress is laid on the importance of the belt of wolfskin in shapechanging tales; such a belt was put on by a man or woman who wanted to turn into a wolf, or put into the bed at night, and is mentioned in a number of Norwegian witch-trials.[22] It is possible that the popular motif of a little dancing warrior with a horned helmet, wearing nothing except a belt but armed with a spear or sword, might possibly represent the warrior in his belt of bear or wolfskin; I have suggested for other reasons that such figures represent the champions of Odin.[23] The belt, as Lid makes clear from later evidence, was held to stand for the skin as a whole.

The link with bear or wolf was a logical one for professional warriors or warrior leaders in the Viking Age. The difference between the two animals is clear. The bear is a lone fighter, an independent champion of tremendous power, with a certain nobility in his behaviour, although when carried away by rage he will strike down anyone in his way. The wolf, however, fights as one of a pack, closely linked with his companions, cunning and utterly ruthless, sparing none. They thus represent two ways of doing battle in the Viking Age and the period before it. The outstanding champion established his reputation by prowess in single combat and courage above the ordinary; he would fight in the forefront of the army against champions of the opposing side, and would scorn to attack an unarmed or weak opponent. The raiding party of Vikings or small force of mercenaries would act as a fierce gang, ruthless in attack, greedy for plunder, supporting one another with loyalty and determination (although also apt to quarrel among themselves) and letting nothing stand in their way. There is plenty of evidence from outside observers that the German warriors and the Vikings after them fought with a savage intensity, an animal ferocity and wildness, which shocked Romans and Byzantines. As late as the tenth century Leo the Deacon watched some of the eastern Vikings fighting with Svyatoslav on the Danube against the Emperor, and commented with disapproval on their methods of fighting, so different from those of the Greeks, who, he said, relied on the arts of war. These men seemed, he claimed, to be driven by ferocity and blind madness, and fought like wild beasts, 'howling in a strange and disagreeable manner.'[24]

There is a vivid account of what might be called a retired berserk in the opening chapter of *Egils Saga*. The grandfather of the famous adventurer and poet, Egil Skallagrimsson, who lived in northern Norway, was called Kveldulf, literally 'Evening-Wolf', and was the son of a man called Bialfi, which means an animal skin. The saga-teller accounts for his name by the fact that he grew sleepy and bad-tempered in the evening; this might seem natural in an ageing man who used to get up very early to do smithying, as we are told Kveldulf did, but here it is clearly associated with shape-changing, for he is said to be *hamrammr*. Although there is no indication that he was ever seen in wolf form, he and his son Skallagrim were at times subject to terrible fits of rage which left them shaken and weak, and when these fits were upon them they would attack anyone they encountered; Egil himself as a young boy narrowly escaped death from his father's violence during a ball game. Egil in his turn showed some berserk tendencies; he attacked a boatload of enemies in Norway in a state of furious anger, and on another occasion bit the throat of his opponent, also said to be a berserk, in a duel.[25]

It may be assumed that those who lived a warrior's life in Scandinavia must have received some kind of training, and we know that there were special spells to be used in battle, and some indication of ceremonial in which fighting men took part; possible suggestions of initiation ceremonies when the troop of berserks admitted a new recruit have already been noted. Another story which might preserve a memory of training of this kind is found in *Vǫlsunga Saga*, a thirteenth century saga which tells the history of the Volsung family, and seems to have made use of earlier sources now lost. In the opening chapters we have the story of how Sigmund reared his son Sinfjotli, training him for the task of vengeance on the king who had killed Sigmund's father and brothers:[26]

> One day they went into the forest to look for plunder, and they found a house, and in the house two men were asleep with thick gold rings on their arms; an evil fate had been wrought upon them, for wolfskins hung above them; they could take off the skins every tenth day, and they were kings' sons. Sigmund and Sinfjotli put on the wolfskins, and were unable to take them off. With the wearing of them went the same nature as before: they spoke with the voice of wolves, and yet each understood what was uttered. They stayed out in the wilds, each going his own way; they made an agreement that each would take on as many as seven men but no more, and that he who was attacked first should cry out as a wolf does. 'We must not depart from this', said Sigmund, 'for you are young and full of reckless courage, and men will want to hunt you down.' Now they went their several ways, and while they were apart, Sigmund encountered some men, and howled, and when Sinfjotli heard him he came at once and slew them all; they parted once more, and before he (Sinfjotli) had gone far in the forest, he met with eleven men and fought them and managed to slay them all.

Sigmund was very angry that Sinfjotli had not called for help:

> Sigmund leapt on him with such force that he staggered and fell, and Sigmund bit him in the throat. That day they could not get out of their wolfskins, and Sigmund picked up Sinfjotli on his back and carried him to the hut and sat over him, cursing the wolfskins.

However Sigmund saw a weasel carrying a leaf which it used to cure another which had been bitten in the throat, and so he healed

Sinfjotli in the same way. Finally the time came when they could take the skins off, and they burned them, praying that no harm should come to anyone else through them. The story ends:

> But in these shapes of bewitchment they wrought many famous deeds in the kingdom of King Siggeir.

This tale contains some of the elements of folktales, but in the agreement about taking on enemies and the reference to warlike achievements in the wolfskins, there seems to be a hint of a different tradition, one associated with young heroes living like wolves in the forest and learning how to support themselves by robbery and killing. Wolves were also identified with outlaws, and the word *vargr*, wolf, was used as a legal term for an outlaw. It may be noted that the Lapp Turi also associated wolves with thieves: he says that in the old days the shamans turned themselves into wolves, and it was easier to do this when they had slain innocent people, like certain Russians who robbed and killed in Lapp territory, until finally with the help of the Uldas or spirits they became wolves and were driven out:[27]

> ... and they went back to Russia, and that is why there are so many wolves in Russia, and wolves so fierce that they eat human beings.

It is interesting that here there is a reversal of the usual rule, and the spirit of evil men enters into the beasts instead of the animal spirit entering a man. Turi declared that there was proof that some wolves had once been men:

> ... Such proofs as finding under certain wolves' hides (while flaying them) things belonging to the people they used to be ... flint and steel and tinder, and sulphur-cups too.

Whereas the bear is a noble adversary, the wolf is a mean and cunning one. Turi believed that he could do magic on a bullet, so that it missed its mark, and could cause those watching for him to fall asleep. He has, says Turi, one man's strength and nine men's cunning, and to hunt him successfully it was necessary to know all his names in the Lapp dialects, and to think of nine different ways of trapping him, using the last in the list.

This picture of the wolf is characteristic of the herdsman and hunter, threatened by invasions on their reindeer and cattle, so that it seems natural to identify a cunning thief and outlaw with a wolf, and the further step of seeing a particularly cunning wolf as a man in wolf shape is not a very difficult one. In the Viking Age the wolf haunted the battlefield, and was one of those which along with birds of prey feasted on the dead, so that he was an even more sinister figure; it was a great compliment to a successful leader to claim that he gave food to the wolves. This helps to explain the symbol of the wolf in dreams in the sagas. To dream of a number of wolves signified an enemy company about to attack, and sometimes a bear was included as a leader. There was much interest in the meaning of dreams in the Middle Ages, and Latin dream-books were known in Iceland.[28] However when a host of attackers is described as a troop of eighteen wolves led by a cunning vixen (a witch in the party), or when a huge bear is seen leaving a house together with two cubs, such symbolism seems likely to be based on native dream lore. The wolf shapes in a dream in *Havarðar Saga* are said to be *hugir* of men. The bear, described as a noble beast with no equal, is said in *Njáls Saga* to be the *fylgja* of Gunnar, the noble hero who was Njall's close friend. In *Ljosvetninga Saga* the brother of the powerful chief Gudmund the mighty dreamed that a splendid ox walked into Gudmund's hall and fell down dead by the high seat, presaging Gudmund's death, and again the word *fylgja* is used for the symbolic animal shape. The most entertaining account of this kind of animal form, visible in dreams or to someone with the power of second sight, is probably told as a jest. It comes in the story of a boy abandoned as a baby and brought up by simple folk.[29] One day he visited the hall where his true parents lived, and a wise old man, the father of the householder, was sitting there. The boy Thorstein

> ... came in with a great rush, as children usually do. He slipped on the hall floor, and when Geitir saw this, he burst out laughing.... The boy went up to Geitir and said 'Why did it seem funny to you when I fell just now?' Geitir answered 'Because indeed I could see what you could not.' 'What was that?' asked Thorstein. 'I will tell you. When you came into the hall, a white bear cub came behind you and ran along the floor in front of you. Now when he saw me, he stopped, but you were going rather fast, and you fell over him—and it is my belief that you are not the son of Krum and Thorgunna but must be of greater parentage.'

It seems likely that such a story is based on popular belief, introduced as a humorous episode by someone who does not take it too seriously. Another example of the use of popular tradition is found in *Njáls Saga* 41, this time the belief that as a man's death draws near he has special powers of perception, and can receive warning of its approach:

> It happened one time that Njall and Thord were sitting outside. A goat used to wander in the home meadow, and no one would drive it away. Thord began to speak: 'Now, that is a strange thing', said he. 'What do you see that you find so strange?' asked Njall. 'It seems to me that I can see the goat lying here in the hollow, all covered in blood.' Njall said that there was no goat there, nor anything else. 'Then what can it be?' asked Thord. 'You are a doomed man', said Njall, 'for it must be your *fylgja* which you have seen; take care of yourself.' 'That will do me little good', said Thord, 'if this is my doom.'

Close parallels to this conception of an animal guardian or companion, to be seen by those with special powers, or in a dream, are to be found in the beliefs concerning the soul or spirit among the Lapps in pre-Christian times, and various other Finno-Ugrian peoples in northern Europe and Asia.[30] In the seventeenth century Forbus, in his account of the Lapps and their beliefs, refers to a *Nemoqvelle*, said to be passed on to a child at baptism, which belonged to his father and grandfather before him:

> . . . and with the name the child also receives the Nemoqvelle, which can often reveal itself and walks before the Lapp near marshes and seas.

This comes from a Lapp word *Namma-Guelle*, meaning 'name-fish', and is used of the name given to a child, which was believed to protect it against evil powers during its life. The reference to marshes and seas suggests a fish which can be seen by the water, but the Lapps also had a tradition of animal spirits of the same kind. A missionary writing in 1726 stated that such spirits were not held to belong to all Lapps, but to a few only, and it seems that the belief was more common among the eastern Lapps. Other names for the accompanying spirit are found among other northern peoples; the Ostyaks had the *jepil*, said to be a visible shadow spirit, the Vogul and Ziryen the *urt* or *ort*, said to dwell as a guardian with the man to whom it belonged; the Skolt Lapps had the *kadz*, and believed that every family, though not necessarily every member of it, possessed such a spirit. Among the Norwegian Lapps the guardian spirit seems to have belonged to the *noidi* or shaman, and might take the form of animal, fish or bird. Here we have something very close to the conception of the *fylgja* in the sagas. It has been suggested that the word is related to ON *fulga*, meaning a thin covering or membrane, and that it may have been used for the afterbirth, as it is in modern Icelandic.[31] The word *ham* in Norwegian dialects can also be used for the afterbirth as well as for a skin. The obvious meaning of *fylgja* however would be 'to follow', and whatever the original significance, this no doubt influenced the meaning, and strengthened the conception of a spirit which followed its owner wherever he went. The connection with the afterbirth would help to account for the idea of a double soul or spirit. Jónasson, writing of Icelandic superstitions, pointed out that the afterbirth was popularly believed to contain some part of the child's soul, so that it must be disposed of with great care and buried in a safe place, such as the threshold of the house, rather than burned or thrown away.[32] The word *hugr*, used of the animal form seen in dreams, seems rather to emphasize the purpose of the person which it represents, since the term can be used with the sense of 'mind', 'wish', or 'foreboding'. Wolves in a dream appear to symbolize the hostile intention of certain men at a particular time rather than to represent their guardian spirits, but obviously it was not difficult for the two conceptions to overlap.

Shamanistic lore from the Lapps and other Finno-Ugrian peoples contains a wealth of stories in which the guardian spirits of the shamans fight in animal form. Among the Lapps these are generally thought to be reindeer, but they might be pictured as bulls, whales, fishes or other creatures, and it is not possible to be sure whether these are the spirits of the shamans themselves, visiting the Other World while their human forms lie in a condition of trance, or whether they should be thought of as the tutelary spirits of the shamans.[33] The episode of the bear in *Hrólfs Saga*, which fought on the battlefield while Bodvar sat in his tent, is an example of such an animal spirit. It was believed that these spirits could be used to work harm to others, and the Skolt Lapps are said still to believe that an evil *noidi* could assume the form of bear, wolf, snake or bird of prey, and be sent out against a victim.[34] We have episodes in the legendary sagas where two men fight in animal form; in one case a Lapp fights another man, and they battle first in the shape of dogs, then as two eagles; in another a man takes on the shape of a walrus and attacks a ship, and he in turn is attacked by a man and a woman in the shapes of a porpoise and a sword-fish.[35] In the second story the importance of the name of the shape-changer is emphasized, recalling the Lapp reference to the 'name-fish'; the man who becomes a sword-fish lies down in the ship under a heap of clothes and forbids anyone to utter his name aloud. The return of the spirit to the body may be a difficult and dangerous process; the girl who took the shape of a porpoise was found afterwards unconscious and very weak, and had to be revived with wine. In another story in *Kormáks Saga* 18 a hostile witch is said to have threatened a boat in the shape of a walrus, and to have been recognized by her eyes; the walrus was hit with a spear and submerged, and afterwards it was said that the witch was seriously ill and that in the end she died from the injury.

The more impressive shape-changing stories seem to be associated with wild creatures rather than domesticated ones. Sometimes men and women take the shape of pigs, but such episodes are of a rather different nature from those concerned with wolves and bears. The wild boar, an animal of great strength and savagery, was certainly associated with battle, and the boar symbol used on helmets, scabbards and swords, while the name of the wedge formation in battle was known among Germans and Scandinavians as the swine formation or the boar's head: *svínfylking* or *caput porci*; it took its name from the tapering head of the boar, with the section in front, where two champions usually headed the attack, known as the *rani* or snout.[36] However the man who takes on boar form seems to do so as a disguise or a means of protection, in the same way as the wearing of a boar helmet appears to be thought of as a means of protection in battle.[37] In the saga stories, the change into a boar or pig is generally used as a means of disguise to avoid attack by enemies, as in the tale of a witch who kept watch in the form of a boar, and woke up those in the house with the news that enemies were approaching, or in that of a man and woman who tried to escape from a burning house in the forms of a boar and a sow.[38] Such stories are of a more conventional kind, and have not the convincing force of the tales of shape-changing discussed earlier.

It is perhaps worth mentioning that there are no stories of shape-changers appearing as horses. Loki was capable of this,[39] but a suggestion that a man might follow his example would be considered a deadly insult, a suggestion of unpleasant and anti-social practices; such as an insult might be offered by erecting a 'scorn-pole' (*niðstǫng*) on which a horse's head was fixed or the shape of a horse carved, along with baleful runes, to bring shame and possibly hurt upon the evil doer.[40] The reason for this practice are too complex to be discussed here, and although relevant to the subject of animal magic, take us outside the realm of shape-changing.

It would seem that on the whole the tales of shape-changers in the sagas are not told 'for true'. Their background may be realistic, but the tales themselves are not; they serve an artistic purpose, bringing in a touch of fantasy, excitement, humour or horror into the saga according to the desire of the teller. They must however have their roots in popular tradition. Werner, discussing the problem of Germanic personal names based on animals and birds, mentions two opposing theories: first, that the names were thought to be lucky, because of the special qualities of the creature chosen; and secondly, because of the important part played by animal names in the diction of heroic poetry.[41] These could not, he said, both be true, but I do not myself see why not. Clearly a long tradition of animal names in poetry helped to emphasize certain qualities associated with the wild creatures which were felt to be proper also to the warrior, so that the bestowal of such names would be felt to bring in an element of power and luck. The background of warrior lore and also that of hunting magic went back into the Germanic past, and it is the wild animals native to the North which inspire the best stories of shape-changing, while the widespread conception of the guardian spirit and of twin souls, found among all the Finno-Ugric peoples and much farther afield, must have extended the popular tales about men appearing as animals still further. Expressions with a metaphorical or psychological significance could easily be given a literal interpretation in a story; similarly a naive popular belief could be used by a skilful story-teller to give his story a deeper meaning. Such expressions and popular traditions have their roots in an assumption of a close link between man and the animal world, and a widespread knowledge and keen observation of wild creatures, such as is natural to hunting peoples. Because of these deep roots, men were prepared to be frightened, amused or mystified by tales of people becoming animals and as always with popular literature, the saga-tellers provided their audiences with what they knew they wanted.

The Social Biology of Werewolves

W. M. S. RUSSELL and CLAIRE RUSSELL

I

We can best introduce the subject of werewolves with a short story, as follows:

'When I was still a slave, we were living in Narrow Street; the house belongs to Gavilla now. There, as the gods will have it, I fell in love with the wife of Terence the inn-keeper—you knew her, Melissa from Tarentum, an absolute peach of a girl. But it wasn't what you're thinking, believe me—no, I loved her for her beautiful nature. If I asked her for anything, she never said no; if she made anything, I got half; if I had anything, I banked it with her, and she never did me. Well, one day her husband died at their place. So I spruced myself up and worked out how to get to her; when you're in trouble, you know who your mates are. My boss happened to have gone off to Capua on some stupid business. So I grabbed the opportunity, and persuaded a man who was staying with us to come with me as far as the fifth milestone. He was a soldier, and brave as hell. We set off about cock-crow, the moon was shining as bright as day. We got to the cemetery; my mate went off towards the grave-stones, while I sat down, humming a tune, and started counting graves for fun. Then, when I looked round at him, he took off all his clothes and dumped them by the roadside. My heart was in my mouth: I stood there petrified like a corpse. He urinated all round his clothes, and suddenly turned into a wolf. Don't think I'm joking, I wouldn't lie about this for a fortune. But, as I was telling you, after he turned into a wolf he began to howl and ran off into the woods. At first I didn't know where I was. Then I went to pick up his clothes: they'd turned to stone! I was ready to die of fright, but I drew my sword and went down the road hacking at every shadow all the way till I got to my girl-friend's house. I came in looking like a ghost. I was at my last gasp. The sweat was running off my crutch, my eyes were glazed, it was all I could do to recover. My girl was surprised I'd been out so late. "If you'd got here sooner", she said, "you might at least have been some use. A wolf got into the grounds, and went for all our animals; he spilled as much blood as a butcher. But he didn't have the laugh on us, even though he got away—our slave stabbed him in the neck with a spear". When I heard all this I couldn't shut my eyes any longer. At day-break I rushed back to my boss's house as fast as an inn-keeper after a guest who hasn't paid his bill. When I got to the place where the clothes had been turned to stone, I found nothing but blood. But when I got home, my soldier mate was lying on his bed like an ox, with a doctor patching up his neck. I understood he was a skin-changer, and after that I couldn't sit down to a meal with him to save my life.'

This story is told by the ex-slave Niceros at the dinner given by his friend, the millionaire ex-slave Trimalchio, in the Latin novel called *Satyricon*. Niceros says in advance he is telling the tale purely for entertainment. The *Satyricon* was written during the reign of Nero (AD 54–68), very probably by the gifted Petronius Arbiter, governor of Bithynia and arbiter of elegance at the imperial court, who was finally forced by Nero to commit suicide, leaving a will in which he characteristically included a blow-by-blow account of the emperor's sex life. The manuscript containing the passage about Trimalchio's dinner was discovered in 1423 by the Renaissance scholar Poggio Bracciolini, but got lost again and was not rediscovered until about 1650; it was finally published in Padua in 1664. As it happened, no werewolf story of this kind was written purely for entertainment between the *Satyricon* in the 1st century and the novel *Monsieur Oufle*, published by the Abbé Bordelon in 1710. This was not because people in the intervening 16 centuries or so had forgotten about werewolves. On the contrary, as we shall see, in Europe in the 15th to 17th centuries a great many literate people were writing about werewolves, not as fiction purely for entertainment, but as sober fact, or at least as what many literate people believed to be sober fact. The werewolf belief was an early subject of discussion in the Royal Society, where, in 1663, Sir Kenelm Digby reported an alleged werewolf case from the Palatinate. As late as 1685, the actual carcase of a werewolf was on display in a museum at Ansbach. Here the citizens had killed a wolf, believed to be an incarnation of a dead mayor of their town. They cut off its snout, added a chestnut-coloured wig, a long white beard, and a mask representing the late mayor's features, and put it on exhibition as a proof of the existence of werewolves. But this was a rearguard action, hardly likely to impress educated citizens of most other towns in north-western Europe, let alone Fellows of the Royal Society. For by that time educated people in these parts had generally ceased to believe in werewolves as fact, and were ready to read entertaining fiction about them again.

The Age of Reason, indeed, had no use for werewolves in fact or fiction, and the Abbé Bordelon's novel of 1710 had no imitators for nearly a century. But with the Romantic revival werewolf fiction revived too, and the 19th and 20th centuries have seen a spate of werewolf stories in print, not to speak of werewolves on the air or the screen. Werewolves appear as episodes in a number of novels on other themes. An early example is the werewolf story in Captain Marryat's fine Flying Dutchman novel, *The Phantom Ship*, published in 1839. In recent times, we may instance a she-werewolf in Poul Anderson's story of Ogier the Dane, *Three Hearts and Three Lions* (1953), a comic werewolf in Sprague de Camp and Fletcher Pratt's delightful excursion into the world of Ariosto, *The Castle of Iron* (1941), and another she-werewolf in Jack Williamson's famous *Darker than you Think* (1948), a veritable menagerie of were-animals including even a were-sabre-toothed-tiger. But in addition there have been some whole novels and many short stories devoted primarily to werewolves. Bibliographical surveys of the werewolf in modern fiction have been made by K. F. Smith (1894), Montague Summers (1933), and E. F. Bleiler (1975); a particularly thorough recent survey is that of Brian J. Frost (1973), in the introduction to his excellent anthology, *Book of the Werewolf*. Here we shall glance at just a few examples of the genre. It is worth doing this by way of introduction to our subject. For, to quote H. R. Ellis Davidson's second Presidential address to the Folklore Society in 1975, 'folklore is an integral part of literature, not an intrusive element in it, something which may affect the language, structure and themes of outstanding works in both poetry and prose'. All authors of good werewolf stories have indeed taken the trouble to acquaint themselves with the folklore of the subject, and a few examples will therefore introduce some of the main themes of the werewolf belief.

Werewolves in fiction may be either simple villains or sympathetic victims of a condition they cannot avoid. For a first example of the simply villainous werewolf, we may take the short story *The Refugee*, by Jane Rice, published in *Unknown Worlds* in October 1943. This is a black comedy about the shortage of meat in occupied France. The resourceful heroine, the daughter of a Pittsburgh butcher, turns the tables on the werewolf by feeding him a chocolate with a silver centre. She had learned about the vulnerability of werewolves to silver by reading Guy Endore's novel *The Werewolf of Paris*, of which more anon.

Cannibalism is certainly an important theme in the study of werewolves; simple murder is another, illustrated by another short story, *The Adventure of the Tottenham Werewolf.* This is one of the many cases of the great detective Solar Pons, of 7B Praed Street. Pons was created in 1928 by August Derleth, after Conan Doyle had refused his request to write more about Sherlock Holmes. Derleth never explained his detective's name, but since *pons* is Latin for *bridge* he may have been designed to bridge a gap, and *solar* is surely a sly reference to a famous analysis of Sherlock Holmes as a solar myth. The Tottenham werewolf is not a supernatural monster but a murderess who plays on the superstition and despatches her victims with a back-scratcher to simulate the claws of the werewolf.

For a sympathetic werewolf we may turn to a memorable story of James Blish, published in 1950, *There Shall be No Darkness.* Blish was one of the rather few science fiction writers to have been a trained biologist rather than a physicist or engineer, and he treats the werewolf condition in a most interesting way as an endocrine disturbance, associated with an allergy to garlic and a metabolic susceptibility to silver poisoning. Though the werewolf is a menace to be destroyed, he is a gifted human being who cannot help his condition, and the story has the unsentimental poignancy characteristic of this author.

A sympathetic werewolf of a quite different kind was created by Anthony Boucher in *The Compleat Werewolf*, a comedy novella published in *Unknown Worlds* in April 1942. The hero is a congenital werewolf, who at first enjoys the transformation, though his troubles begin when he finds himself trapped in his wolf form.

He is completely free of predatory impulses, rescues a strayed child, who takes him for a nice dog, foils a gang of Nazi spies, and finally joins the F.B.I., which in those days was a popular organization. The best episode, depicted by the great illustrator Edd Cartier, concerned the problem of clothes. We have seen that Petronius's werewolf had to strip before transforming, but werewolf accounts vary on this point. On the morning after his first adventure, Boucher's hero recalls 'the wonderful, magical freedom of changing, ... the boundless happiness of being lithe and fleet and free'. Forgetting that on that occasion he had taken off his clothes first, he attempts another transformation. It works. 'He flexed his limbs in happy amazement. But he was not a lithe, fleet, free beast. He was a helplessly trapped wolf, irrevocably entangled in a conservative, single-breasted gray suit'.

We shall now consider three full-length werewolf novels. The first deserves mention not so much for its merit as for its phenomenal success. This is *Wagner the Wehrwolf*, by George William MacArthur Reynolds, first published as a serial from November 6th, 1846 to July 24th, 1847. The son of a flag officer in the Royal Navy, Reynolds began a lifelong war with the establishment when he was released from Sandhurst in 1830. He spent the next eight years in France. Between 1848 and 1851 he was a prominent leader of the Chartist movement; after the movement collapsed into internal dissensions, he spent some time feuding with a rival editor in the labour movement called Ernest Jones, one of whose contributors was 'a German exile who wrote under the name Charles Marx' (E. F. Bleiler). But Reynolds was chiefly known as a prolific journalist and writer of fiction for the masses: Henry Mayhew found he had an enormous and devoted following among the London costermongers. His most popular books were scandalous, almost pornographic mystery stories about the upper classes. This kind of literature flourished in mid-19th-century Britain and France, and attracted illustrators as distinguished as Gustav Doré. One of Mayhew's informants told him: 'I have known a man, what couldn't read, buy a periodical what had an illustration, just that he might learn from someone, who *could* read, what it was all about'. In 1933, Max Ernst produced his famous series of collages based on these lively and lurid illustrations, though we do not know if he used any pictures from Reynolds's own books.

Wagner the Wehrwolf is a typical Reynolds production. While there cannot be said to be never a dull moment in the book, there is certainly never a quiet one. We have not actually counted, but Reynolds conveys the impression of averaging at least one murder, abduction or torture scene in each of his seventy-seven chapters. The werewolf is a basically sympathetic and unfortunate hero, who is finally released from his condition by a merciful if macabre death.

Alfred H. Bill's novel *The Wolf in the Garden*, published in 1931, presents a complete contrast. This is a simple story, admirably well told, set in a small town in New York State at the end of the 18th century. The werewolf, however, is a refugee French aristocrat. He is a sadistic villain, effects his transformation by putting on a belt of human skin, and gets his come-uppance from a couple of silver bullets and the full charge of a musket.

Reynolds spent eight years in France and soaked himself in French culture; Bill made his werewolf a Frenchman. The links with France are not fortuitous, for in western Europe France is above all the country of the werewolf. The link is still clearer in the most interesting of all modern stories on the subject, S. Guy Endore's *The Werewolf of Paris*, published in 1933. The British Museum catalogue credits Endore with several novels, translations of French and German works, including a French book titled *Beasts called Wild* and a German book called *The Human Face*, and substantial biographies of Casanova and Joan of Arc: all these were published before *The Werewolf*. We also possess a fictionalized but clearly well researched biographical novel by Endore about the Dumas, father and son, published in 1956. *The Werewolf* itself reveals an extensive knowledge of 19th-century France.

The werewolf of Endore's novel is called Bertrand Caillet, and is plainly derived from the real historical case of Francois Bertrand, a non-commissioned officer in the 1st Infantry Regiment of the French army, who was tried in 1849 for breaking into a number of graves in Paris cemeteries. Nobody supposed him to be a werewolf, but his case was unusual: he had an overwhelming compulsion to tear to pieces the corpses of women and girls. Since his crime was without precedent, he got away with one year in prison. Charles Fort, that indefatigable collector of newspaper reports, found one about Bertrand in the *San Francisco Daily*

Evening Bulletin, June 27th, 1874: 'Bertrand the Ghoul is still alive: he is cured of his hideous disease, and is cited as a model of gentleness and propriety'.

Bertrand Caillet in the novel is an outright werewolf, but his condition is represented as a kind of congenital disease. He has a compulsion to kill as well as to tear corpses, he fights against it in vain when he falls in love, and he dies miserably in an asylum run by a crook. Among many interesting features of the book, three may be mentioned. First, Caillet is a priest's bastard: this is good folklore, for it was commonly believed in the Perigord region that priests' bastards inevitably became werewolves; the belief is referred to in a novel of Zola's. Second, Caillet commits incest with his mother; this is of great interest in relation to an aspect of the werewolf belief we shall consider later. Third, when transforming the ghoul Bertrand into the murderous werewolf Caillet, Endore has moved the setting of the story, not in space but in time. Even the years of the Second French Revolution and the *coup d'état* of Louis Napoleon were evidently not violent enough, in Endore's view, as background for the career of a werewolf. So he has set Caillet's crimes in the years 1870 and 1871, a period of intense population crisis in France, marked by the Franco-Prussian War and the Paris Commune. This is behaviourally sound, for, as we have written elsewhere, 'the background of tension and violence in a society provokes and stimulates the mass-murderer to his work', as well as often providing opportunities for it. We gave as examples the mass-murders of Haarmann in Germany in the early 1920s, those of Petiot in German-occupied Paris, and a mass-murder in Chicago in 1966, a year of severe riots in American cities. The setting gives Endore the opportunity for ironic comment, as he describes the historically authentic atrocities on both sides during the suppression of the Commune. His hero, the werewolf's guardian Aymar Galliez, holds a minor post under the Commune, in the Department of Fine Arts, and therefore finds himself among the Communard prisoners being marched through Versailles in June 1871, when they are horribly beaten by an upper-class lynch mob, an event that really happened. 'And Aymar chuckled. "More werewolves!" he exulted, oblivious of the blows that rained upon him. "The world is full of them. How is it that I once thought they were rare?"'

We cannot leave the subject of modern fiction without some

reference to two stories of Robert Louis Stevenson—*Dr. Jekyll and Mr. Hyde*, published in 1886, and *Olalla*, published in 1885. *Olalla* is about an English officer in the Peninsular War, convalescing from a wound in the home of a family of mother, son and daughter, the last remnant of a line of inbred and degenerate grandees. The daughter, Olalla, is virtuous and intelligent; the son is mentally retarded and given to sadistic impulses; the mother is so excited when she sees blood on the officer's hand that she seizes it and bites it to the bone. Though the word *werewolf* is never mentioned, the local peasants clearly believe the mother is one, and plan to burn down the house. As for the greater and more famous story, in the words of K. F. Smith, 'Stevenson's *Dr. Jekyll and Mr. Hyde* offers a curious analogy to the werewolf story without, in so many words, suggesting it'. The bodily transformation of the tall and virtuous Jekyll into the short, hairy, murderous Hyde is certainly an echo of the werewolf belief. Now in his essay *A Chapter on Dreams*, Stevenson describes how scenes from some of his stories were acted before him in his dreams. Clearly when a writer tells stories he has actually dreamed, he is close indeed to folk belief; to quote Davidson again, 'as Derek Brewer has been demonstrating in his lectures, there is a marked parallel between the imagery of the folktale and romance and that of dreams'. It is therefore interesting that Stevenson only gives two examples of stories directly inspired by dreams—*Jekyll and Hyde*, and *Olalla*. In the case of *Jekyll and Hyde*, Stevenson had indeed been trying for some time, in his words, 'to find a body, a vehicle, for that strong sense of man's double being, which must at times come in upon and overwhelm the mind of every thinking creature'. In Stevenson's night nursery there had stood a book-case and a chest of drawers made by Deacon Brodie, a famous Edinburgh character hanged in 1788, after living for some years as a respectable cabinet-maker by day and a burglar by night. Stevenson wrote a play about Brodie when he was only 13, and kept coming back to the subject till he collaborated with W. E. Henley on a play which ran in Bradford, Aberdeen and London, without much success, between 1882 and 1884. So by 1885 he was ready to dream of Jekyll and Hyde. 'In the small hours of the morning', wrote his wife Fanny, 'I was awakened by cries of horror from Louis. Thinking he had a nightmare, I awakened him. He said angrily, "Why did you wake me? I was dreaming a fine bogey tale" '. Three days later, he read a draft of the novel to Fanny and his step-son Lloyd Osbourne. Osbourne 'listened to it spellbound', but Fanny had reservations. In the words of her biographer, Margaret Mackay, Fanny felt Stevenson 'had made Dr. Jekyll a bad man who posed as being good, whereas he was really "Everyman" who had both a good self and a bad self'. 'Stevenson', wrote his step-son, 'was beside himself with anger. He trembled; his hand shook on the manuscript'. There was an appalling scene, which ended in Stevenson burning the manuscript and starting all over again, to produce, in the next three days, the novel as we know it. He had realized that Fanny was absolutely right. And this remarkable episode sums up the whole conflict between the views of werewolfery as a simple crime or as a complex illness, a conflict that runs through modern fiction and governed the actual treatment of supposed werewolves in an earlier age.

2

So much for modern werewolf fiction, which with all its variety follows always the pattern set by Petronius. Medieval literature, as we shall see, treated the werewolf in a rather different way. But now we must turn to the werewolf belief in deadly earnest, and especially to that period of intense population crisis in Europe, from the late 15th to the middle of the 17th century, when the belief was widely held, not only by illiterate peasants, but by literate scholars and lawyers. It seems to be well established that the English word *werewolf* and its counterparts in other Germanic languages means *man-wolf*. The form *wehr-wolf*, used by Reynolds in his Wagner novel, is probably just a variant, only accidentally related to the German word *wehr* (armour). The French word *loup-garou* is apparently derived from French *loup* (wolf) and English *werewolf*, so it contains a repetition and means *wolf-man-wolf*. Eastern Europe has some special characteristics. In most Slavonic languages the vampire is denoted by a word such as *vampiru*, from which comes the English word, while a werewolf is denoted by a word such as the Polish *wilkolak*. In Serbian, alone of the Slavonic languages, the corresponding word *vukodlak* means a *vampire*. This is not altogether surprising, for the two ideas are closely connected among all Slav peoples, it being supposed that werewolves become vampires when they die. In the 6th and 7th centuries AD, the Slavs poured into Greece, occupying the Peloponnese as far as Sparta; they were eventually assimilated, but they have heavily influenced the culture of the modern Greeks, to whom they have transmitted the word *vrykolakas* in the sense of *vampire*, and apparently also their connection between the two beliefs. This mix-up of vampire and werewolf does sometimes appear in western Europe, for instance in the case of the mayor of Ansbach and in a belief in Normandy that King John of England became a werewolf after his death. On the whole, however, the werewolf appears in the west in relatively pure form, as a living man who becomes a wolf at night, and we shall therefore confine our study to western Europe.

In his book *The Way of the Sacred*, Francis Huxley prints a German woodcut of 1685, 'showing a werewolf driven into a well, and another hanged from a gibbet'. The wolf being driven looks an ordinary beast, but the one who is hanged, though his muzzle and all four paws are wolf-like, is smartly got up in a suit of clothes, with a hat and a wig. At first sight, 1685 seems a little late for such affirmation of the belief, but a village in the background is labelled Eschenbach, and this turns out to be a few miles from Ansbach, so this woodcut is clearly based on propaganda from the Ansbach museum. However, it rather clearly expresses what a great many learned men believed less than a century earlier.

In his vastly erudite book *The Werewolf*, Montague Summers has listed a number of writers who wrote about werewolves giving it as their opinion 'that the demon can really and materially metamorphose the body of a man into that of an animal'. The most famous of these was Jean Bodin, publishing in 1580, but they also included Ulrich Molitor (1489), Jean de Sponde (1583), Henri Boguet (1590) and Pierre de Lancre (1613). The belief also appears plainly in the wording of court proceedings in the numerous trial proceedings of the period, and in such unofficial accounts as a pamphlet of 1591, which describes the case of Peter Stump (or Stubbe), executed at Bedburg, near Cologne, in the previous year. The Stump pamphlet is accompanied by a cut in the form of a strip cartoon, in which Stump appears first as a wolf from head to waist and a man from waist downwards, in the process of transformation; then as a wolf committing his depredations (he was accused of killing and partly eating at least two men, two pregnant women and thirteen children); finally as a man being tried and executed: he was torn with pincers, broken on the wheel, beheaded and the headless corpse burned, along with his unfortunate mistress and daughter, who were burned alive. It may be noted that Stump was also accused of incest with his daughter.

The werewolf trials were involved in the great outburst of witch-hunting that developed in intensity as the European population crisis worsened in the later 16th and early 17th century, against a background of famines, epidemics and religious wars. The werewolf accusations were, however, quite specific, and the werewolf trials can be clearly distinguished from those of other witches and warlocks, though all were supposed to be in league with the Devil. Werewolves were also the subject of special proclamations, such as that of the Parlement of Franche-Comté in 1573, concerning their punishment and apprehension. We have analysed 21 trial cases described in detail by Summers. Two occurred in Germany, two in Switzerland, and 17 in France. Three occurred in the 1520's, one in the 1550's, one in the 1570's, five in the 1580's, eight in the 1590's, and three in the first decade of the 17th century. The 1590's, when werewolf trials were most frequent, were a time of bad weather and bad harvests all over Europe. Also to be noticed is the prevalence of werewolves in France: we shall return to this. In all these trials, the accused were convicted; they were usually sentenced to be burned alive. Seven of these werewolves were women.

A famous but typical case is that of Gilles Garnier of Lyons, burned at Dole in 1573. He was believed to have made a pact with a demon who promised to change him into any animal shape, but advised him 'that since the wolf was the least remarkable of savage beasts this shape would be the more conformable'. In his wolf form, Garnier killed and partly ate three children, according to the trial account. Finally he was caught with the body of a boy he had just strangled. And at this point a note of real horror enters the sober record. 'The said Gilles Garnier was then and at that time in the form of a man and not of a wolf, yet had he not been let, hindered and prevented he would have eaten the flesh of the aforesaid young boy, notwithstanding that it was a Friday'—for of course on Fridays eating people was wrong and one should stick to fish.

Behind the writings of the scholars and lawyers, there was of course a large body of peasant folklore, especially in France. The chief difference was that ordinary people sometimes believed werewolves were victims of an unavoidable condition, as in the case of priests' bastards in Perigord, whereas the learned believers all regarded them as sorcerers who had become werewolves from choice by making a pact with the Devil. Otherwise the literate and illiterate had generally similar beliefs, and our knowledge of werewolf folklore is in part obtained from the trials themselves, supplemented by the usual kind of folklore collections.

To begin with, how do you recognize a werewolf in his human form? First, his eyebrows meet in the middle over the bridge of the nose. This belief is attested from Denmark, France, Germany and Scotland; Gilles Garnier had such eyebrows. Second, at least in France, the werewolf has hairy palms. Other alleged signs are pointed ears and a loping walk. Boucher mentions a long index finger, but we have not been able to find an authentic source for this sign. Brian Stableford tells us Boucher took it from another work of werewolf fiction, Seabury Quinn's *The Phantom Farmhouse* (published in *Weird Tales* in October 1923), and that Quinn was apt to invent such details. It is, of course, not unknown for modern literature to act as a *source* of folklore belief, as E. M. R. Ditmas has shown in the case of Drake's drum, but we do not know if this has happened yet in the case of werewolves.

To return to authentic werewolf folklore, there are a variety of methods for effecting the transformation from man to wolf. Moonlight is often a necessary, and in Perigord and Sicily a sufficient condition for the change. Spells were sometimes recited. It was not always necessary to strip naked, like Petronius's werewolf. Pierre Burgot and Michel Verdun were colleagues in werewolfery; they were tried together at Poligny in 1521. Yet whereas Burgot had to strip before he could change, Verdun was transformed from a clothed man to a naked wolf. None of the historical werewolves are reported to have suffered from the predicament of the hero of Boucher's novel. The case of Verdun, however, was a rare one, for it was usually necessary to strip in order to carry out other requirements. Rubbing with a special ointment was often reported in the trials, and we shall return to this. Some werewolves made the change by dressing in a wolf's skin; more often it sufficed to wear a girdle made either of wolf's skin or human skin, preferably that of a condemned criminal. A variety of other methods are recorded, but the ointment and the girdle or skin were those usually favoured.

Urination occurs only in the Petronius story, and both Summers and Smith interpret it as having nothing to do with the transformation, but serving the purpose of a magical protection for the werewolf's clothes. Both in Italy and in India urinating round something has been believed to create a magical barrier. In this connection, Francis Huxley quotes a pertinent observation about animals by the naturalist Bilz: 'Excrement and the image conveyed by it frighten and even terrify the intruder to a territory. Is not this similar to magic? ... The scent banner unfurled against a tree stump by a dog continues to strike terror even when the animal has long since ... gone to live on another farm'. Thus Petronius's soldier suggests the marking of territory by urine in lower mammals.

Returning from wolf to human form is a simpler matter, effected usually just by taking off the skin or girdle, sometimes by washing or rolling in dewy grass. It may happen automatically if the werewolf is wounded in wolf form. The wound or mutilation will then appear on the human body. This is called repercussion, and evidently appears in the Petronius story, where the wolf is wounded in the neck and the soldier shows the same wound. Repercussion is recorded in several of the accounts of werewolf trials, for instance in the case of Michel Verdun (1521). Some kinds of wound will permanently free an involuntary werewolf from his transformation, for instance carving a cross on his forehead; such a cure can also be effected, according to some tales, by striking him with a key or calling his Christian name three times. These cures belong to folklore proper rather than the courts, as do a few special beliefs. Georges Sand, in a book on French folklore she published in 1858, discusses the *lupins* of Normandy, strange wolf-like beings that chatter and howl as they stand by the walls of country cemeteries at night. Her artist son Maurice provided a gruesome illustration of *lupins* for the book. The werewolf belief itself persisted in popular folklore long after its disappearance in literate circles. Summers, publishing in 1933, recorded its recent occurrence in Italy and the highlands of Scotland, where a man with eyebrows meeting was described to him as a reputed werewolf. There was even a reported case of repercussion in France as late as 1879, when a miller was blinded in one eye after his wife had struck in the eye a large animal she saw in their courtyard in the early morning. Finally, in 1925, a policeman at Uttenheim, near Strasburg, was tried for shooting dead a boy he believed to be a werewolf. Nor indeed had the werewolf belief by then *entirely* disappeared even in literate circles, for the extraordinary Montague Summers, who combined vast erudition with unlimited credulity, was himself firmly convinced of the literal truth of most of the things reported in the trials of witches and werewolves. A reviewer in *The Times Literary Supplement* actually thought one of his books was a hoax, but Summers himself, in a biographical note supplied to a reference work, maintained that he had 'an absolute and complete belief ... in witchcraft', and there is no doubt he was equally firmly persuaded of the reality of werewolves.

About 2400 years before Summers was writing, a much more modern view was expressed by the historian Herodotus, when he was describing the Neuri, a people living in what are now Poland and Lithuania. 'There is a story', he writes, '... that once a year every Neurian turns into a wolf for a day or two, and then turns back into a man again. Of course, I do not believe this tale'. Sturdy scepticism of this kind has persisted in parallel with the wildest werewolf beliefs, even right through the period of the trials in France. Lambert Daneau wrote a book called *Les Sorciers*, which was translated as *A Dialogue of Witches* by Thomas Taylor in 1575. 'Daneau has nothing new to offer', writes the indignant Montague Summers, 'in his consideration of metamorphosis but is trivial to a degree with his easy prattle of "meere tryfles and oulde wyves tales"'. The question is, of course, what was the background of these meere tryfles and oulde wyves tales: and that is what we shall investigate in the remainder of this paper.

3

A number of explanations have been advanced for the werewolf belief, but there is certainly no reason to regard them as mutually exclusive. There are, in fact, so many factors working to produce such a belief that it is no wonder the belief appeared and persisted, and we may suppose that all these factors have worked together at various times and in various combinations. It is these factors that together make up the social-biological background of werewolves.

Were-animals are found all over the world, and we shall consider later the relevance of this for the werewolf belief in Europe. There are, however, a number of special factors in the specific case of werewolves, and we may conveniently begin with these. Even those 16th-century scholars and lawyers who firmly believed in the werewolf's pact with the devil did not all believe in his literal transformation to wolf shape. Two alternative explanations were offered. One was that the werewolf's body lies somewhere in a trance, while either his own spirit or a demon familiar takes possession of the body of a real wolf, and uses it to raven on livestock and human beings. This view was favoured in the books of Pierre Mamor (1490) and Gaspar Peucer (1553). The second explanation was called 'glamour': the Devil casts a spell that makes the werewolf appear both to himself and others to be a wolf, though he really remains a man. This view was favoured in the books of Nicolas Remy (1595) and Francesco Guazzo (1608). Summers himself admits that both these mechanisms may occur, as well as sheer transformation. These theories are of interest because they point in the direction of the only two possible rational explanations of the killings listed in the trials. It is impossible to believe that none of these killings occurred at all, and the two obvious possible explanations are slaughter by real wolves and murder by real men or women.

In Europe and northern Asia, by far the most dangerous animal to man and his livestock has been the wolf. 'From Scotland', writes Colin Matheson, 'where priests offered the prayer ... for deliverance ... "from wolves and all wild beasts", to Russia where peasants pronounced ... the recurring plea, "God grant the wolf may not take our cattle", the wolf was the great destroyer, the despoiler of flocks and herds and man's chief enemy in the animal world'. France, in particular, according to John Pollard, 'has probably suffered more from wolves than any other country, not excluding Russia'. The menace presented by wolves may be judged from the effort expended against them, especially in France, where there was a special government institution for wolf control from at least the reign of Charlemagne (AD 768–814) to the 20th century, and bounties were usually paid for dead wolves: at the end of the 18th century, the substantial sum of 150 francs was paid for a rabid wolf. Occasionally, solitary man-eating wolves have caused large numbers of deaths. In 1764–7, in the south of the Auvergne, on the most cautious estimate, some 60 people seem to have been killed by a single animal, known as the Beast of Gévaudan. It was finally shot by the hunter Jean Chastel in

June 1767, and is said to have had the collar-bone of a young girl in its stomach. By that time, in Matheson's words, the episode is 'estimated to have cost the State well over 29,000 livres—a considerable fortune for that period'. Most deaths of livestock and people, however, have probably been caused by wolf-packs. Livestock depredations have sometimes been on a considerable scale. In 1923, in the neighbourhood of Tsaritsin (now Volgograd), 1500 head of livestock were taken by wolves, and a single village, Dvoinoia, lost 160 horses. More recently, in 1962, according to Erkki Pullainen, in North Karelia, wolves killed 149 sheep, 9 cows, 15 calves and 3 horses, besides an unspecified number of cats and dogs. Killings of human beings by wolf-packs have been reported in France (1900) and Eastern Europe (1946–7), and in Siberia the whole village of Pilovo was only saved from a concerted attack by a wolf-pack in 1927 by a military operation, after a number of people had died. These are only some of a number of incidents of wolves killing human beings assembled by Colin Matheson, James Clarke and John Pollard.

Some zoologists have expressed scepticism about these accounts, and claim there are no authentic incidents of this kind in recent decades. However, it is difficult to believe that all the past accounts, often highly circumstantial, are legendary, and the sceptics appear to overlook three important points. First, modern wolves have had many generations' experience of fire-arms, and are likely to be more cautious than their ancestors. According to Anthony Dent, wolves can tell an armed from an unarmed man, and in fact a large proportion of the reported victims have been women and children. After the royalist rising in La Vendée in 1793 the inhabitants were forbidden to carry arms: wolves became such a menace that the government had to authorize a number of people to carry muskets as a defence against the animals. Second, wolf attacks have always been said to increase in hard winters, when the (then much larger) wolf populations were short of other food, and particularly in times of war and anarchy, when normal social arrangements broke down and communities were vulnerable to attack. In Matheson's words, 'war has always been associated with an increase in the numbers and ravages of wolves'. In France in 1439, during the frightful civil war between the partisans of the Count of Armagnac and the Duke of Burgundy, wolves came right into Paris and once ate 14 people in a fortnight. During the War of the League of Augsburg (1688–97), wolves attacked women and children up to the gates of Orleans, and when the city militia returned from the war they had to be used in a campaign against the wolves. Wolf depredations increased markedly during the first French Revolution in the 1790s, and again after the Franco-German War of 1870, and the last two human deaths ascribed to wolves in France occurred during the First World War (1914–18). After Cromwell's terrible campaign in Ireland in 1649, wolves increased so much there that a bounty was offered of no less than £5 per wolf. A third factor which the modern sceptics may underestimate is the possibility of man-eating individual wolves, which may well behave in a way uncharacteristic of the species as a whole. It is hard to believe the government of Louis XV spent more than 29,000 livres on a folk-tale. In 1970, H. Suomus reinvestigated some 19th-century Finnish data, and concluded that during the years 1880–1 a single wolf killed 22 children in southwestern Finland. Wolves such as this one and the Beast of Gévaudan cannot have been rabid, because they lived so long. In any case, nobody disputes that rabid wolves have killed human beings, of which more anon, and nobody disputes the enormous depredations of wolves on livestock. 'The most ardent exponents of fauna protection', writes Matheson, '—fortunately an increasing company at the present day—will see in the reduction of the wolves only a necessary step in man's control of the environment'.

In view of all this, it is no wonder the wolf has been the object of enormous fear and hatred in Europe. As the sinister Isengrin he appears in a cycle of medieval satiric poems, beginning with *Ysengrimus*, composed about 1150 in Latin, and continuing in the next three centuries with the many stories about Reynard the Fox; as Kenneth Varty has shown, these were lavishly illustrated in works of art in churches. The wolf is also the villain of numerous folk tales, including the European versions of the wolf and the kids (Type 123) and Red Riding Hood (Type 333 of Aarne and Stith Thompson). In the Anglo-Saxon calendar, January was Wolf-month, when the wolves formed packs and hunted large prey. In Norse mythology, the wolf Fenrir is the ultimate enemy of the gods, and the slayer of Odin himself. In St. Matthew's Gospel (vii, 15) there occurs the famous warning: 'Beware of false prophets, which come to you in sheep's clothing, but inwardly they are ravening wolves'. Now it is interesting that in the poem *Pierce the Ploughman's Crede* (about 1394), when this passage is quoted, the word used is *wer-wolves*. In the Laws of Cnut (King of England 1016–35), bishops and priests are urged to defend their flocks from the *werewulf*—here clearly a fierce wolf used as a metaphor for the Devil. The poet Alexander Montgomerie, in 1582, uses *warwoolffs* to mean simply fierce wolves. In books on hunting from the 14th to the 17th century, *loupgarou* and *werewolf* are used in the specific sense of a real wolf who has acquired a taste for human flesh, a man-eater. In 1508, Dr Johann Geiler von Keysersperg preached a sermon at Strasburg on werewolves. The whole sermon is concerned with man-eating wolves, and much of it is straightforward natural history. All this raises the question how many killings ascribed to werewolves were done by ordinary wolves. If ever there was a well-authenticated case of a killer wolf, it was the Beast of Gévaudan, yet even this was suspected of being human. A well-to-do, respected farmer testified before a magistrate that he had seen the Beast leaping through the air, and remarking: 'You must admit that's not a bad jump for an old man of ninety'.

In north-western Europe the wolf was gradually exterminated, first in England and probably Wales and the Scottish lowlands in the 16th century, then in Ireland and the Scottish highlands in the 18th century, then in Denmark, Switzerland and most of Germany in the 19th century. As Anthony Dent has observed, 'it is hard to imagine the weight that was lifted from the flock-master's shoulders once the wolf was no more. Like being in the dairy business and waking up one morning with the assurance that there would never be another outbreak of foot-and-mouth or contagious abortion—never again'. By about 1950, the wolf was believed to be extinct in France, but in 1968 wolves appeared in the Landes district of Aquitaine. It is no wonder the werewolf belief took such firm root in wolf-haunted France. As L. Illis has observed, extinction of wolves was soon followed locally by a more humane and rational attitude to alleged werewolves. James VI of Scotland was not noted for his humane and rational attitude to witchcraft in general. His *Daemonologie*, published in 1597, is full of savage and superstitious beliefs about witches. But in this same work he diagnosed alleged werewolves as suffering from depression and delusions, and ascribed stories of actual shape-changing to 'uncertaine report, the author of all lyes'. The reason, as Illis has noted, is evident: wolves were no longer a menace in most of Britain. At about the same time, at Labout in the wolf-ridden Pyrenees, some 200 human werewolves were burned.

There were two special features of wolves which helped to deepen the horror of the wolf image. First, wolves gain an added terror from their deceptive resemblance to their domesticated relatives, dogs. 'After dogs became domesticated', writes John Paul Scott, 'selection by man for various traits of appearance and behaviour began. One trait that distinguishes dogs from their wild relatives is an upturned tail, ranging from a sickle shape to a tight curl. This characteristic, a mutation that probably goes back to the original stock of domestic dogs, points to a common ancestry for all types of dogs'. We have suggested that the tail-up characteristic was consciously or unconsciously selected by the first dog-breeders because they had every incentive to make dogs recognizably different from the wolves that remained wild (for it is generally agreed that the first dogs were domesticated wolves). The difference between upturned and down-turned tail is scrupulously recorded in ancient representations of dogs and wolves, for instance in the charming clay figures of dogs from Jarmo in Iraq, dated to the 7th millennium BC. We have heard of a zoologist who took a hand-reared wolf on a voyage by ocean liner, registering it as an Alsatian; many passengers watched the fine dog with approval as he exercised it on deck. No ancient peoples familiar with wolves would have been deceived. But in dark or mist the distinguishing mark of the tail could not always be easily seen, and the European peasant or shepherd was subject to the terrifying risk of confusing man's best friend with man's worst enemy. In a Gothic tale published in 1838, there is a reference to twilight as 'that darking time ... which explains the diabolical sense of the old saying "'Tween dog and wolf"'; and the French, significantly, still use the phrase 'entre chien et loup'.

Both in Old Welsh and Old Irish, *wild dog* means *wolf*. The Welsh story of Prince Llywelyn and his dog Gelert is worth recalling in this context. The prince goes off on a raid, leaving his baby son in his tent, guarded by the hound Gelert. When he returns, he finds the tent collapsed, and Gelert sitting beside it covered with blood. Jumping to the wrong conclusion, he kills the poor dog, only to hear the cry of a baby, and find his son safe and sound under the tent, with the carcase of a huge wolf, slain by the faithful Gelert in defence of the baby. Now this is a widely distributed tale (Type 178): there is a version from India with a mongoose as hero and a snake as villain. But the Welsh version surely gains an added dimension from the special relationship between the dog and the wolf.

It was sometimes remarked by trial witnesses that werewolves in their wolf form had no tails: this was reported, for instance, of the werewolf Perrenette Gandillon in 1584. Now as Katharine M. Briggs has observed, when witches changed into animals of any kind, it was 'supposed that an actual transformation of member for member took place, and therefore witch creatures must be tailless ... This limitation made toads particularly useful creatures to shape-shifters'. Hence the First Witch in *Macbeth*: 'and, like a rat without a tail, I'll do, I'll do, and I'll do' (Act I, Scene 3). Werewolves clearly conform to the general rule for witches, and some authorities took a similar view of their transformation. Nevertheless, for peasants and shepherds accustomed to distinguish dogs from wolves by their tails, the absence of tails in werewolves must have had an added significance. Nor is the dog-wolf confusion entirely absent from the reports. In 1603, a young girl of 13, Marguerite Poirier, of Saint-Paul in the Landes region, fought off a creature later identified with the werewolf Jean Grenier: she described it as not unlike a huge dog.

Theo Brown has shown that dogs in folklore may be either protective or menacing. We have just seen them in their protective role, contrasted with wolves. When we turn, however, to a second terrifying feature of wolves, it is one they share with dogs. This is the appalling disease of rabies, which is transmitted to man by wolves as well as by dogs and certain other animals. By a careful comparison of Greek and Hebrew medical literature of various dates, R. H. A. Merlen, of the Royal Veterinary College, has established the course of events in the early history of the disease. In the ancient Mediterranean, rabies was a common disease of dogs, but before the 1st century BC man was not susceptible to it. By the 1st century AD, however, people in the Mediterranean countries were dying of the disease after being bitten by rabid dogs. During the 1st century BC, large numbers of dogs from northern Europe were imported into the Mediterranean lands, and it seems likely that they brought with them a type of rabies virus that was fatal to man. Presumably this virus type had evolved in northern Europe, but for lack of written records we have no means of knowing how long it has been present there. From the beginning of the Christian era, rabies was one of the most dreaded of all diseases throughout Europe, and by the time of the medical writer Soranus of Ephesus (2nd century AD) it was being transmitted to man by wolves as well as dogs. The first detailed record of a rabid wolf was in 1166, at Carmarthen in Wales: the animal is said to have bitten 18 people, most of whom died. Numerous cases are recorded from France in the 18th and 19th centuries; for instance, in 1839 in the Department of Puy-de-Dome, 28 people are said to have been bitten by a rabid wolf, and 12 of them died within periods of up to 39 days after the bite. It was not until 1885 that Louis Pasteur developed a vaccine against rabies. In 1886, he treated 19 Russians from Smolensk, who had been bitten by a rabid wolf, and succeeded in saving all but three.

Nearly a century after Pasteur's discovery, rabies is referred to as 'the most terrifying disease known to man' in the *TV Times* of 19–25th July, 1975, in an account of a programme describing the serious rabies problem in France and Eastern Europe, and the potential dangers for Britain. A useful modern account of the disease is given by D. A. Robinson in the March 1976 issue of *Update* (the Journal of Postgraduate General Practice). The disease can be averted if the wound is disinfected or vaccine administered soon after the bite of a rabid animal; once the disease has taken hold, it is virtually incurable—'only two proven cases of paralytic rabies are known to have survived'. The symptoms include painful spasms of the throat, which make it impossible to swallow and result in a phobia of water, an alternation 'between manic activity and calm but distressed lucidity', and eventually paralyses and convulsions. 'The fact that the patient may retain full insight right to the end despite his suffering makes rabies not only a barbarous death but a most harrowing and indelible experience for those who have to look after him'.

It is hard to imagine the fear aroused by rabies in earlier times, when the only remotely rational treatment known was immediate cautery of the wounds inflicted by a rabid animal. Pasteur's own first encounter with rabies occurred at Arbois when he was nine years old, in 1831: he witnessed the cautery, by a red-hot iron in the local smithy, of wounds inflicted on a farmer by a rabid wolf that had invaded the village. The shocking symptoms made the disease particularly frightening. All this must have added greatly to the terrors surrounding the wolf; for a rabid wolf is obviously far more difficult to fight off than a rabid wild animal of a smaller species, or all but the largest rabid dogs. Moreover, a wolf is likely to inflict serious wounds; and 'severe tissue damage increases the likelihood of a large dose of virus being inoculated, and shortens the incubation period' (Robinson).

The occurrence of a terrible disease transmitted from wolf to man, providing a sinister linkage between the two species, may well have contributed to the werewolf belief. It is even possible that some of the convicted werewolves may have been suffering from rabies. Though the vaccine had to wait for Pasteur, rabies in man has been the subject of rational discussion by medical writers ever since its appearance in the Roman Empire; in 1583, at the height of the werewolf scare, an account of rabies was published by Petrus Salius at Bologna. Nevertheless, Montague Summers (writing in 1933!) had apparently never heard of the disease. He mixes it up with lycanthropy (of which more later), ascribes the phobia of water to demoniacal possession, and relates it to the water ordeal inflicted on witches, in which they were thrown into a pond or stream to see whether 'the water shall refuse to receive them in her bosom' (James VI). Some of the 16th- and 17th-century judges may well have been as ignorant and confused as Summers, and sent the victims of rabies to the stake as witches or werewolves.

4

We have considered the contribution of the wolf to the werewolf belief; we must now consider the contribution of the purely human factor. The simplest way to account for the killings recorded in the werewolf trials is to ascribe them to mass-murderers, who may sometimes have been the werewolves themselves, and sometimes person or persons unknown who got away with their crimes while the unfortunate werewolves were convicted. The importance of mass-murder for the werewolf belief was much emphasized by that versatile folklorist, the Reverend Sabine Baring-Gould, in his *Book of Werewolves* (1865); among other examples of mass-murderers, he mentions in particular Gilles de Rais (Bluebeard) and a Hungarian noblewoman who, from his description, is evidently Erzsebet Bathory, Countess Nadasdy.

The characteristics of mass-murderers have been studied in modern examples by William Bolitho, and we have elsewhere summarized these in relation to still more recent examples. The crimes of the werewolf trials seem very like conventional modern mass-murders. It comes naturally to modern writers and journalists to describe a mass-murderer, picturesquely, as a werewolf. Paul I. Wellman, for instance, in his account of the Harpe gang, who terrorized the American frontier at the end of the 18th century, has a chapter headed *Werewolves in the Wilds.* 'Like werewolves', he writes at one point, 'the two blood-mad murderers had begun to kill for the sheer lust of killing'. We have shown that Adolf Hitler 'fits all the specifications' of the mass-murderer, and it is interesting that the Nazis saw themselves as werewolves. As the war in north-west Europe drew to a close, there was a rumour in the British 2nd Army that the more fanatical Nazis were planning to disband the party and operate as individual mass-murderers, under the name of *werewolves.* One of Hitler's military headquarters, near Vinnitsa in the Ukraine, was officially called *Werewolf.*

Detailed study of Gilles de Rais and Erzsebet Bathory shows Baring-Gould's acuteness in picking on these cases. The despotic powers of some great European land-owners in the 15th to 17th centuries afforded special opportunities for mass-murder; but both the French Marshal and the Hungarian Countess conformed closely to the behaviour of modern mass-murderers, notably in the repetitiveness of their crimes and in their growing megalomaniac disregard for the restraint and discretion necessary even for great European land-owners: so that Gilles de Rais ended up on the scaffold and Erzsebet Bathory walled up in her bedroom. Both of them managed, despite enormous possessions in France and Hungary, respectively, to squander so much money that they were eventually in serious financial difficulties. Gilles de Rais (1404–40) was a Marshal of France, the heir to great estates on the borders of Brittany, and for a time a person of influence at the French court. Between 1432 and 1440 he butchered an unknown number of boys, certainly hundreds. Erzsebet Bathory (1560–1614) belonged to an enormously influential Hungarian noble family, which included kings of Poland and Transylvania. They were, however, highly inbred, and by Erzsebet's time included a number of insane sadists. Erzsebet herself outdid them all; between 1604 (possibly earlier) and 1610, she tortured to death something like 600 girls, often bathing in their blood. It is interesting that both De Rais and Bathory have wolf associations. A Breton song about Bluebeard, recorded in the 19th century, includes the line: 'the ravening wolf is not more terrible than the wild Baron'. One of De Rais's servants believed his master had summoned up the Devil in the form of a large dog or wolf: Gilles himself described it as a big black dog. There was a legend that Erzsebet Bathory was followed about by a she-wolf. The Bathory coat of arms showed three wolf's teeth: the three teeth, embedded in a vertical jaw-bone, are used to represent the E of Erzsebet in a surviving portrait of the Countess.

The connection between wolves and violent crime is an old one. When a Roman was convicted of matricide, his face was covered with a wolf-skin. The term *wolf* or *wolf's head* was used to mean *outlaw* in the laws of the Franks, the Normans, Cnut, Edward the Confessor and Henry I; and in medieval Europe a wolf was sometimes hung on the gallows beside a human criminal. Several authors have drawn attention to this association of wolves and human outlaws as one basis for the werewolf belief.

The werewolf trials make several references to the eating of the victims. Baring-Gould connects this with the occurrence of cannibalism. This is found as a regular practice only among peoples living on starchy crops and liable to be short of protein, chiefly in the Pacific, Africa and Central America (where the Caribs gave their name both to cannibalism and the Caribbean). It has, however, been not uncommon in Europe as a result of sheer starvation, in sieges and serious famines—it occurred on a large scale in the terrible famine of 1315–17.

More to the point, cannibalism is sometimes found as a regular accompaniment to mass murder. In the early 1920s, when Germany was suffering from severe food shortage, there were cases of mass-murderers peddling their victims' flesh as ordinary meat, in Berlin, Hanover and Munsterberg: as William Bolitho comments, 'the days of werewolves and anthropophagi were brought back in Europe'. In this connection, we may also mention a wood-cut by Lucas Cranach, that we saw on March 27th, 1975 in an exhibition of his works in the National Museum of Fine Arts in Valletta, Malta. The cut, produced about 1512, shows a naked man, dishevelled and crawling on all fours with a screaming small child in his jaws: two dismembered corpses of women lie in the background, and another child is running away. Though the central figure is a perfectly ordinary male human being (with rather long hands and feet), the cut is entitled *The Wolf.*

It is against this background of metaphor and association that we must consider the factor of 'glamour'—that is, in rational terms, of hallucination on the part of either the witnesses or the accused. Suggestion alone, in a suitable setting, can produce remarkable results. The psychoanalyst Nandor Fodor mentions a report, dated March 23rd, 1933, by Dr. Gerald Kirkland, formerly Government Medical Officer in what was then Southern Rhodesia. 'Dr. Kirkland had seen a native jackal dance and *could almost swear to it that two natives actually transformed themselves into jackals*' (Fodor's italics). Hallucinations on the part of *witnesses* of werewolf doings can therefore not be ruled out. Hallucinations of all kinds were occurring throughout the Middle Ages in Europe, and they may have had more specific causes than the recurrent stresses of the period. The disease of rye called ergot is produced by the fungus *Claviceps purpurea.* In medieval mills the grain was normally divided into two piles—one free of ergot infection, the other infected. The clean grain was reserved for nobles and clergy, the ergotized grain left for the peasants. Ergot produces a number of poisonous substances; it was used as a rough-and-ready abortifacient, often with lethal results. In 1943, Albert Hofmann, working with derivatives of ergot, isolated the substance lysergic acid diethylamide (LSD), a fantastically potent hallucinogenic drug. It now seems likely the fungus periodically produces this or very similar substances under natural conditions, and that this accounts for severe epidemics of ergot poisoning that have occurred in Europe at intervals since AD 857, often resulting in thousands of deaths. The most recent outbreak, described in detail by John G. Fuller, occurred in 1951 in the village of Pont-Saint-Esprit on the Rhône, when ergotized rye was mixed with wheat in a consignment of grain. Nearly three hundred people were poisoned, five died, and many others never fully recovered. The most ghastly feature of the epidemic was the flood of terrifying hallucinations experienced by the victims. One man thought red snakes were eating his brain, another saw the hospital attendants as great fishes with gaping mouths, ready to eat him alive. A little girl and a labourer both felt they were being attacked by tigers: the labourer, a powerful man, broke seven strait-jackets, lost all his teeth biting through a leather strap, and bent two thick iron bars in a hospital window, in his struggles to escape from the tigers. This modern episode casts a lurid light on the medieval epidemics. Clearly it would only need a few such episodes to give currency to a belief in the actual transformation of werewolves.

When we come to hallucinations experienced by the accused werewolves themselves, we are on still firmer ground. In a number of the werewolf cases, the accused were said to have smeared themselves with a special ointment before being transformed into wolves: this was reported of Pierre Burgot and Michel Verdun (1521), Gilles Garnier (1573), Pierre and Georges Gandillon (1584), Jaques Roulet (1598) and Jean Grenier (1603). Now according to Johann Weyer (1579), this ointment was the same as that employed by ordinary witches before they went to a Sabbat. Throughout the period of the witch and werewolf trials, a large number of writers were suggesting that the supposed experiences of witches at their Sabbats were really hallucinations resulting from the drugs contained in the ointment. These writers included Alphonso de Torado, Bishop of Avila (1451), Gerolamo Cardano, the great mathematician and physician (1554), Giovanni Battista Porta (1560), the Johann Weyer we have just mentioned (1579), the Sieur de Beauvoys de Chauvincourt (1599) and Jean de Nynauld (1615). Weyer, de Chavincourt and de Nynauld specifically suggested the ointment could produce hallucinations of being transformed into a wolf. The composition of the ointment was well known: recipes were published by Cardano, Porta, Weyer, de Nynauld and Francis Bacon. The ingredients included several plants of the Solanaceae, the nightshade family, notably henbane and deadly nightshade. These plants contain powerful drugs: deadly nightshade is still grown as a source of scopolamine and atropine. In 1545, the physicians of Pope Julius III tried out the ointment taken from a sorcerer on a woman suffering from a nervous disease: she reported strange hallucinations. Experiments have been made right up to modern times with the application of the ointment, which includes a fatty base to facilitate absorption, and is most effective when applied to hairy, thin skin; hallucinations have usually been obtained. In addition, there is a large modern literature on the effects of scopolamine and atropine. The hallucinations thus produced match the reported experiences of the witches, including, for instance, sensations of flying through the air. Bernard Barnett, in a paper on witchcraft and hallucinations published in 1965, notes the striking fact that people accidentally poisoned by nightshade substances have imagined themselves to be changed into animals, with a vivid sensation of growing fur. In view of all this, anyone in the 16th and 17th centuries who smeared on the ointment with the expectation of becoming a wolf could easily have hallucinated the transformation, and confessed to it afterwards as a fact.

Besides such transient hallucinations, we have also to reckon with the fixed delusion of being a wolf. It was this that James VI had in mind when he wrote of deluded individuals who 'have thought themselves verrie Woolfes indeed'. The delusion was well known in his day, and was generally called *lycanthropy*, from the Greek words for *wolf* and *man*. It is well described in Act V Scene 2 of John Webster's *The Duchess of Malfi* (printed 1623):

Doctor: A very pestilent disease, my lord.
They call lycanthropia.
Pescara: What's that?
I need a dictionary to't.
Doctor: I'll tell you.
In those that are possessed with't there o'erflows
Such melancholy humour they imagine
Themselves to be transformed into wolves;
Steal forth to churchyards in the dead of night,
And dig dead bodies up: as two nights since
One met the duke 'bout midnight in a lane
Behind Saint Mark's church, with the leg of a man
Upon his shoulder; and he howled fearfully;
Said he was a wolf, only the difference
Was, a wolf's skin was hairy on the outside,
His on the inside; bade them take their swords,
Rip up his flesh and try....

A real-life case strikingly like this had been described by Job Fincel in 1556; it occurred near Padua in 1541. A farmer, who believed himself to be a wolf, attacked and killed several people, tearing them with his teeth. When captured, he explained his fur was inside his skin. Whereupon, as Summers well puts it, 'some of the bystanders, showing themselves to be more cruel wolves than he, actually made deep wounds in his arms and legs to test the truth of his frantic imaginings'. After they had cut off his arms and legs without finding any trace of wolf-fur, they handed him over to the surgeons, but not surprisingly he soon died. This case was almost certainly known to Webster. In another similar case, the patient was fortunately rescued by a doctor before the peasants flayed him to test his belief. We cannot rule out ergot poisoning in these cases, for one of the victims at Pont-Saint-Esprit in 1951 cried out: 'Please, Sirs, cut my skin. Cut my skin! I'll feel better. Get me a bicycle and cut my skin!' However, cases of chronic lycanthropic delusions have been described in medical literature from the early 14th century (Bernard de Gordon) to 1852, when a certain Dr. Morel described a patient completely convinced he was a wolf, who eventually died in the asylum at Mareville. James VI was not the only writer in the wolf-free parts of Britain to interpret the continental werewolves as sufferers from lycanthropic delusions: the same conclusion was reached by Reginald Scot (1584), William Camden (1586), and Randle Cotgrave (1611). In this connection it is worth noting that a delusion may, through the power of suggestion, bring about something approaching repercussion. There is a well-authenticated story, dated to 1919, concerning a certain Saiyi of Zumethi, employed in the Civil Works Department of Assam, who believed he had a special relationship with a wild tiger. On learning that this tiger had been shot, he took to his bed. Before he died in Kohima Hospital, according to C. P. Mills, 'he said he was suffering terrible pains in the abdomen owing to the wound inflicted on his tiger, and showed an inflamed swelling on either side of the stomach, corresponding, of course, to the entrance and exit holes of the bullet which had hit the tiger'.

Besides the behaviour disturbance, the disease of lycanthropy in its typical form included a number of physical symptoms. These were first described in a monograph written early in the 2nd century AD by the highly respected physician Marcellus of Side (in what is now Turkey); he was followed by a large number of other medical writers of the Roman Empire and the 16th and 17th centuries, listed and quoted by Summers. Now in this connection a most important discovery has been made by L. Illis. He first noticed that some of the detailed accounts of werewolf cases involved partial transformations, in which only the hands and teeth of the accused became wolf-like: Garnier, for instance, was said to have killed one of his victims with his teeth and hands, seeming like paws. Next, Illis compared the symptoms of lycanthropy listed by the medical writers with the physical characteristics ascribed to werewolves by the legal writers and court records: he found a close agreement. (Summers himself notes the dry eyes mentioned by the medical writers, and relates this symptom to the reputed inability of witches to weep, but he seems to have wanted to prove lycanthropes were werewolves, rather than the converse!) Illis sums up the usual symptoms of both lycanthropes and werewolves as follows: a tendency to wander about at night, a yellow complexion, hairy skin covered with sores, red teeth, frightening facial deformities, and disturbed behaviour. He has shown that all these symptoms may occur in sufferers from the inherited disease called congenital porphyria. The patient's skin becomes sensitive to, and damaged by light (which could well result in a preference for going out at night), the skin may be yellow and hairy, red pigments appear in the teeth and urine, there may be disturbances of behaviour, and ulcers sometimes cause severe deformities of the face and hands, which may indeed come to resemble a wolf's paws. Blood-red teeth and urine, hairy wolf-like faces and hands, disturbed behaviour and nocturnal wanderings would certainly have aroused alarm and suspicion in the period of the werewolf trials, and the occurrence of one or two violent deaths (however caused) would be enough to bring about the trial and execution of the unfortunate sufferer from porphyria.

5

We have now considered both the wolf and the human factors contributing to the werewolf belief; to complete the picture, we must consider the composite figure of the man-wolf as such. We find at once that the werewolf is only one example of a category of were-animals found in folklore all over the world. In any given region, the species chosen is generally the mammal most dangerous to man and/or his livestock. For instance, in Asia we find were-tigers, in Africa were-hyenas, in Central America were-coyotes; in New Zealand, for lack of indigenous mammals, we find were-lizards. The source of all these monsters is ultimately to be found in the system of beliefs and behaviour called totemism.

We have elsewhere given an up-to-date account of totemism; here a brief summary will suffice. The system was discovered in its simplest form among the Australian aborigines and the Melanesians of the islands off New Guinea. Aspects of totemism are, however, universal in human societies. The system seems to have appeared in the Old Stone Age, and (as Jack Lindsay especially has shown) it has influenced the cultural evolution of all civilizations up to the present. In its most complete form in a tribal society the system is as follows. The tribe is composed of several clans (kinship groups), and each clan is intimately associated with one species of animals (sometimes one species of plants or one kind of natural object). The members of a clan are forbidden to mate among themselves, and forbidden to eat animals of their totem species except on special ritual occasions. They believe their first ancestor or ancestress was a being with 'the characteristics of both men and animals, which were not then distinct' (B. A. L. Cranstone). This human–animal was the ancestor or ancestress of both the totemic clan and the animals of their totem species. On special ceremonial occasions, this human–animal ancestor or ancestress is represented by members of the clan, wearing appropriate masks and disguises.

The realization that mankind is one species, unique and different in important ways from all other animals, is actually a very recent achievement: it had been established for less than a century when Darwin explained the *real* sense in which mankind *as a whole* is descended from animal ancestors. We are now so familiar with the notion of man as unique, and separate from the animal world, that we cannot easily imagine how readily people thought until recently in terms of animal–human monsters. Were-animals, and werewolves in particular, are obviously a highly stress-laden expression of this confusion. Their sinister character is due in part to accumulations of stress in the societies concerned, and in part to changes in patterns of kinship and social organization, such that earlier forms come to be seen as monstrous and criminal. Since werewolves are eventually regarded as breaking the most sacred taboos currently observed, it is entirely appropriate that Endore makes his fictional werewolf commit incest.

In examining the totemic origins of the werewolf, we may begin with some ancient Greek stories. The god Apollo seems to have been associated with a wolf clan: his mother was in the form of a she-wolf when she bore him, and he himself sometimes took wolf form. Later mythographers rationalized his name of *wolf-god* by claiming that he offered protection against wolves: the shrine of the Lyceum at Athens, where Aristotle taught, was sacred to the god in this aspect. More clearly relevant for the werewolf are a group of legends, told in various forms by a number of ancient writers, about some sites in Arcadia (in the central Pelopponese) with names from the Greek root *luk* (wolf): Mount Lycaeus, with its temple of Zeus Lycaeus, and the nearby town of Lycosura. It was said that a king called Lycaon made a human sacrifice there, and according to some, a cannibal feast: for this crime, he was turned into a wolf by the gods. It was also said that, after each subsequent sacrifice to Zeus Lycaeus, the officiating priests took off all their clothes, swam across a lake, and became wolves. After nine years, they could recover their clothes and turn back to men; but if they had meanwhile tasted human flesh, they remained wolves for life. In 1931, these stories were convincingly explained by Sir William Ridgeway as arising from 'the circumstance that as the medicine-men of modern totem clans often get themselves up like their totem animal, so the priest who officiated at the Lycaean rites may have arrayed himself in a wolf-skin'. The wearing of animal masks and costumes by sacrificing priests is very well attested. In the earliest representation of a human sacrifice, a cave engraving of the late Old Stone Age at Addaura, near Palermo, bird-masked officiants supervise the strangling of human victims. Wall-paintings of the late 7th millennium BC, in the farming town of Catal Huyuk (in what is now Turkey), show human beings in vulture costumes surrounding headless human victims. Among the Tupinamba of Brazil, the executioner at a human sacrifice wore an elaborate feather costume. In the words of Francis Huxley (who lived among the related Urubu people in 1951 and 1953), the executioner danced 'round the clearing ... imitating the act of a falcon striking down its prey'. So it is entirely plausible that the Lycaean priests wore wolf-skins. Now the Urubu executioner, after the sacrifice, had to observe a number of taboos, and 'go into seclusion for many months' (Huxley); so it is quite conceivable that the Lycaean priests may have had to withdraw into the wilderness (like wolves) for a fixed period. Moreover, the Tupinamba sacrificer was not allowed to touch the flesh of his victim, which was eaten by the other tribesfolk. It is therefore possible that the Lycaean priests had a similar taboo, and that if they broke it they became outlaws for life. In this way we can trace the whole complex of Arcadian stories back to totemic practices; at the same time, these stories have obvious affinities with werewolf tales (notably the point about the clothes); and in the early Middle Ages we hear of werewolves condemned to remain in wolf form for a fixed period—seven years, in the case of two Irish werewolves described by Giraldus Cambrensis in 1188.

In the course of cultural evolution, through conquest, assimilation, or other means, some totems became emblems of social units much larger than clans, and eventually of whole peoples. Two famous peoples had wolf totems—the Turks (who called themselves the Sons of the Wolf) and the Romans. In view of the influence of Rome on the cultural evolution of western Europe, it is worth considering the Roman wolf in some detail. The myth of the she-wolf that suckled Romulus and Remus was probably well established at Rome in the 4th century BC, for a statue of the wolf and twins was set up there in 296 BC. Though there were Greek precedents for choosing a wolf, there is no reason why the wolf should not have been the totem of one of the clans contributing to the ancestry of the Roman population. At all events, the wolf was soon clearly identified with Rome in the minds of friend and foe alike. In the words of Michael Grant, the wolf-and-twins scene 'appears on coins of c.269 and was reduplicated thousands of times on visual representations for century after century'. When the Italian cities and tribes revolted against the Roman League (91–87 BC), they adopted the bull as their emblem, and struck coins of the Italian bull goring the Roman wolf. The Roman Emperor Hadrian (AD 117–38) was a great lover of Greek civilization, and cordially endorsed the famous observation of Horace that conquered Greece had taken her conquerors captive, by her enormous cultural influence on Rome. He expressed this gracefully by setting up statues of himself in Greece (there is one in the Agora at Athens), wearing a cuirass decorated with a Greek goddess standing on the Roman she-wolf as she suckles the twins.

The notion that Romulus, the ancestral hero of Rome, was suckled by a she-wolf is a thin disguise for the idea of a totemic ancestral human-wolf. For the most self-consciously patrilineal of ancient peoples, the *she*-wolf, clearly a totemic ancestress, was an embarassing relic of matrilineal descent. The scholars of the later Roman Republic tended to rationalize the story in terms of the two meanings of the Latin word *lupa*—*she-wolf* and *prostitute*. It is, of course, quite characteristic of patrilineal culture to misinterpret the behaviour of a woman in an earlier matrilineal period as the equivalent of prostitution. At the same time, it is very interesting that by the time of Petronius (1st century AD) the werewolf conception appears fully formed. Certainly by this time plenty of stress had accumulated in Roman culture. But the sequence also suggests that the werewolf can represent a former totem become disreputable, a matrilineal symbol reinterpreted in the terms of a patrilineal society under stress.

The transition from matrilineal to patrilineal culture took place somewhat later in northern Europe, so it is now of interest to look at the history of the werewolf in that region. Though wolves are depicted rather rarely in early Celtic art, they appear to have been Celtic totems. One whole Irish tribe claimed descent from a wolf, and the Irish hero Cormac was suckled by a wolf, and kept a band of wolves always with him—presumably his clan. The great Welsh collection of stories now called the Mabinogion contains several tales of 11th-century or 10th-century composition, with material probably far older: there are plenty of matrilineal elements. In the story of Math, son of Mathonwy, the brothers Gwydion and Gilfaethwy are punished for rape by being turned into a he-wolf and a she-wolf, respectively, for a year: but when the year is up they resume human form, and the cub they have produced becomes a boy and is carefully reared. We are here on the border between totemic ancestors and werewolves. The werewolves Burgot and Verdun, it may be noted, were accused of coupling with real she-wolves.

In northern Europe, therefore (and this seems to be true of Germanic as well as Celtic peoples), the werewolf long remained an acceptable expression of old totemic beliefs. This accounts for two striking facts. First, in the Dark Ages and early Middle Ages, church authorities regarded the *belief* in werewolves as sinful, evidently because it harked back to an older system of social organization. The werewolf belief was condemned, for instance, by St. Boniface in the 8th century, Bishop Burchard of Worms in the early 11th century, and Pope Gregory VII in 1080 (in a letter to King Harald of Denmark). This attitude was still being expressed in a Lubeck handbook for penitents published as late as 1484. This is the more striking as a few decades later it was widely regarded as sinful *not* to believe in werewolves—by then regarded as evil sorcerers.

Second, in medieval literature, and in one stream of north European folklore until recent times, werewolves were treated as sympathetic. We have mentioned the case of the two Irish werewolves discussed (as an authentic incident) by the Welsh ecclesiastic Giraldus Cambrensis in 1188. These two were a married couple, cursed by a saint and condemned to be wolves for seven years. In this story even a priest sympathized with their plight: he gave the wife, who was ill, Holy Communion, and in return the male werewolf led the priest and his attendant out of the wood where they had been benighted. The case naturally gave rise to much discussion by Church authorities.

In this account the werewolves appear as sympathetic. In medieval fiction, the werewolf could even be a hero, 'the innocent victim of a malignant power' (K. F. Smith). This trend even resulted in one story (written in 1258 by Philippe de Novare) in which the *wolf* Isengrin figured exceptionally as hero instead of villain. There were several romances with werewolf heroes: *Arthur and Gorlagon*, the *Lai de Melion*, Marie de France's *Bisclavret*, the *Histoire de Biclarel* and *William of Palerne* (Palermo). They were all intricately connected. Irene Pettit McKeehan has discussed these connections, and the derivation of the romances from a Celtic folk-tale, from the stories of the Irish hero Cormac, and even from the Roman she-wolf. The most successful was *William of Palerne*, which she aptly describes as a medieval best-seller. It began as a French poem in the late 12th century (loosely based on an earlier work in Latin), was translated as an English poem in or soon after 1350, and was rewritten as a French prose romance in the 16th century. The story tells of a prince, William, who is stolen as a child by a werewolf, Alphonse, to save him from a murder plot. Besides saving and caring for him in childhood, the werewolf later helps him to elope with the girl he loves, Melior. During their flight, the lovers are disguised, first as bears, then as deer—further totemic elements. Alphonse himself has been turned into a wolf by his stepmother, the Queen of Spain: William, who finally becomes Emperor, forces the wicked queen to disenchant his benefactor.

This theme of the hero turned to wolf by a stepmother is not only Celtic: it occurs in a Swedish folk-tale (from Uppland) called

The Werewolf, where the tables are finally turned on the enchantress (here the stepmother of the princess who loves the hero), when she and her daughters are turned into werewolves after the hero recovers his human form. *William of Palerne* must therefore have appealed to all the peoples of western Europe. Wicked stepmothers are of course matrilineal ancestresses trying to foist their offspring in place of the legitimate patrilineal heir or heiress. But as patrilineal descent became fully established in western Europe at the start of the 16th century (when surnames derived from the mother ceased to be used), it seems the werewolf itself fell into disrepute as a survival of the earlier totemic system. The expansion of silver coinage about this time may be connected with the vulnerability of werewolves to silver, a conception that first appears in Germany, where most of the silver was mined until the Spaniards began to import it from the New World. Meanwhile, under the stress of two successive crises of overpopulation, the wolf and human factors we have discussed came fully into play, and the terrible epidemic of werewolf trials broke out. In popular folklore, however, some werewolves at least continued to be sympathetic victims of enchantment.

In the urban societies of modern Europe, where people no longer have any dealings with real wolves, the old totemic attitude has reappeared in the form of a remarkable sentimentality about these animals. This tendency was crystallized by Rudyard Kipling, in what his biographer, Charles Carrington, calls 'the first and second *Jungle Books*, the best-sellers among his works'. Kipling began work on these stories in 1892, after reading a scene in a book of Rider Haggard's, where 'in a riot of supernatural fantasy' (Carrington), the hero runs with a pack of wolves. In Kipling's stories of talking animals, set in India, a boy is raised, Romulus-like, by wolves, and educated by the wise pack-leader wolf Akela; the wolves are idealized, and the monkeys (man's *real* relatives) systematically denigrated. In considering these enormously influential stories, we may notice that Kipling also expressed a new British attitude to *Rome*. In the 17th century, Rome was of course the source of all villainy for British Protestants, and the wolf was still an unpleasant memory, so the wolf emblem of Rome took on a new lease of life. This revival of old symbolism appears in *Lycidas*, where Milton is castigating the negligent shepherds of the Church of England:

The hungry sheep look up, and are not fed,
But, swoln with wind and the rank mist they draw,
Rot inwardly, and foul contagion spread;
Besides what the grim wolf with privy paw
Daily devours apace, and nothing said.

Members of the flock lost to the wolf were, of course, conversions to the Church of Rome. A grimmer expression of this equation was to be seen in Cromwellian Ireland, where the same bounty (£5) was offered for the head of a wolf or the head of a Roman priest. In the 18th century, when the Protestant succession was ensured, the British upper classes looked fondly back to the Rome of the Republic and early Monarchy, and liked to see themselves in togas. But this nostalgia was for Roman law and civilization, not for anything so Gothic as a wolf totem. With Kipling, we find yet another attitude, a highly emotional expression of affinity between the Roman and British Empires (both seen in a somewhat sentimental light). It seems therefore entirely appropriate that Kipling should have given definitive expression to the revival of the wolf symbol.

Though there is not much documentation on the subject, it is known that Kipling heartily approved of the Boy Scout organization founded by his friend Baden-Powell: he visited a scout camp, and in 1909 he wrote a 'Patrol Song' for the scouts. The wolf-cubs are, of course, definitely derived from the *Jungle Books*: the cub-leader, standing beside a wolf's-head standard, is called Akela, like Kipling's pack-leader. Thus generations of urban children have been familiarized with the wolf totem. This may help to explain the appearance in recent years of movements to conserve wild wolf populations, and even reintroduce them into regions where they have been exterminated. Whether or not healthy wolves kill human beings, there is no doubt about their depredations on livestock, and wolves are certainly particularly dangerous carriers of rabies. To propose conserving them in the wild is therefore analogous to suggesting the conservation of desert locusts or malarial mosquitoes; it can surely only be explained by something like totemic survivals. We may note at this point that a totemic clan is obsessed with the need to conserve its totem species, and performs many ceremonies magically supposed to contribute to this. The taboo on killing the totem species really does, of course, help conserve it. So long as all totems were valuable food species, the totemic system was ecologically sound. However, as Sir Baldwin Spencer showed among Australian aborigines, 'with the development of the totemistic idea, this gradually spread until it embraced a variety of objects, many of which were of no actual service to the natives'. The conservation of a pest species is, therefore, intelligible in totemic terms, though obviously not in terms of rational ecology. The sentimental attitude to wolves is not shared by modern peoples (especially herders) who have anything to do with them in real life. The introduction of the Boy Scout movement among reindeer-herding Same (Lapps) encountered an unexpected resistance; the Lapp children were quite prepared to be called animals (say, lemmings), but objected strongly to the name of Wolf-cubs.

We cannot close the subject of the Man-Wolf without some reference to the Wolf-Man. This is the name traditionally used by psychoanalysts since the 1920s for a patient treated between 1910 and 1914 by Sigmund Freud. The case is exceptional because more material is available about it than about any of Freud's other cases. This material includes Freud's own case history, the Wolf-Man's own memoirs and his recollections of Freud, a case history of his later treatment by another analyst, and accounts of interviews with him in later life: all this material, edited by Muriel Gardiner, was published as a single book, called *The Wolf-Man and Sigmund Freud*, in 1972. The Penguin edition of 1973 has a jacket decorated with a photograph of Freud and an inset montage of a man with a wolf's head.

The Wolf-Man was a Russian nobleman, who was ruined by the First World War and the Revolution. Both his traditional title and the jacket picture of the Penguin edition are oddly, and perhaps significantly, inappropriate. For the Wolf-Man was not a lycanthrope, and had no delusions of being a wolf. On the contrary, he had an extreme fear of wolves. When he was a little boy, his elder sister teased him by promising to show him the picture of a pretty little girl. When she took away the piece of paper she had used to cover the picture, the boy saw, 'instead of a pretty little girl, a wolf standing on his hind legs with his jaws wide open, about to swallow Little Red Riding Hood'. He screamed and had a temper tantrum. However, he owes his title chiefly to a famous dream analysed by Freud. This dream occurred just before one Christmas, when he was nearly four—his birthday was on

Christmas Eve. He was lying in his bed at night. 'Suddenly the window opened of its own accord, and I was terrified to see that some white wolves were sitting on the big walnut tree in front of the window.'

Claire Russell has recently re-examined the Wolf-Man case, and this dream in particular, in the light of her studies of the evolution of kinship and its symbols. Her reinterpretation of the dream is given here only in bare outline. To begin with, we have seen that when kinship patterns change, behaviour natural under the earlier system comes to be regarded as sinful. This appears also within the family. Now totemic themes may be introduced even in early childhood through the medium of fairy stories. For reasons connected with early stressful sexual experiences, the Wolf-Man felt himself to be sinful; and in his dream the totemic animals of the fairy tales appeared to threaten him with punishment for his sin.

Freud had already pin-pointed the disappointment and shock in the dream: 'the content of the dream', he wrote, 'showed him his Christmas box, the presents which were to be his were hanging on the tree. But instead of presents they had turned into—wolves'. But this interpretation can be taken further. The dream tree does indeed stand for a Christmas tree, but the Christmas tree itself stands for the family—it is a *family tree*. At one level, the child might expect presents on the tree, at another level he might expect reassuring family figures, such as mother or father; but instead there are wolves.

Now a typical matrilineal community is made up of a succession of females, with the mates they receive from other such communities in each generation. Most of the community's own males go elsewhere to mate when they become mature. A few, however, the brothers of females of special seniority, remain in the community and effectively govern it. These priests, as we may roughly call them, when engaged in ritual, typically wear animal masks and disguises representing the clan totem. Now such a community may also be represented as a tree. The females that make it up may be represented simply as themselves, as female human beings; but the community male priests may be represented as totem animal heads or masks. A beautiful example of this coding procedure is afforded by a Moghul miniature depicting the fabled 'speaking tree' discovered by Alexander the Great in India. This is clearly a large social unit made up of many clans: the great branching tree is hung with fully human women, and with the heads of a variety of animals.

The priests of tribal societies are typically concerned with the training of the young, and their initiation into the customs of the tribe as a whole. In carrying out these functions, they often wear masks and disguises (for instance among the Pueblo Indians and in many African tribes); we can see a relic of this in the wolf's-head totem standard of the pack-leader of the wolf-cubs (called Akela) in the Boy Scout movement. As trainers and initiators of the young, the priests may be seen as a kind of *social parents*, and they also exercise a supervisory social-parental role over the males brought into the community from outside as mates. Such social parents are the object of social emotions, as opposed to real parents within the family, the object of family emotions. Some females (perhaps the priests' consorts) may have figured as social parents, symbolized by animal heads like the male priests: hence the animal-headed mother figurines found in New Stone Age contexts in both the Old and New Worlds. Social parents may show relaxed behaviour under favourable conditions, but when there is stress in a society they will inevitably express it; initiations in tribal societies have often involved torture and terror, and sometimes outright murder of the most independent-minded children. Moreover, it is these social parents of the outsider males who may kill them as human sacrifices, with a specious promise of acceptance into the clan after death, as happened regularly among the Tupinamba and the Urubu; and in this capacity, as we have seen, the priest also wore a mask or disguise. Now under sufficient stress, as we have discussed in detail elsewhere, even real parents may behave increasingly as stressful social parents, replacing affectionate family emotions with more or less hostile social emotions. And this could well be coded as a transformation from the human face of the family parent to the animal mask of the stressful social parent, ready for cruel initiation or even merciless sacrifice.

So if the Wolf-Man dreamed of wolves in the tree, and these wolves were really representative of his family—mother, father, elder sister—they no longer came under family emotions, but under stressful social emotions of terror and distress. The transformation appears at its most extreme in that story of Little Red Riding Hood that the Wolf-Man's sister used to frighten him. The grandmother is a member of the heroine's family, a human being, a parental figure. But when she goes to visit her, the grandmother has turned into a wolf that is going to eat her. And so we may appropriately end this account of werewolves, in all their sinister complexity, with a poem by Claire Russell called *In Memoriam: Variations on a Theme of Little Red Riding Hood*:

> Grand-mother, with a wolf face, sat up in bed,
> And her hungry devouring eyes,
> Half-hidden predatory spies,
> Belied all she said.
>
> I was frightened of the change;
> Why should Granny be so strange?
>
> But suddenly Granny dropped dead,
> Shot by a hunter's gun;
> And then she jumped out of bed,
> And the hunter and Granny and I—we all had lots of fun.
>
> But the episode is uncanny;
> I'm no longer so sure of my granny.

ANIMAL IMAGES

Birds and Animals in Icon-Painting Tradition

VENETIA NEWALL

'It is inevitable', writes Anne Ross, 'that animals, like birds, should play some part in the religious traditions of all peoples'.[1] Neither is central to the study of icons, but there are certain important themes which deserve closer attention.

Angels are so familiar to Christians of every denomination that their obvious ornithomorphic associations tend to be overlooked. Orthodox iconography portrays them with a frequency which reflects their significance in Eastern Church doctrine. An Orthodox Christian prays regularly to his guardian angel, for they 'fence us around with their intercessions and shelter us under their protecting wings of immaterial glory'.[2] God and the Saviour are never alone, but attended by great choirs of the heavenly host, and, during the liturgy of the Eucharist, when 'Holy, Holy, Holy, Lord God of Hosts' is sung, they enter the church and join with priests and congregation in the great hymn of praise. This is why icons of angels have a specially allocated position in the sanctuary and on the iconastasis—the screen of pictures which separates it from the main body of the church.[3]

At the 7th Ecumenical Council in 787 Tarasius, Patriarch of Constantinople, declared that it was permissible to paint angels because they 'had appeared to many in the form of men'; but many of the Church Fathers did not accept that angels have bodies.[4] Whichever view is taken, they are, as represented, folkloric. On the one hand they are not shown 'in the form of men'; on the other hand, they are depicted corporeally. Various biblical texts provide a basis for presenting angels with wings, for example, *Daniel* IX. 21: 'the man Gabriel . . . being caused to fly swiftly', and in *Psalm* 104. iii, God Himself 'walketh upon the wings of the wind'.

In folk tradition birds are often messengers of the gods and the word angel, from the Hebrew *mal'ach*, is translated in the Septuagint as *angelos*, meaning 'bringer of tidings', 'emissary'. It can be applied, in a broad sense, to priests, prophets and the Messiah, as sent by God.[5] Icons often show John the Baptist with wings, because he was the forerunner, the messenger of God, the angel sent to prepare the way;[6] sometimes he holds a chalice containing the Infant Christ. John is significant in iconography as the prototype of the hermit,[7] and traditionally he is represented dressed in animal skins, with tangled hair and an emaciated face. The effect, in conjunction with the wings, is suggestively ornithomorphic. A striking example in Yaroslavl Art Museum, dating from the 16th century and executed in egg tempera on wood, shows the Baptist surrounded with scenes from his life, and holding a platter containing his head—a narrative icon, foretelling his martyrdom.[8]

Christ Himself is occasionally represented with wings, signifying 'the great angel of the will of God', 'He who is sent to announce the deep counsels of God' and 'the Angel of the Great Counsel', a phrase used to describe the Messiah in the Septuagint version of the prophecy of *Isaiah.* This icon portrays theological doctrine in visible form. The figure should be surrounded by a wheel of light, ringed with angels, and accompanied by the inscription: 'I have come out from God; I have not come of myself, but it was He who sent me', and the words from *Isaiah*, 'the Prince of Peace'. There are various examples on Mount Athos, but the type is rare elsewhere.[9]

Sometimes Christ appears in the form of the Crucified Seraph, a pseudo-mystic didactic icon; an example in the Recklinghausen Icon Museum is Russian and dates from the second half of the 16th century. His Body on the Cross is covered by a seraph's wings and only the extremities of the arms and legs are shown. Above the head is a red figure armed with a sword; behind this, God the Father, in bishop's robes, clasping a similar weapon and, at the highest point of the composition, a medallion containing a symbol of the Holy Ghost in the form of a dove.[10] At a Moscow Church Council, convened in 1554, Secretary of State Ivan Mikhailovich Vishkovati voiced his objections to this type of the Crucifixion, on the grounds that it represented a 'latin heresy'. That cherubim had covered the naked body of Christ he had often heard in conversation with Latins—the reference is to Roman Catholics. Such icons were too difficult for ordinary people to understand and represented a departure from tradition. His views were ruled unacceptable by the Church Council and he was obliged to retract.[11]

The red figure represents Sophia, Divine Wisdom, as personified in Christ, and the sword it clasps is the Sword of the Spirit 'which is the word of God'.[12] The concept, usually personified in winged form, involved the relationship between cosmos and creator and was popular in Russian doctrinal icons. Byzantine tradition identified Divine Wisdom with Christ, *he Hagia Sophia*, the Incarnate Word of God: hence the famous church of St. Sophia in Constantinople. Russian Orthodoxy at first followed in this and 11th-century cathedrals in Kiev and Novgorod were dedicated to Divine Wisdom. But later there came a broadening into native Russian interpretation, more cosmic in outlook. Now Hagia Sophia is an angel enthroned, to make the point that the world was created in Wisdom.[13] The winged figure is usually represented flanked by John the Baptist and the Blessed Virgin Mary in reverent attitudes, the figure of Christ directly behind the halo, and angels hovering above.[14] St. Sophia, who died in about AD 138, was, according to a Roman tradition, the mother of the virgins, Faith, Hope and Charity, who were martyred during the reign of Hadrian. Their mother died 3 days later, while praying at their graveside. *The Book of Saints* suggests an Eastern origin for the story, which has also been regarded as an allegorical explanation of the cult of Divine Wisdom, from which proceed Faith, Hope and Charity.[15] The whole is a thinly veiled pagan concept, visually presented in ornithomorphic form.

More explicit are the subjects of two mid-eighteenth century Russian icons in the Recklinghausen collection: the Paradise Bird Alkonost and the Paradise Bird Sirin. Both are mythical creatures with human and zoomorphic characteristics. The Paradise Bird Alkonost is a composite, the upper part consisting of a crowned head and halo, a torso dressed in robes, arms, and golden wings like those of an angel. A finger of the right hand points towards Paradise. The lower parts are formed by a bird's feathered body, a feathered tail, and thick legs ending in 4 sturdy claws. The Paradise Bird Sirin also possesses a human head with a halo and a pair of angel's wings. But it does not wear a crown, has no arms, and, in place of a robe, its torso is covered in feathers; the legs resemble those of Alkonost. The background of each icon is a wilderness of brown rocks.[16]

It is possible to detect here a connection with the *lubki*, cheap pictorial prints on sale in Russia from the end of the 17th century. Originally specializing in everyday scenes from ordinary life, the *lubki* were later mass-produced to make popular tales and literary masterpieces in pictorial form available to the uneducated. Sirin derives from the sirens of Greek mythology, and Russian texts accompanying these pictures stress the strength of the bird's song. Those who enter Paradise hear it when they see the trees and realize the joys of the holy life there. God has prepared all this for those whose eyes and ears are able to appreciate it.[17]

Alkonost, according to folk belief, lives near Paradise and makes regular visits to the source of the Euphrates. Her songs, which describe the joys of Paradise, comfort the old. But it is dangerous to approach too near: the soul will leave the body, a role closer to classical belief concerning Sirin. Her prototype is Halcyone, wife of Ceyx in Greek myth, who threw herself into the sea when she learned of his death and was changed into a bird, which was named halcyon (kingfisher) after her. For 14 days in winter, when Halcyone broods on her nest, her father Aeolus restrains the winds and the sea is calm. Halcyone is a Greek word which means 'brooding on the sea', because it was anciently supposed, incorrectly, that the kingfisher prepared a floating nest of fish-bones in which its eggs were laid. The word *alkonost* entered the Russian language through a distortion of the old Russian saying: '*Alkion est 'ptitsa*', meaning 'Halcyon is a bird'.[18]

Russian folk tales are rich in composite animals like the bird woman, and Alkonost and Sirin occur in religious folk songs, legends and religious publications. Their proximity to Paradise implies an identification with the soul, often represented as a bird in traditional Russian belief: traces of this concept occur in funeral laments. Dead children were thought to return in the springtime as swallows, to console their sorrowful parents with their chirping, and in some districts breadcrumbs were put on the window sills for 6 weeks after a death: the soul, in the form of a bird, would return and feed. After death there was a difficult journey to make. A common form of this involved climbing the glass mountain—a folk representation of the land of the dead—with the aid of animal claws like those of Alkonost and Sirin. Peasants in Old Russia carried parings from an owl's claw, enclosed in a ring or an amulet, for this purpose, and Lithuanians burn animal claws on their funeral pyres.[19]

A Mazovian legend of the final journey is based on another bird attribute, feathers. A pilgrim who saw a ladder of birds' feathers in the air, climbed it, and reached the Garden of Paradise. Slav conceptions of Paradise are worth comparing with a passage in Herodotus concerning the Eastern Slavs. He refers to the Issedones, a people who lived near a fabulous land of gold, guarded by gryphons; creatures represented as part eagle and part lion and, in appearance, not unlike Alkonost and Sirin. Pettazzoni locates this region east of the Urals, in the basin of the Iset and the Tobol.[20] A further comparison might be made with the Hebrew cherubim, who protected the Garden of Eden with flaming swords. One Biblical text implies that they were wind-spirits: 'He rode upon a cherub and did fly: yea, he flew swiftly upon the wings of the wind' (*Psalm* XVIII 9.10). But the *Encyclopaedia Biblica* suggests that they were a type of gryphon of the kind associated with the Hittites of Syria: a composite creature, part eagle, part lion.[21]

An orthodox variant of a more overtly Christian representation of the final journey is the Ladder to Paradise, a common iconographic subject. St. John Climacus, a sixth to seventh century monk, who became Abbot of Mount Sinai, was author of a devotional work *Ladder to Paradise*. *Klimax* is a Greek word meaning 'ladder', so the Abbot's name, John of the Ladder, evidently derives from the title of his book. It is set out in 30 chapters, each describing a vice and its corresponding virtue, and the author uses the image of a ladder with 30 rungs. So popular did it become that it influenced Byzantine monasticism for centuries and created a new theme in iconography. Monks ascend the ladder and a choir of angels waits to welcome the righteous. Grotesque winged beings, demons with animal attributes—claw feet, horns, tails and distorted faces—wait on each rung to drag the monks off the ladder and down to hell.[22]

In Western Christian religious art demons are commonly represented in animal, or semi-animal form. Similar motifs occur in Jewish tradition. *Mahzorim*, the festival prayer books, sometimes show, next to the *shofar*-blower, a horned, claw-footed devil; the blower rests his foot on a three-legged stool, since it was thought that a 3-pointed object would keep away evil spirits.[23] Traditional Judaeo-Christian notions of the devil are thought to derive from Assyro-Babylonian remains.[24] The classical satyr was also significant and several biblical references support this. Isaiah, prophesying the fall of Babylon, says, 'His houses will be full of howling creatures ... and there satyrs will dance',[25] and 'wild beasts shall meet with hyenas, the satyr shall cry to his fellow'.[26] To the influential St. Augustine, satyrs, fauns, Bacchus, Pan and other pagan deities were all demons: 'The malignant devils, which those peoples regard as gods ... the Greeks thought of themselves as the servants of such divinities'.[27] There is no single fixed form for demons in either western or eastern art, but the animal attributes are almost invariably present and derived from a wide variety of unpopular creatures.[28]

St. Seraphim of Sarov writes of the fallen angels: 'They are hideous; their conscious rejection of divine grace has transformed them into angels of darkness and unimaginable horrors'.[29] Demons, then, must be ugly. Icons endeavour to amalgamate theology with art and to use theological ideas in their construction.[30] On the subject of evil, the Orthodox church teaches that it does not exist, or rather that it exists only at the moment in which it is practised. It can only become a reality through the will and is a negation of being.[31] Something of this transient nature of evil is portrayed in an icon type of that well-loved saint, Nicholas, in his role of defender of the faith: exorcising a devil from a well, striking a pagan tree to release demons, and smashing pagan images from which the evil spirits flee. In the era of St. Nicholas pagan elements were still active in the Byzantine Empire and idols were worshipped.[32]

The mouth of hell, a zoomorphic conception, is much used in Byzantine iconography, chiefly in representations of the Last Judgement, a popular subject in Eastern Church art. A Russian 16th-century icon in private hands, reproduced by Skrobucha, shows a winged sin-worm: the head almost touches the feet of Adam as he kneels below the aureole of Christ. The body winds downwards, passing through twenty blue and red discs, each guarded by a demon representing the chief sins and stations of purification—a conception which parallels the devotions of St. John of the Ladder. A description of each sin is written beside the appropriate disc. The fiery trail passes into the red sea of hell and the mouth of a two-headed monster, with Judas seated on its back. Sometimes the hell-mouth is greatly enlarged and resembles the head of a ferocious animal.[33] In western tradition Leviathan recurs in early medieval representations of hell. Hughes, who suggests that *The Vision of Alberic* was the chief source, traces its derivation to eastern sea dragon myths, which appeared in this guise in the Old Testament.[34] By the early 12th century Leviathan, the apocalyptic beast, was identified with hell mouth. The theme is widely used in sculpture and in medieval religious drama, where hell was commonly represented by the head and throat of a terrible dragon, on a lower level.[35]

Some conceptions of hell mouth portray it as the head of a dog, a convention occasionally applied to representations of St. Christopher in Eastern art. A Greek icon in the Byzantine Museum, Athens, dated 1685, is inscribed:

> 'St. Christopher
> Dog-headed
> Valiant in faith
> Fervent in prayer
> Thou soldier of Christ
> Raised to sanctification
> O victorious Christopher
> Feared by the king of idols
> And glorified by the songs of Angels
> Thou paragon of martyrs'.[36]

Examples of the type, showing the saint's head in a variety of animal forms, survive on Mount Athos, though at least one has been painted out by the monks; the tusk portrayed on another is, according to tradition, preserved as a relic of Dionysiou.[37]

The legend of St. Christopher as the Christ-Bearer, which has no historical foundation, is well known in the West. But *Britannica*, *The Book of Saints* and *The Dictionary of Saints* are all silent about the Eastern version of the dog-head. Christopher, a fine-looking Roman soldier, who found his attractiveness to women a continual temptation, prayed to be relieved of it, and was given a dog's head; some versions say that he wore a dog's mask. The *Synaxaristis*, a Greek collection of the *Lives of the Saints* rationalizes the story. Christopher began life as a pagan youth named Reprevos, who was converted and martyred during the reign of

Decius. He came from a country of cannibals, the Cynocephali, who lived in the Land of the Anthropophagi:

> 'And of the cannibals that each other eat
> The Anthropophagi, and men whose heads
> Do grow beneath their shoulders' (*Othello* I. (iii))

and was captured in battle. So savage was the prisoner that he could not speak until an angel had touched his lips, but he converted his nation to Christianity, hence his name, Christopher. Dog-faced was only a metaphorical way of saying that his people, who lived on the edge of the world, were cannibals, but foolish painters had taken this literally.[38]

The Gnostic 4th-century Egyptian *Acts of St. Bartholomew* refer to Christianus, a dog-headed cannibal converted by St. Bartholomew and St. Andrew, who helped them with their missionary work in Parthia. The 6th century *Passio* also describes him as dog-headed, and an Irish variant of the same text links a martyr in the reign of Decius with the motif of the miraculous flowering staff. According to other versions of the legend, he was converted by Christ in a shower of rain, resisted Dagnus, a mythical pagan king, and was imprisoned. There he was tempted by 2 women, whom he converted, suffered torture, and was martyred.[39]

Inscriptions from 5th-century Bithynia are helpful in tracing the cult there. It spread through Egypt, Syria, Palestine, into 6th-century Sicily, and, during the Middle Ages, through Romania and Russia, into parts of Germany. It continued into the 18th century and was vigorously opposed in Russia by the Metropolitan of Moscow, Arseni Matsievich. The Romanian Rabbi, Moses Gaster, sometime President of the Folklore Society, had in his own library a Romanian chapbook, printed at the Monastery of Neamtz by permission of the Metropolitan of Moldavia, which is illustrated by the dog-headed figure. This suggests that it was evidently not unknown in popular art of the period.[40]

The earliest eastern portraits of St. Christopher are all of the dog's head. None are earlier than the 15th century, and it may be that others were destroyed by iconoclasts. Ameisenowa, the leading authority on this subject, found only two examples in the West—one in Usuard's mid-12th century *Martyrology*, housed in Stuttgart Town Library, the other in a 16th-century window of

Angers Cathedral. Here the type of the Western Christ-bearer has merged with the Eastern dog-headed figure.[41]

The Icon Museum at Recklinghausen contains 7 examples of the animal-headed Christopher: 4 are currently on display. A Greek 18th-century icon shows Modestos, Patriarch of Jerusalem, standing beside a pig-headed Christopher holding his staff, and bearing the Christ Child on his shoulder. This combination of both legends, also mentioned above, is very rare. A second 18th-century Greek icon portrays Archdeacon Stephanos with Christopher dressed as a soldier, in a red cloak, emblem of a saint, and armed with shield and spear. In this icon he is wolf-headed.[42]

The horse-head type, possibly associated with the cult of Saints Florus and Laurus, which will be discussed later, is mainly found in Russia. The example in the Recklinghausen collection also dates from the 18th century. The figure is dressed in uniform: red cloak, corselet, white breeches and high black boots. The background is plain brown, and empty, except for a small figure of Christ high in the upper left-hand corner. An early 19th-century Greek example of the horse-head type in the same collection shows the saint dressed as a soldier, with a red cloak and shield, but clasping the flowering staff in place of a weapon. It is a biographical icon and the central figure is surrounded by vignettes of the Saint's life—an angel blesses the animal-headed figure, he enters the heathen army of the prince, converts and baptises the heathen warriors, is summoned before the king to account for his behaviour. Torture of various kinds follows. He is hanged by the hair, stabbed, burned with torches and finally beheaded; the body is then burnt.[43] Christopher can also appear in this form in icons of other saints. A Russian 18th-century icon of St. Nicholas, exhibited in London in 1970, shows the saint flanked by medallions of Christ, the Blessed Virgin Mary, and miniatures of 2 saints: one is the horse-headed St. Christopher.[44]

Since these other animal types of St. Christopher exist, it is unlikely that the figure is connected with Anubis, as suggested by Ameisenowa, especially, as pointed out by the Director of the Recklinghausen Museum, in view of the recent work done by Loeschcke. Animal-headed figures with human bodies and dogs' heads seemed to the ancients to have a genuine existence. In portrayals of Paradise they are shown with satyrs, centaurs and sirens, in an intermediate world between the human and the animal.

In representations of the pouring forth of the Holy Spirit there is sometimes an animal-headed figure shown standing near the crowned cosmos, to signify that these beings will also have benefited by having the Gospel brought to them. Early literary evidence for the animal-headed Christopher is to be found in the Moz Arabic liturgy of the late 6th century. Here the special grace of God is stressed: it has loosened his tongue and given him the power of speech.[45]

The legend of the dog-headed figure is not confined to St. Christopher. There is a Coptic tradition that the father and grandfather of St. Mercurius were out hunting when they met two cynocephali, who killed and ate the older man; the younger was saved by an angel, which descended and surrounded the savage creatures with fire. As the heat increased, they repented and, under God's influence, became Christians and accompanied the saint's father wherever he went. Not long after this the child Philopator was born and he grew up to be a great soldier. The cynocephali went with him everywhere and fought the enemy in battle with great ferocity. Philopator's skill in war earned him the name Mercurius. Aided by an angel, he helped Decius defeat the Persians, but would not celebrate their victory by sacrificing to the gods, and was beheaded. He was venerated as a martyr in Cappadocian Caesarea and is one of the group of warrior saints. An icon showing the two cynocephali in conventional Roman dress is housed in the Coptic Museum of Old Cairo.[46]

Ameisenowa points out that animal-headed gods feature in the mystery religions of Rome, and we may compare in this connection the figure 'Man with the Cock's Head' on a 3rd-century mosaic pavement in a Roman villa at Brading in the Isle of Wight.[47]

Animal-headed sacred figures also occur in Jewish tradition. Zoomorphic representations of the Patriarchs appear from the 13th century onwards in Hebrew bibles and manuscripts, and Ameisenowa refers to a prayer book in which the archangels Gabriel and Michael are animal-headed.[48] A liturgical manuscript in the Bodleian Library, portraying the Giving of the Law on Sinai, shows the principal characters wearing the obligatory Jewish pointed hat, introduced after the Lateran Council of 1215, but with birds' heads. The famous German Birds' Head Haggadah of about 1300 shows the male birds in conical hats, the females in contemporary fashionable hair-nets and jewelled pins. The ostensible aim of such figures was to evade the prohibition of the ten commandments against making a 'graven image'. Raphael states that representational art was clearly somewhat questionable at that early period in Germany. One feels tempted to ask why. These figures are surely much more suggestive of idolatry than the human face. The whole subject in any case deserves further investigation, since a haggadah manuscript in the Bezalel Museum, Jerusalem, for example, only applies this distortion to representations of Jews. Gentiles appear, sometimes in the same picture, with human heads.[49] The *Leipzig Mahzor*—the festival prayer book—provides the figures with birds' beaks instead of nose and mouth. But those responsible for decorating the later *Tripartite Mahzor* did not appreciate the reason for such distortions, and portrayed male figures with human heads, females with those of animals.[50]

South German Jewish manuscripts before 1300 consistently use animal-headed figures. The earliest surviving European Hebrew manuscripts are from that country, and the style is similar to Latin illumination. Other distortions of the human face practised in 13th-century Germany include covering it with an item of headgear—a helmet or a kerchief—and representing the figure from behind. All three devices occur in the Ambrosian Bible prepared for Rabbi Moses of Ulm in the 3rd decade of the 18th century.

Bezalel Narkiss in the *Encyclopaedia Judaica*, admitting that the reason for this curious representation is not known, since there is no direct prohibition against portrayal of the human form in illuminated manuscripts, suggests that, while possibly owing something to a common origin with the Christian practices, it primarily developed as a self-imposed offshoot of the 12th-century pietistic movement of Judah and Samuel be-Hasid.[51] This was puritanical, restricting embellishments in general and forbidding the decoration of manuscripts. This argument fails to convince, in the present writer's view. The bird and animal-headed manuscripts referred to are elaborately decorated in a way that surely would not have appealed to those who disapproved of decoration. Inevitably it seems that we should look to folk tradition, rather than to religious dogma, for the explanation. It is also worth noting that Germany is a country which knew something of the animal-headed Christopher tradition, and the likelihood of some common source should not be under-estimated.

The figure of St. Christopher is usually horse-headed in Russia and there may be some ideological link here with the cult of Saints Florus and Laurus, patron saints of horses and horsemen. The animal occupies an important position in Russian folk tradition and—as in the well-known story of the humpback horse[52]—a magic steed is the hero's most usual helper in Russian folktales.[53] The cult of patron saints of animals can be traced back to ancient times, but there is little direct expression of it in art. Florus and Laurus, whom some authorities have unsuccessfully attempted to identify with the Dioscuri, are an exception. They are usually portrayed with the winged Archangel Michael conferring on them the patronage of the herd. He presents each with a saddled and bridled horse. Below this scene appear three mounted Cappadocian horse-herders: Persipp, Elasipp and Mesipp, meaning horse-scout, horse-breaker and black horse; Skrobucha glosses their names as Eleusippos, Melesippos and Speusippos. Alpatov relates their iconography to an origin in the three Magi. Representations of these saints, which were closely associated with peasant beliefs, were very popular in 14th-century art of the Novgorod region, which, according to Alpatov, would account for their archaic features. Florus and Laurus, martyrs from Illyria, who probably never existed, are healing saints in the Orthodox Church, known as *anagyroi*, 'those who accept no money'. They were associated with a specific trade. Greek tradition says they were stone masons, drowned in a well on the order of the Emperor Licinius. It was later, in the 14th century, that they became associated with horses. Their cult spread from Georgia and Cappadocia to Russia, France and Spain.[54]

Also in northern Russia there are iconographic traces of the cult of St. George as protector of stables and cattle. Some authorities believe this reflects aspects of the ancient Slav deity, Volos, guardian of herds and cattle. He was especially venerated in Novgorod, where such icons were most numerous.[55] There are also examples from Romania, where he was revered as keeper of livestock,[56] and from Macedonia.[57]

Other saints served in the role of protectors of domestic animals. St. John was another guardian of livestock in Romania,[58] and St. Blaise and St. Spiridonus are sometimes included in Russian icons of Saints Florus and Laurus, blessing herds of cows, sheep and goats.[59] In North Russia the Samoyeds venerated St. Nicholas as protector of their animals, smearing his icon with reindeer blood and fats.[60]

Ascetics are sometimes associated with animals in legend. St. Sergius of Radonezh possessed not only protective, but miraculous powers—animals obeyed him, even in their wild state, because he was filled with the Holy Spirit. He lived in the forest as a hermit and shared his bread with a bear cub—shown in biographical icons of the saint—which became tame; bear stories of this kind are relatively common in legends of the saints.[61]

St. John Koukouzélis, a 13th-century monk who led a simple life tending goats on Mount Athos, is a figure with Orpheus-like characteristics. He was a gifted Albanian singer, who renounced a distinguished career at court in favour of an ascetic existence, and an icon on the peninsula shows him surrounded by dancing goats.[62]

The self-denial of St. Barsumas the Naked, who lived 20 years with a serpent, is more overtly didactic. The serpent was a demon which uttered false prophecies. Exorcised by the saint, they remained companions in the crypt of a church in Old Cairo. Icons of this 13th- to 14th-century hermit represent him as naked, except for a loin-cloth, trampling the serpent beneath his feet.[63]

The iconography of St. Mamas, another hermit and one of the best-known Cypriot saints, is purely allegorical. He is shown riding a lion and clasping a lamb, a clear echo of the famous passage from *Isaiah*. Legend says he was on his way to be tried before the Duke for non-payment of taxes, when he saw the lion about to attack the lamb and intervened. The astonished Duke relieved him of financial obligations for the rest of his life—which he devoted to milking lions and preparing their cheese to feed the poor.[64]

A mid-16th-century Russian icon in the Tretyakov Gallery, Moscow, shows St. Gerasimus drawing a thorn from a lion's paw.[65] Gerasimus, who founded a monastery near Jericho, is mentioned in an early 7th-century work, *The Spiritual Meadow* by John Moschus. The book describes how he assisted the wounded animal, which became tame and helped the monks as if he were a servant. When his master passed away, the creature died of grief. The Latin form of St. Jerome's name, Hieronymus, has been confused with Gerasimus; hence the anecdote recounted of the other saint. It resembles the story of Androcles and the Lion, an international folk tale, which is part of the cycle of grateful animal stories and appears in Aesop, the *Gesta Romanorum* and other famous collections. The earliest accounts of such animal miracles come from the desert fathers, and lions are of course characteristic of a desert area. St. Mary of Egypt, another ascetic, is frequently represented in her icons as being buried in the desert by a lion.[66]

In representations of St. Ignatius of Antioch the lion's role is purely supportive. This early martyr, who flourished less than a century after Christ's ascension, emerges from his famous letters as a gentle, dedicated personality. A 19th-century Bulgarian icon in the Art Gallery at Elena depicts his death at the public games in Rome. He stands, a tranquil figure, with arms outstretched in a gesture of acceptance, while 2 lions bite at his shoulders—an object lesson in the ability of the spirit to rise above the flesh.[67] Here the lions are given the same physical stature as the saint, though the expression of repose on his face discounts this. In Daniel in the Lion's Den, a 16th-century Novgorod icon, the biblical hero is tall and ethereal, towering above the tiny lions which crouch at his feet, a different method of expressing the same idea.[68]

The lion is of course the symbol of St. Mark, though in Eastern tradition he is sometimes assigned to St. Luke.[69] A representation of St. Mark in the 8th-century Godescalc Gospels, a manuscript from Charlemagne's scriptorium, thought to derive from a Byzantine source, shows the Evangelist writing, and turning to look up at his lion symbol, hovering in the air. This attitude has been copied for the Mark of the somewhat later Soissons Gospels from the same scriptorium, which are distinguished by contemporary Byzantine elements. Here the Evangelist turns more obviously to gaze at the lion symbol, floating above him and clasping a document.[70] We may compare the attitude of St. John the Evangelist in a 16th-century Russian icon of the Recklinghausen collection. An angel, symbol of inspiration, hovers above his shoulders and whispers in his ear, and a red lion is also a part of the composition.[71] St. John of the Silence,[72] a variant of this type, sits meditating, fingers raised to his lips to indicate contemplation. Later the angel, whispering words of the gospel, or his symbol, the eagle, were added. An 18th-century North Russian example represents him with both bird and angel.[73]

Fabulous animals often feature in legends of the saints. The best known is of course the story of St. George and the Dragon, a common theme and very popular in iconographic tradition, especially in Novgorodian art. The story is an ancient Oriental legend, absorbed into Christian hagiography, expanded and enriched by popular tales, and medieval stories of knights-errant and their adventures. In the earliest Greek legends he is a martyr, and the story of the princess rescued from a dragon was added during the late Middle Ages, when it was popularized in the West by *The Golden Legend*.[74] Some examples show the saint in the act of striking down the dragon, often represented as a winged serpent-animal composite;[75] others show the princess obeying the command of the saint. He has overpowered the monster and ordered her to bind it with her belt, and lead it like a tame dog into town, where it is finally slain.[76]

The dragon fight occurs in Russian folk-tale traditions, where Christian influence subsequently identified the monster with the devil and transformed it into a clear statement of the conflict between good and evil.[77] MacCulloch notes that the Devil appears as a dragon in the 3rd-century *Acts of St. Perpetua* and *Acts of St. Thomas*, a conception which originates from *Revelation* XX. 2, and continued into the Middle Ages.[78] The rise of nationalism personified the dragon in Russian folk tradition as the enemy country and, in one folk tale from World War II, it is identified with fascism, a modern restatement of an earlier theme.[79]

In some instances the dragon-slayer is opposed to purely physical forces: St. Haralambios, a popular subject in Romanian glass icons, overcomes the plague, often in the form of a dragon.[80] But more often a moral combat is implied. A Russian 15th-century icon from Rostov shows St. Ignatius of Gangra, a tall, stern figure, clasping by the throat a serpent, which is his equal in height, and brandishing a cross in its face.[81] In seizing the creature, the saint has already indicated who the victor will be. The dragon may represent a pagan cult.[82] St. Demetrius, the most famous military martyr of the East apart from St. George, is shown in a 17th-century Bulgarian icon, crushing a scorpion beneath his foot, right hand raised in blessing.[83]

Other saints are represented iconographically with animals and these examples can only be a selection. But they show the role of the animal in relation to the saint to be very varied: symbolic, moral and didactic, anthropomorphic, inspirational, allegorical, personifications of moral attitudes and states of mind.

Zernov has pointed out that, before Russia's encounter with the West in the 18th century, it was preferable to express theological ideas in icons, rather than in essays on theology.[84] Such icons were a notable peculiarity of Russian culture. We have already seen that I. M. Vishkovati, at a synod in the mid-16th century, objected to the Crucified Seraph type icons of Christ. He also criticized the portrayal of the Saviour as a Lamb, instead of in human form, which occurs, for example, in representations of the Trinity of Angels, with the Lamb of God in the chalice. Rublev's painting provides a famous example.[85] In his view the use of symbols confused the uneducated, who would be unable to understand complex mystical didactic icons.[86]

The mosaics in the Mausoleum of Galla Placidia at Ravenna, pre-dating Vishkovati by over a thousand years and falling outside the Russian tradition, nonetheless strikingly illustrate the type of symbolism of which he disapproved. Doves and stags drink at a fountain, representing souls thirsting for truth imbibing the fountain of Christianity.[87] More acceptable, since more overtly explicit, would have been the Christ of the Unsleeping Eye, a Russian icon of about 1500 in the Recklinghausen collection, based on the text of *Psalm* 121: 'He that keepeth Israel shall neither slumber nor sleep'. Christ is compared to a young lion, and the Blessed Virgin Mary and Archangel Michael flank Him on either side; many small birds decorate the scene.[88] The point is made even more definitely in an example at Philotheou, Mount Athos: the blessed Virgin and two angels adore Christ, portrayed as a sleeping boy. Nearby is a symbolic lion, illustrating the text in *Genesis* XLIX. 9: 'He couched as a lion, and as a lion's whelp who shall rouse him up'.[89]

The symbolism employed is often far from obscure. In a mid-14th-century Russian hagiographical icon of Saints Boris and Gleb, those beloved national saints, in the Tretyakov Gallery, a *klayma*, one of the smaller marginal pictures, shows Gleb asleep in his white tent, a black beast, which is death, poised centrally above him.[90] The colours enhance the contrast implied between saintliness and the treachery of murder at a brother's hands. Again, we find clear-cut theological symbolism in a detail which occurs in many full-scale representations of the Last Judgment. A good example can be seen on the western façade of the Monastery Church at Voroneţ, with wild animals regurgitating those they have eaten, so that all may appear before the Judge on the Final Day.[91] A 16th-century Russian icon in private hands, reproduced and described by Skrobucha, includes this same detail which, he says, is taken from the words of Ephraem the Syrian.[92]

The Dove, of course, with its theological symbolism, is a commonplace in icons. In Southern Albania, which used to be orthodox, at Epiphany the church icons were traditionally 'sold for the day' in some communities, a means of raising funds for the church. The Dove icon[93] was thought to possess special significance because of its symbolic connection with the baptism of Christ; this is why it fetched the highest price. The purchaser took it to his home for the occasion and was thought to receive a special blessing.[94]

Today, like Albania, Russia is officially a non-religious Communist society. But, although icon-painting no longer exists on any significant scale, its traditions persist in a secular form, with a strong emphasis on animals. Today the skill of the former icon-painter is reserved for lacquer boxes, referred to by Dr. Carmen Blacker as 'the only beautiful things to come out of the Soviet Union'.

The Klyazma river, with its source north of Moscow, provides a geographical link between 4 Russian villages noted for their lacquer paintings. Fedoskino, nearest to Moscow, was the first to achieve widespread fame. As early as 1804, nearly a third of the *objets d'art* produced there were sold for export, the paintings mostly decorating snuff boxes or other small containers.

Ilyin, in his book *Russian Decorative Folk Art*, gives a brief description of the method: 'papier-mâché objects were saturated in drying oil and oven-dried, after which miniatures were painted in oils against a black background of lacquer. Later the miniatures were imposed over gold or silver leaf. As the oils were thinly laid on, the colours were extremely brilliant, the effect being enhanced by a coating of varnish'. This technique derives partly from icon-painting and, from the establishment of a workshop at Fedoskino, right on through the 19th century many of the masters were unemployed icon artists, put out of work by new styles and methods of production. A snow-scene entitled 'The Ravens Have Arrived' and showing ravens as traditional harbingers of spring, is among Fedoskino's most popular products. Ravens, if only one symbolic bird, were commonly reproduced in icons of Elijah in the Wilderness.[95] The feeding of ravens was a favourite subject because the Prophet was considered to be an Old Testament prototype of Christian monasticism.[96]

Palekh was a painting village at least two centuries before Fedoskino. Goethe, seeking information on icons through Queen Elisabeth of Württemberg, was, in an indirect way, informed by the Suzdal clergy about Palekh, Kholui and Mstera, icon-painting villages in their vicinity.[97] Like Palekh, Mstera became an artistic co-operative in the mid-1920s—Kholui followed some ten years later—and all three experimented first with papier-mâché boxes brought from Fedoskino. Each now has its own papier-mâché producing workshop, though Fedoskino's technique still provides the basic painting method. However, with a more direct link to icon-painting in these comparatively remote villages, the materials used vary accordingly—egg tempera, for example, is still used.[98]

Kholui, which lies between two other villages, has had some difficulty in establishing a distinctive style, and many of the earlier paintings resemble post-revolution Mstera work. An example in the writer's collection, the magic squirrel in Pushkin's *Tsar Saltan*, painted in the 1970s by Zaitsev, incorporates elements of a picture of the same scene (1934) by the Palekh master, Kotukhin.[99] The Kholui version is more formal and exhibits not only stylistic differences but important variations in conception. A clerk's figure, on one side of the picture, is reminiscent of a priest in dress and hair style, and a cathedral has become the dominant feature of the palace in the background. The outsize, centrally placed squirrel undoubtedly owes something to a tradition in icon-painting: it was customary to stress the central theme of an icon in this way. Pushkin's writings, especially those based on folk-tales, have been a special inspiration to Russian lacquer painters.

An example from Mstera, also in the writer's collection, is painted by Gromov, and it too owes a less obvious debt to icon-painting. It shows a scene from the tale of Ilya Muromets, and the flowing red cape of the hero, also typical of Palekh art, might echo the decorative role of angels' wings. Such red cloaks are a frequent feature. In old Russian the words for red and beautiful were the same, and red symbolized good fortune. Stylistically Mstera drew on *klaymi*—the miniatures forming the surround of biographical icons. Another influence were the *lubki*, the cheap prints mentioned earlier, first on sale at the end of the 17th century. The popularity of literary subjects among Palekh and other lacquer artists following the revolution must be traceable in part to these *lubok* illustrations. The Posrednik publishing house sought out the village market and a century ago a pedlar's stock-in-trade included picture-book versions of works by Pushkin, Gogol and other writers.[100]

The Mstera example referred to shows the moment when Ilya Muromets (Ilya of Murom) found and captured Nightingale the Robber. Murom is south of Mstera, about 60 miles distant, but it was on the Chernigov–Kiev road that the Nightingale had his nest. His encounter with Ilya, described in Russian folk epics in numerous versions, supposedly took place in the reign of Vladimir I. This was St. Vladimir, baptised in 988, and Ilya delivered the chained robber at court in Kiev one Easter day in the years which followed. Though Nightingale (Solovei) is often described as part bird, part man, the fully human figure in the writer's example varies from most of the epic versions. Professor Alexander argues, in fact, that the Nightingale, sometimes described with various dragon-like qualities, is a modified descendant of the fiery monsters in Russian fairy-tale tradition, and here there is a link with the St. George legend.[101]

A Palekh painting, the work of Elkhavikova in 1960, and also the writer's property, is based on 'Battle with the Dragon' by Ivan Vakurov, one of the masters who has worked in lacquer since the first years of the Palekh co-operative.[102] His painting, rather as in St. George icons, stresses the combat between the hero and the dragon, but the creature is of monstrous proportions; traditionally, as part of its negative characterization, it would have been smaller than the saint. Vakurov did, however, make his dragon, which is red, more snake-like in shape, and therefore more typical. Its very beautiful wing is that of an angel—models can be seen in icons at Yaroslavl. The tale is common in Russian folklore and the scene corresponds with a version collected by Afanas'ev in the mid-19th century.[103] Bilibin, whose lovely illustrations of the *skazki*—traditional tales—were done about 50 years later, popularized a realistic portrayal of the multi-headed monster.

In Afanas'ev's version, the Princess, held captive by the dragon, is to be sacrificed to the Tsar of the Waters, a fate from which Prince Ivan saves her. Another picture belonging to the writer, painted by Babafov at Palekh in 1963, shows the Neptune-like Tsar commanding the ocean. Rimsky-Korsakov's opera *Sadko*, basing its story on folk themes, has made the Tsar of the Waters known to a wider audience. It is possible that the conception portrayed in this example of the sea-borne troika, a sharp-prowed curricle drawn by 3 horses, is pictorially related to Elijah in his chariot.[104] This was earlier a common subject for icon painters, who often depicted it drawn by red winged steeds. Thus Zinoviev[105] states specifically that Golikov's piece 'The Troika' is based on the traditions of 17th-century Stroganov painting. An identity between the prophet and the important Slav thunder god Perun—because of the fire on Mount Carmel and his fiery ascension—has often been pointed out, as well as the singular devotion to Elijah,[106] Russia's weather saint.[107] This and numerous other troika-like paintings from Palekh were inspired by Ivan Vakurov's *Devils* (1935), a richly symbolic work illustrating the Pushkin poem, and incorporating a portrait of the poet.[108]

Various aspects of iconographic art were easily adaptable to progressive themes. Artistically, as Bazhenov showed in his 'On Guard for the U.S.S.R.' and Golikov in 'The Third International', a Soviet star can provide the same emphasis as a nimbus. In one, a soldier is backed by a star comprising factories, power stations, oil wells and other symbols of industrial might; in the other a worker, peasant and soldier reach out from a star to embrace all nations in racial harmony.[109] Rays behind the fire-bird, another popular theme, may show traces of the same idea. This miraculous bird, which appears in numerous Russian folk-tales, parallels the phoenix, a pre-Christian element adopted into Christian mythology.[110]

The exquisite miniature work involved harks back, as has often been pointed out, to the Stroganov school of icon painters. At their most inspired from about 1580–1620, they continued to flourish long afterwards. The name is that of their employers, an important family based round Solvychegodsk, and it is odd to find icons of such elegance associated with so remote a place.[111] But the school's most distinctive contribution was probably the introduction of realistic animals and vegetation into their work. A lacquer miniature by Golikov, 'Beasts', surely draws on traditional representations of animals in the wilderness with John the Baptist,[112] just as a lacquer by Vakurov, dated 1930, 'The Wood Goblin and the Girl' clearly draws on earlier representations of the anthropomorphic devil. So, equally strikingly, does a painting by Butovin (1935–6) to illustrate Pushkin's 'Tale of the Priest and his assistant

Baldiev'.[113] Indeed the whole tradition of painting animals harks even further back to the iconoclastic movement and the Byzantine Emperors, who encouraged the portrayal of flowers and animals as an antidote to excessive veneration of icons; they were accused of transforming the churches into aviaries and stables.[114]

Some of the most influential Stroganov masters, so it is believed, were trained in Novgorod, a background which blended well with the family's interest in oriental art. Commenting on a late 15th-century Novgorod icon of Saints Florus and Laurus, patrons of horses, Richard Hare notes the eastern style in which the animals are painted. They could, in fact, be part of a Russian miniature and, as the same writer observes: 'This strange movement away from strict Byzantine towards the ornamental art of non-Christian Eastern neighbours became a striking feature of the later Stroganov school. It also characterized elaborately decorative icons of the late 16th-century and early 17th-century Yaroslavl school'.[115]

Time and again the beautiful Novgorod horses, or animals painted in the same tradition, appear in Palekh paintings. Two examples in the writer's collection illustrate the point: the 3 chargers in the instance mentioned earlier, the Tsar of the Waters, and a scene from Yershov's *The Little Humpbacked Horse* (1834)—a popular theme—a tale in which the fire-bird also appears. The whole story is a poetic version of folk material and describes many marvels. Here the horse is the hero of the central scene. It is a magic creature, which brings about the fool's transformation into a match for a princess, following his forced immersion in boiling water. The illustration in this case was painted in 1964 by V. Smirnova, a woman artist. Women never painted icons, and seem first to have worked at Palekh during World War II.[116]

Purists, Richard Hare points out, saw the 18th century as the end of Russian icon-painting: gone were the local variations of Byzantine themes, usurped by Western models. But religious art continued as a peasant tradition, especially in areas where the best wood was specially grown for making seasoned panels, and where local craftsmen were used to working together in co-operative groups, as at Mstera, Palekh and Kholui.[117]

In viewing the modern work of Palekh we are reminded of the 16th century stricture: 'He that shall paint an icon from his own imagination shall suffer endless torment'[118] Palekh students must copy miniatures by I. P. Bakurov, I. Golikov and other masters, in order to learn the traditional elements of the old Russian painting in lacquer work,[119] and they must be 'totally familiar with icon-painting techniques'.[120]

The Palekh icon-painters were dispersed by the First World War into different towns and their workshops in the village no longer functioned.[121] When the fighting was over they turned to farming in order to make a living. They were glad of any opportunity to paint again. Zinov'yev, a member of the group, has described how he began by painting portraits of Lenin.[122]

After preliminary tentative efforts 'The Palekh Workshop of Ancient Painting' was established in December 1924. Golikov, in consultation with a colleague, proposed using icon-painting techniques and 'The Bear Hunt' was the first miniature that he produced. When Zinoviev became interested in the project and visited Golikov in his workshop, the master stressed the importance of turning back to the severity of icon-painting: 'In this work we must preserve our traditional icon-painting style—it's the most valuable asset the new Palekh possesses'.[123]

The writer Maxim Gorky was very interested in Palekh art: as a boy he had worked in the icon-painting studio of the Palekh craftsman Salabanov in Nizhny Novgorod. One of the Palekh artists decided to realize the dream of Zhikarev, most gifted painter in the studio of Silabanov—a man whom Gorky greatly admired, and described in his story *Among the People*—and he painted Lermontov's *Demon*.[124] A plate by Kochupalov, dated 1972, shows the heroine Tamara's body being carried up to heaven, the only undisguised representation of an angel that I have seen in modern Palekh work.[125] Pushkin apart, Gorky became Palekh's writer and they illustrated many of his works.[126]

The writing of Pushkin himself is rich in animal themes popular with the Palekh artists: Prince Gvidon and the Swan, a scene from *The Tale of Tsar Saltan*; the squirrel and the golden nuts, from the same work; and *The Tale of the Golden Cockerel.*[127] The first of Pushkin's works to attract the interest of Palekh artists was *The Tale of the Fisherman and the Gold Fish*, possibly in part because it lent itself to the type of treatment familiar in hagiographical icons. A central picture, in this case the old man and old woman, is surrounded by small historical vignettes, readily comparable to the *klaymi* of pre-revolutionary icons. From the start there seems to have been a desire to include animals in the purely decorative miniatures of Soviet Palekh, and, in one way or another, animals formed a fairly commonplace feature of these *klaymi*.[128] The instance of St. Sergius and the Bear has already been cited.

The appreciation and understanding of icons has come far since, in a standard *History of Art* published in the 1920s, Cotterill epitomized them as 'Apostles and saints, and Madonnas with orange or brick-red face tinged and shaded into cadaverous green, set against a background of gold and decked out with gilt ornaments and gorgeous apparel'. Eastern Church painting, he felt, was 'incapable of developing into a living form'.[129] To a considerable extent rejection of such ideas stems from the respect for popular traditional art which has developed, particularly since the war. An official exhibition of Croatian art in Berlin in 1943 contained only a few naive paintings, the genre for which the country was, within a decade, to become internationally famous.[130] In a comment on the subject not many years later, Oto Bihalji-Merin wrote: 'The richest collections of naive art will be found among the votive pictures in churches ... In the Montenegrin church of Our Lady of Škrpjel, on an island in the Gulf of Kotor, I saw an impressive scene of this sort—a small miracle room full of awe, visions, hope and mercy. I contemplated this modest anonymous art: it consists of childish fantasy and the genuine feelings of people whose fate is linked with the perils of the sea.'[131]

In the pre-industrial world, and in much of rural society today, the natural world is the major force with which man must contend, and which he must attempt to harmonize. The role of animals and semi-bestial creatures in Orthodox Church art is an example of this process. Among the most pressing aims of the Soviet system is the full control by man of his natural environment and, in the hierarchy designed to bring this about, Palekh artists enjoy an esteemed position. It is interesting, therefore, that in their scheme of artistic expression, animals appear largely as adjuncts of human society or as purely historical figures, illustrating archaic or mythological events. This is in strong contrast to typical Balkan naive art in which, although technically there is some debt to the same earlier traditions, western influence is much more apparent. Bihalji-Merin alludes to this, as well as to the Aesopian characteristics of Slovene beehive paintings, precursors of the genre dating from the second half of the 19th century.[132] From various points of view, then, Palekh and two neighbouring villages doing similar work are the most notable successors to the Orthodox iconographic tradition.

*Animal Fossils as Charms**

KENNETH P. OAKLEY

From the earliest days of the emergence of our own species *Homo sapiens* the discovery of animal fossils, whether on the surface or in earth falls or in diggings, has been treated as like finding a 'marvel', something outside the range of normal experience. This generalization is based on two kinds of evidence.

(1) In recent times and up to at least 3,000 years ago Australian aborigines are known to have observed and transported fossils for considerable distances (in one case it was as far as 280 miles from the source).[1]

(2) There are several examples known of fossils that were evidently observed and transported by early Palaeolithic people, for example Swanscombe man (*Homo sapiens steinheimensis*).

Therefore it is little wonder that these natural marvels acquired associated beliefs such as, that they had fallen from the sky with lightning or claps of thunder, or that they insured good luck in hunting game, or good fortune in courtship. In other words fossils have for long been widely and systematically used as amulets or charms. In this paper I will indicate some of the more notable examples of animal fossils so used, whether in prehistoric or later times. When the same kind of fossil was repeatedly discovered it gave rise to explanations mainly in the form of myths. For convenience I will deal with the examples of animal fossils in the order of our familiarity with their living equivalents, but I shall

* When this paper was presented on April 3rd, 1976 in the University of Reading (at the joint Conference there of the Folklore Society and the Reading Department of Sociology), both invertebrate and vertebrate fossils used as charms were discussed. In view of space limitations, only that part of the paper dealing with fossil invertebrates is published here. For an illustrated account of vertebrate fossils used as charms, see K. P. Oakley 1975 (in the references that follow these Notes).

start by giving an account of an exceptional animal fossil with no modern equivalent.

In sedimentary rocks of Eocene age there are fossils occurring quite frequently which look like coins. They are giant protozoans known as *Nummulites*. They occur commonly for example in the limestone quarried near the foot of the Great Pyramid at Gizeh, Egypt. A chalky white nummulite was found in the rock-shelter deposits containing late Mousterian implements at Tata in Hungary.[2] There can be no doubt that it was brought to the site by Palaeolithic man, probably *Homo sapiens neanderthalensis*, although it is possible that early members of our own sub-species *Homo sapiens sapiens* influenced the Tata culture.[3] Scratched on one side of the nummulite is a simple cross formed by two lines crossing at the centre of this circular fossil. The diameter of the nummulite is 21 mm. Radiocarbon dating of associated burnt bone is recorded as about 33,000 years old.[4] This is unquestionably the oldest known use of the cross as a symbol. The late Dr. László Vértes, who was responsible for the discovery, showed me the original specimen in the National Museum at Budapest in 1965, and gave me permission to reproduce his photograph (Plate 1). He thought that from the cross on the nummulite one might infer that the Tata people were familiar with the right-angle, perhaps through using boughs in the building of their huts. Was the nummulite a hut-charm as N. H. Field suggested was the case with the fossil helmet-urchin (p. 234)?

I shall now deal with animal fossils in order of our familiarity with their living equivalents. You will all know the bivalve (lamellibranch) and the univalve (gastropod) molluscs whose shells were extensively used by early man particularly in the Upper Palaeolithic period, but mainly, one infers, for ornamental purposes. Fossil examples were used to supplement the available supplies of shells of recently living molluscs collected on the contemporaneous sea-shore. For convenience I call these latter 'recent' shells; although as they were used more than 10,000 years ago geologists would count them as fossils. When I refer to 'fossil' shells in this paper I mean shells which were already fossils when they were used by the Upper Palaeolithic people, and mostly many millions of years old.

Whether fossil or recent there was often more to the use of shells than mere decoration. For example, in one of the Grimaldi caves

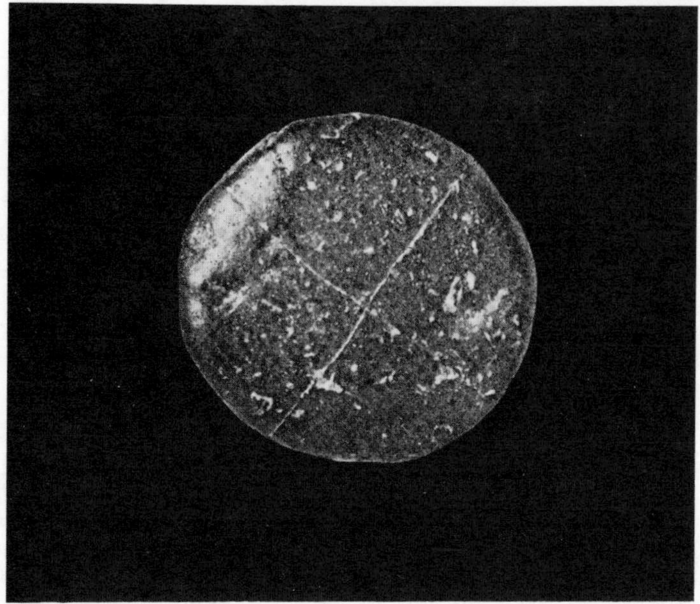

Plate 1. An Eocene foraminifer, *Nummulites perforatus* (de Montfort) found in Mousterian occupation layer at Tata, Hungary. On one surface two finely cut lines intersecting at almost 90° form a cross, the possible significance of which is discussed on p. 209. The other surface of the nummulite is unworked. Diameter 21 mm. Original specimen in Magyar Nemzeti Muzeum, Budapest. Photograph reproduced by permission of the late Dr. László Vértes.

near Mentone there was a cache of 8,000 small shells all of one species and mixed with red ochre—a powerfully symbolic substance. The Grimaldi cave-dwellers used shells for necklaces, bracelets and head-dresses. The shells were usually perforated and strung together with vertebrae of salmon and the canine teeth of male deer. From the point of view of the present study, the interest of the shell necklaces is that a certain percentage of the shells were *fossils.*[5] Apparently there was a regular trade in shells recent and fossil among the Upper Palaeolithic tribes of Europe. Inland settlements in Southern France were supplied with recent shells from both Mediterranean and Atlantic coasts, and with fossil shells from nearby sources as well as from far afield.

One of the Abbé Breuil's imaginative drawings,[6] based on a detailed knowledge of the excavator's finds, showed the Grimaldi cave-dwellers bartering shells for Gravettian flint knife-blades. It is interesting to note that gastropod shells, particularly the pointed spiral forms and cowries, were the kinds most favoured. They were always more abundant than the bivalves in Upper Palaeolithic shell jewellery. Possibly the fact that they are stronger than bivalves when pierced was one factor, but subsequent development of interest in gastropod shells, for example cowries, suggests that their 'symbolic' appeal had an early beginning.

The fact that the Grimaldi people supplemented their local supply of recent shells with *fossil* shells brought from considerable distances, indicates that special significance attached to fossil shells. One of the most conspicuous fossil shells recorded in the Grimaldi caves by Fischer[7] was the Eocene gastropod *Cerithium cornu-copiae* Sowerby, a species originally described from Eocene deposits in southern Britain, but only known from one locality in France, namely Valognes (Manche).

One of the four movable objects of culture found in the Lascaux caves is a fossil gastropod shell with a saw-cut slit for threading[7A]; it was identified by M. Jean Roger with the fossil species *Sipho menapiae* Harmer known previously only from the Pliocene shell beds of Wexford and the Isle of Man. Probably the shell was obtained from some unrecorded French source.

Fossil gastropod shells of helicoid form are known colloquially in some parts of England as 'screws', for example casts of *Cerithium* in the Portland Beds of Dorset and in the Great Oolite near Bath.[7B]

Miocene gastropod shells have been found in the deposits of the so-called Neolithic temples of Malta (e.g. *Conus* was found by Dr. David Trump during his excavations at Skorba); but more remarkable, carved limestone helicoids modelled as copies of internal casts of Miocene fossil gastropods have been found in some of these temples.[8]

The straight, narrow cone-shaped shells of the gastropod *Dentalium*, recent and fossil, resemble fangs, that is to say, canine teeth. They were much favoured by early man. They were used in necklaces by Gravettian hunters of Moravia,[8A] and by the Natufians of Palestine. They have also been found in a Middle Bronze Age barrow near Winterbourne Stoke.[9] The tendency to interpret early man's selection of such objects as phallic emblems is often I believe misguided. To primitive hunters at any rate the resemblance of a natural object to a tooth or weapon probably appeared more significant, and the direct aesthetic appeal of many fossils must not be overlooked.

I have stressed that bivalve molluscs [9A] were not sought by early men to the extent that gastropod shells were. However *Pecten* or scallop shells, recent and fossil, served for decoration, occasionally as food utensils and as symbols. In historic times, scallop shells were carried along routes followed by pilgrims to the shrine of St. James of Compostella. These tracks were possibly based on prehistoric shell-trade routes.

Any fossil bivalve shell filled with rock matrix to form an endocast in Jurassic or Cretaceous rocks is colloquially called 'heart of the stone'. Examples of this category have been found in Bronze Age tombs in Cyprus and in Britain.

In passing, it is worth noting that *Gryphaea*, the fossil curled-up oyster common in Jurassic marine clays, has long attracted country folk, and is generally known in England as the Devil's toe-nail, and in Scotland as *clach crubain* or crouching shell.[9B] Some 17th- and 18th-century writers in Scotland said that they were reputed to cure pains in the joints—a clear case of sympathetic magic, because these shells have a contorted appearance. Examples of *Gryphaea* shells have only rarely been reported from early sites: one was found in a mound at the Celtic Iron Age village of Glastonbury, and another at a Gravettian hut site at Kostienki in the Ukraine.

Brachiopods are 'bivalve' shells, but not molluscan: they belong to a different Invertebrate Phylum. Recent brachiopods are commonly known as 'lamp-shells' because they resemble in shape miniature Roman lamps with the hole for the stalk or pedicle corresponding with the opening for the wick. They occur in all modern seas but not very abundantly, whereas as fossils in many Jurassic and Cretaceous marine rocks they are extremely numerous.

Fossil brachiopod shells were occasionally used by early man. Fossil *Terebratula* shells obtained from the Tertiary rocks of Southern Moravia were used in the shell necklaces of the Gravettian mammoth-hunters of Dolni Věstonice (Fig. 3). Similar globose terebratulid shells, but filled with rock, occur in the Oolites of the Cotswolds, and in the childhood of William Smith, 'Father of English Geology', they were called *pundibs*, and used as marbles and in the game of *dibs*, or 'five-stones', often played with sheep knuckle-bones which are easier to hold. The double or more numerous pleats in a terebratulid shell (Fig. 1) facilitate holding it in the crotch between two fingers.

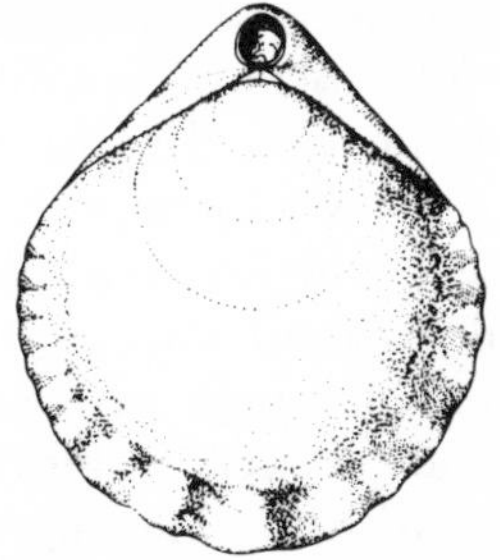

Fig. 1 Two views of *Terebratula fimbria* J. Sowerby, (now referred to *Plectothyris*). From the Inferior Oolite, Cotswolds. Natural size. Drawing by M. L. Holloway.

It is possible that these fossil brachiopod shells were most frequently noticed by inhabitants of the Cotswold region as soon as tilling of the soil became common practice, that is to say during the Bronze Age. The terebratulas would have been frequently seen in the soil while it was being tilled. Also, at this time pulses became an important component of diet, so that terebratula shells would have acquired symbolic value on account of their pod-like pregnant appearance.

During excavation of Ivy Lodge Round Barrow near Woodchester, Mrs. E. M. Clifford found within the construction of the mound a 'nest' of a hundred and twenty fossil terebratula shells,[10] all of the same species (Fig. 2), obtained from the local Inferior Oolite, and this 'nest' was covered by a layer of red clay. Clearly these terebratula shells had some symbolic significance. Much of

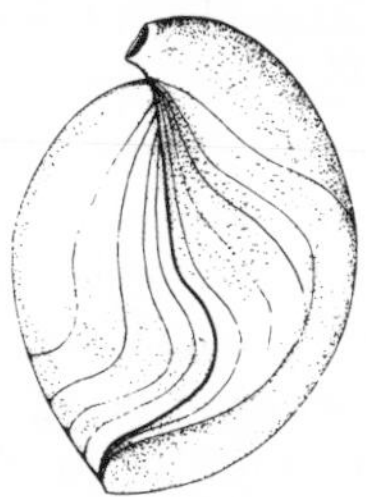

Fig. 2 Lateral view of *Terebratula globata* J. Sowerby, (now referred to *Stiphrothyris*). From the Inferior Oolite, Cotswolds. Natural size. Drawing by M. L. Holloway.

the folklore of fossils indicates that animistic beliefs have been widely held since prehistoric times, thus, the terebratulas may well have been regarded as imbued with immaterial anima—we would call it 'soul substance'. It is worth recalling that at a Magdalenian occupation site in the department of Côte d'Or, France, a fossil terebratula shell was found with the engraving of a human face on it.

In the Fossil Brachiopoda Collection at the British Museum (Natural History) there are some beads of Indian origin (see Frontispiece), which have been carved in very light wood and correspond precisely in form to three species of Upper Jurassic terebratulid shells. They have all been gilded to some extent and also painted in bright colours, mainly in reds and greens, in accordance with the Kashmiri decorative style, known for utilizing the cone-form, better known in India as the *buta* pattern. I suggest that in Buddhist modes of thought a terebratula shell (with an upper and a lower valve) would be subject to symbolic equation with the carapace of the tortoise regarded in India as a version of the Cosmic Egg, which came from the Seed or Golden Germ.[11] To some extent therefore, these gilded beads support the author's hypothesis that the builders of the Ivy Lodge Round Barrow in Gloucestershire viewed terebratula shells as imbued with 'soul substance'.

The other fossil brachiopods quite frequently used, either for decorative purposes or as amulets are the rhynchonellids. In the typical genus *Rhynchonella* the shell is biconvex, round or triangular, and ornamented with numerous radial ribs. The anterior margin like that in terebratula is distinguished by angulate pleating. Rhynchonellids were quite commonly used by the Upper Palaeolithic people of Europe. They were among the ornamental fossils used by the cave-dwellers of Grimaldi on the western borders of Italy. *Rhynchonella vespertilio*[12] from the Upper Chalk was found amongst pierced shells accompanying Magdalenian artifacts at La Grotte de Rochereil in the Dordogne (Fig. 3). The specific name informs us that the shape of the shell is reminiscent of a bat. The fact that many rhynchonellids have a winged appearance has led much more frequently to their being likened to small birds. Examples from the White Jura in the Schwaben Alps have the folklore name *täubli*, an Austrian word meaning 'little doves',[13] and occasionally, in that part of Europe they are worn on a thread round the neck. There is a Permian rhynchonellid occurring in

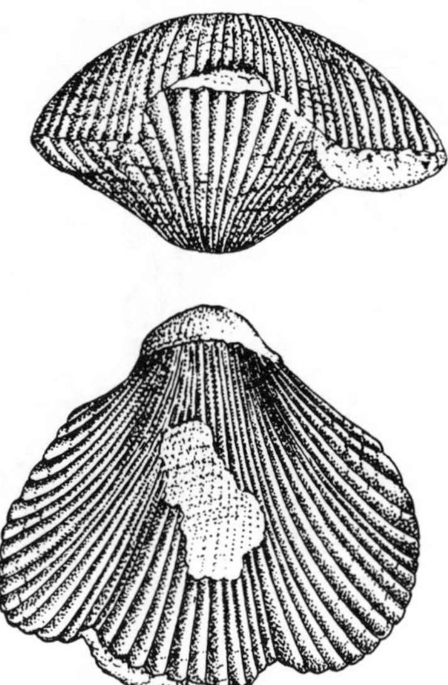

Fig. 3 *Rhynchonella vespertilio* Brochi (now referred to *Cyclothyris*). Upper Chalk. Found with pierced shells in Magdalenian occupation layer, La Grotte de Rochereil, Dordogne. Twice natural size. After Jude 1960. Drawing by M. L. Holloway.

the Eastern Alps which was named *Camarophoria spiriti-sanctus* in honour of the Holy Ghost,[14] because when viewed from in front (Fig. 4) it appears very much like a dove hovering with outstretched wings, and as we know the dove is a very ancient emblem for the Holy Spirit (Matthew III, 16).

Shells of the Palaeozoic brachiopods of the genus *Spirifer* (and allied genera) also resemble birds with outstretched wings (Fig. 5); and at least from the 4th century AD have been known in China as 'stone swallows', the Chinese name being *shi-yen*. In that country there is an extensive folklore on these fossils. One

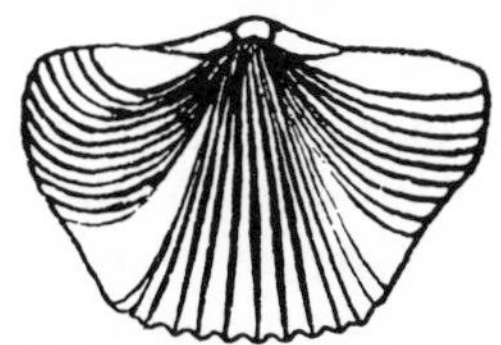

Fig. 4 Permian brachiopod, *Camarophoria spiriti-sanctus* Schellwien, from Carnic Alps. Natural size. After O. Abel.

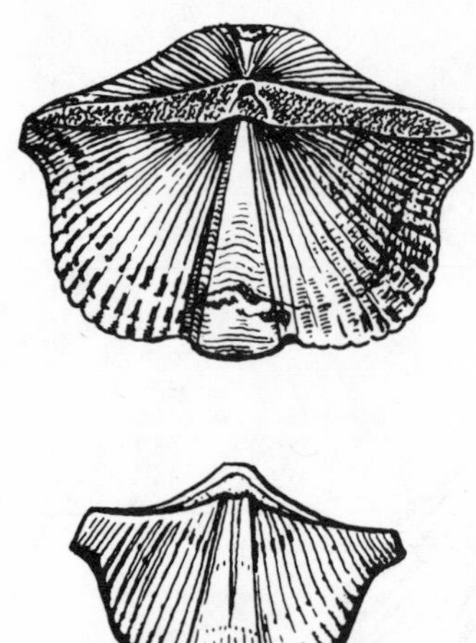

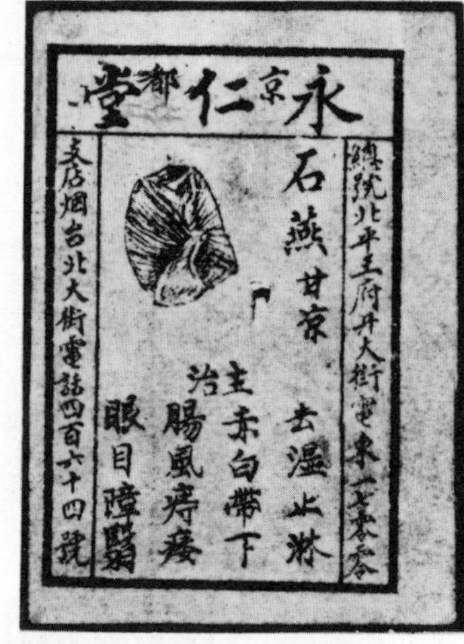

Fig. 5 Devonian spirifers (*Sinospirifer*) obtained on request for *shih-yen* ('stone swallows') at pharmacy in Singapore. Natural size. Leaflet supplied with this drug describes it as 'sweet and cooling, good for rheumatism, skin diseases and eye troubles.' G. H. R. von Koenigswald Coll., British Museum (Nat. Hist.).

Chinese author writing in the 5th century quoted an earlier writer as saying that 'During thunder-storms shih-yen fly about as if they were real swallows'.[15] Tom Harrisson suggested to me that the Chinese were probably confusing swallows with swiftlets (*Callocallia*) of the Borneo Caves, one of the sources of edible birds' nests, and known to react to storms in just this way. He said that there was archaeological evidence of trade between China and Borneo during the T'ang dynasty, and possibly earlier.

'Stone swallows' (*shih-yen*) have been used in medicine since the 13th century. In 1959 Dr. Helen Muir-Wood at the British Museum (Natural History) made a statement that can only have meant that all the Chinese spirifer type-specimens described up to that date had been obtained from medicine shops (drug stores), and none directly from outcrops. Although spirifers commonly occur in some Devonian and Carboniferous marine rocks in Europe, as far as I know none has been reported from any archaeological site. However, the shell of *Spirifer verneuli* in a flattened condition is a common fossil in the Devonian slates quarried since the 16th century at Delabole, west of Camelford in Cornwall, and has become known as the Delabole Butterfly.[16]

Probably the most familiar of all fossil invertebrates are the ammonites. They are an extinct order of the class of molluscs known as Cephalopoda which include some well-known living forms, nautiluses, octopuses, cuttlefish and squids. The only cephalopods which concern us in this paper are those having shells and therefore readily preserved as fossils. The extinct ammonites like the living pearly nautilus and numerous extinct nautiloids had *external* shells, mostly coiled in a plane spiral. The extinct belemnites in common with their living relative the cuttlefish had *internal* shells. Other generalities about cephalopods that are worth mentioning before dealing with the fossil forms which have attracted so much attention are their being almost exclusively marine and almost entirely carnivorous. In life they had a well-defined head with central mouth surrounded by fleshy appendages which were derived in the course of evolution from the snail-like feet of their crawling ancestors. The French zoologist Cuvier called these molluscs 'cephalopodes' because he thought (quite wrongly) that their fleshy appendages were used *as* feet, whereas in fact, they are used for seizing prey. Cephalopods forcefully eject water from an inner cavity and thus travel through the sea-water by a kind of jet-propulsion.

Palaeozoic nautiloids were among the fossils collected by Australian aborigines. It is suggested that the Ordovician nautiloid called *Calhounoceras* collected in Queensland (cf. Fig. 6), attracted the aborigines because its corrugated rod-like form reminded them of a cyclone,[17] so familiar in Australia, and very awe-inspiring.

A strange fish-like humanoid head (Fig. 7) carved out of a large nautilid (*Solenochilus*) from the Carboniferous Limestone, County Limerick, Ireland, has been described by Mr. J. G. Jackson.[18] It was discovered under the staircase of a house in Newcastle West about the turn of the 19th century; the ears, eyes and hair are very clearly cut, evidently with a sharp metal tool. Although the workmanship is unlikely to be more than a few centuries old, the carving even if only 'doodling' is reminiscent of the Celtic head made out of an ammonite and preserved at Devizes Museum. In each instance, whoever selected and carved the fossil was surely recognizing that such a 'formed stone' was imbued with 'soul substance'.

The *Ophites* of the Greeks was a term almost certainly applied to ammonites, but Pliny used the name in a different sense, to

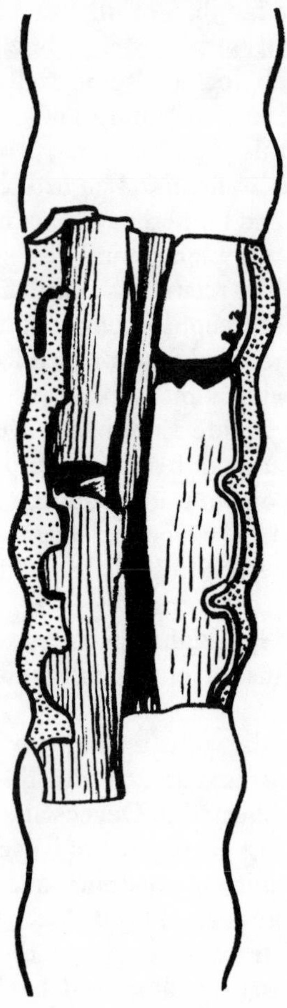

Fig. 6 Part of inner tube or siphuncle of Ordovician nautiloid, *Calhounoceras* from the Arctic. After C. Teichert. $\frac{3}{4}$ natural size. A similar specimen was carried around by an aborigine in Queensland.

include pebbles of serpentine. Anyone who has handled one of the black 'salagrama' of India (see below) will have little doubt that an ammonite was being referred to when the 3rd-century poet writing under the pseudonym of Orpheus refers to *Ophites* as 'the vocal stone ... in which dwells a soul, round, roughly black, hard; all over its circumference run sinews, like unto wrinkles'. This stone served as an oracle. Before consulting it 'the seer kept

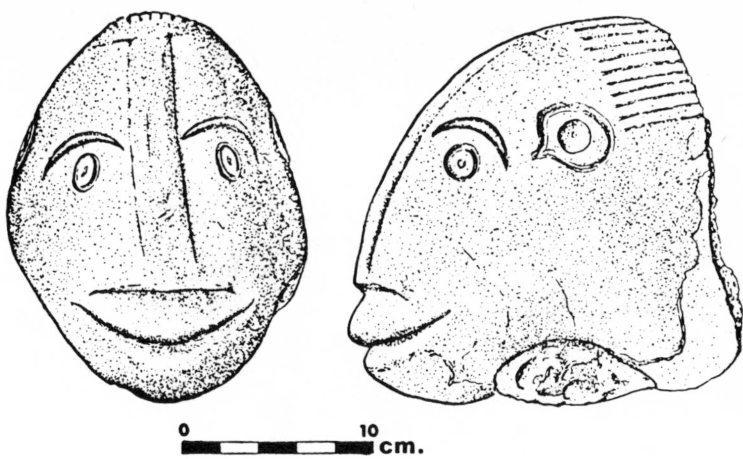

Fig. 7 Fish-like humanoid head carved out of nautilid shell (*Solenochilus*) from Carboniferous Limestone, County Limerick. Natural size. After J. G. Jackson.

a fast, bathed it in running water, wrapped it like an infant, set it in a shrine, inspired it with life by chanting spells'.[19] It was alleged to serve as a protection against serpents, and to be a cure for blindness, impotence and barrenness.

The plane spiral, distinct from helicoid, evidently has a deep-rooted significance for man, possibly because it is the form taken by the coiled snake. Its graphic representation is found in the Bushman rock art of South Africa, and in the Mesolithic rock art of S.E. Spain. The drawing of a spiral is an essential feature of the secret ritual of the 'Old Men' in some Australian aboriginal tribes. In the form of ammonites, the plane spiral was of interest to the Upper Palaeolithic peoples of Europe.

Thomas Kehoe has suggested that the interpretation of ammonites by Blackfoot Indians of the Plains, as sleeping buffaloes, would be more consonant with the mode of life of Upper Palaeolithic hunters in Europe than the historic identification of these fossils with snakes. When an ammonite is found by a Blackfoot Indian it is recognized by him as an *iniskim*, or 'Buffalo stone'[20] (Fig. 8). Wrapped in a sacred bundle, containing bison hair and other objects of ritual significance, the iniskim was believed to have the power of helping the owner to gather buffalo into the *pis'kun*, a corral-like pound. The owners of *iniskims* were actually shamans,

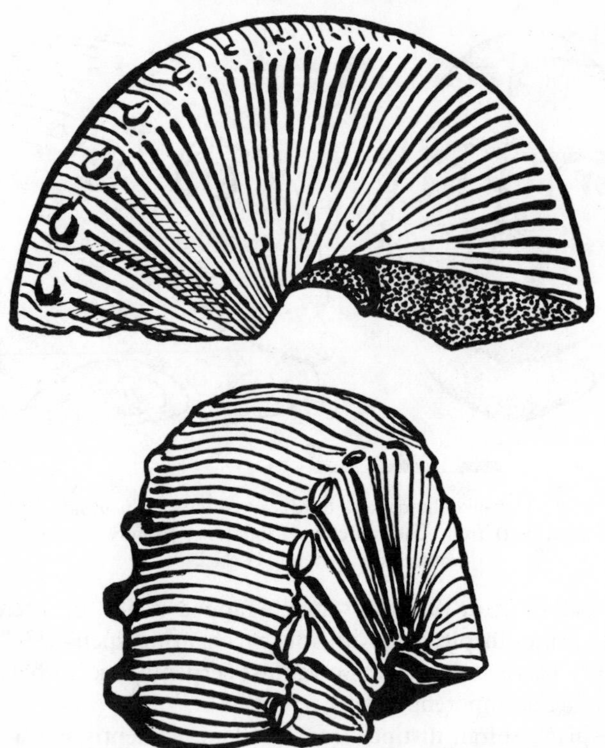

Fig. 8 'Buffalo stone', Cretaceous ammonite (*Hoploscaphites*) from Saskatchewan, used by Blackfoot Indians as charm in buffalo drives. British Museum (Nat. Hist.). Natural size. Drawing by R. Powers.

Indians with special powers, who were expected to perform the buffalo-calling ritual whenever the tribe was in desperate need of more meat. Grinnell has recorded a story of the use of an iniskim by a Blackfoot shaman and it has been related by Kehoe. 'He would take the rock and put it in his lodge close to the fire, where he could look at it, and would pray over it and make medicine. Sometimes he would ask for a hundred buffalo to jump into the pis'kun and next day a hundred would jump in. He was powerful'. In one iniskim bundle from the Blackfoot Indian Reservation in Montana, there were three Cretaceous ammonites: one was quite large, another of medium size and the third tiny. The Indians believe that a 'mother' buffalo-stone will procreate, so that 'baby' stones hatch out within the bundle. Bruce McCorquodale has suggested that this belief may have arisen through the ease with which ammonites break into segments along their septa or suture-lines.

In the folklore of Britain ammonites have long been termed snakestones. Preoccupation with snake-bite in England, where poisonous snakes are rare, is not easy to understand. Possibly in the pre-Christian religion of Western Europe snakestones were equivalent to the salagrams of India (see below). Two centres of snakestone tradition exist in Britain: Keynsham and Whitby. At Whitby in Yorkshire ammonites from the Lias, with heads carved on, have been used as amulets since Elizabethan times. These fossils are supposed to have been living serpents until St. Hilda (Latinized form of Saxon Hild) destroyed them when she founded the convent. We read in Scott's *Marmion* (II, 13):

> When Whitby's nuns exalting told,
> Of thousand snakes, each one
> Was changed into a coil of stone,
> When Holy Hilda pray'd:
> Themselves, without their holy ground,
> Their stony folds had often found.

Hilda was founder and first abbess of a monastery at Whitby which she ran as a double house, for nuns and monks, from AD 657–80. 'The relics of the snakes which infested the precincts of the monastery were, at the abbess's prayer, not only beheaded, but petrified, are still found about the rocks, and are termed by Protestant fossilists, *Ammonitae*'.[21] Superstition accounted for ammonites being without heads as the result of St. Cuthbert's curse; but some of the Whitby dealers felt that their headlessness was inconvenient, and compassionately supplied some with carved heads (Fig. 9). There is a similar legend at Keynsham in Avon.[22]

Perisphinctid ammonites from the Upper Jurassic rocks on the north-west side of the Himalaya, mainly Spiti or Niti Pass region, have for long been traded to all parts of India. They are used throughout India as charms, and placed in Hindu temples as fetishes, being regarded as the embodiment of the god Vishnu, and spouse of the basil plant. They are called 'salagrams', or 'salagrama'[23] (Fig. 10). A draught of the water in which one of the sacred ammonites has been steeped is supposed to wash away sin and secure temporal welfare. This form of the Vishnu cult can be traced back on literary evidence to the 5th century BC.

Fig. 9 Whitby snakestone: ammonite from the Upper Lias (*Hildoceras*) with snake's head carved in early 19th century. British Museum (Nat. Hist.). Natural size. Drawing by R. Powers.

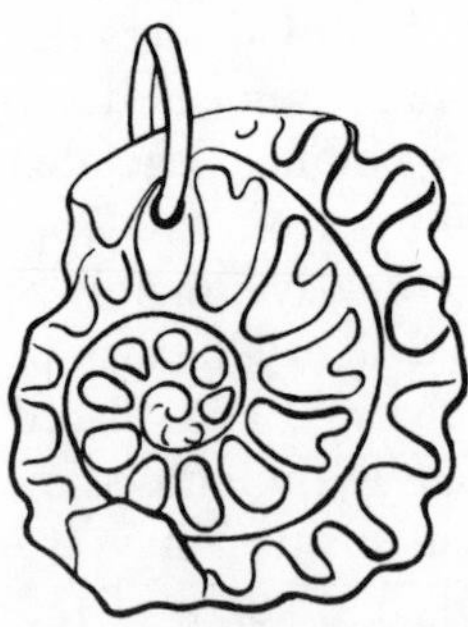

Fig. 10 Salagrama charm: external mould of the umbilical region of perisphinctid ammonite (*Spiticeras*) from Lowest Cretaceous division of Spiti Shales, Kashmir, India. E. J. Begg Coll., Pitt Rivers Museum, Oxford. Drawing by R. Powers.

In one of the stone uprights forming the entrance of the Stony Littleton long barrow near Bath, there is the impression of a large ammonite, *Arietites* cf. *bucklandi* (Fig. 11). According to Professor D. T. Donovan[24] the slab of Lias limestone containing this fossil was quarried about 5 miles away and transported by the Neolithic barrow-builders, so it must have been regarded by them as an object of great magical power. The ammonites at Keynsham which formed the basis of the snakestone legend of St. Keyna included *A. bucklandi*.[25]

Fig. 11 Stony Littleton long-barrow, Avon. External mould of Liassic ammonite *Arietites* cf. *bucklandi* in left-hand stone upright flanks the SE-facing entrance to the chambered gallery of this Neolithic communal tomb, *c.* 3000 BC. Height of visitor 5 ft. 8 in. (1·73 m.). Drawing by Christine Court.

In Britain small ammonites from the Lias were extensively used from the 19th century as jewellery, possibly because in some circles it was fashionable to be familiar with Darwin's evolutionary theory of which fossils were visible evidence. In the collection at the Pitt Rivers Museum, Oxford, there are a number of examples of ammonite jewellery, dating from Victorian times, that were obtained in London Street markets by the late Miss E. J. Begg, F.S.A. One of the most remarkable pieces is illustrated in Fig. 12. This is a small ammonite, probably *Dactylioceras*, which was cut in half laterally and one surface polished to expose the inner chambers with their crystalline infilling. The silver ring containing the ammonite was mounted on pivots within a castellated silver hoop, ornamented with silver spheres (now worn down) and with a loop for suspension. When worn as a watch-fob the ammonite could be swivelled round so that either the polished interior, or the ribbed exterior was visible. According to Mrs. Shirley Bury in the Metal-

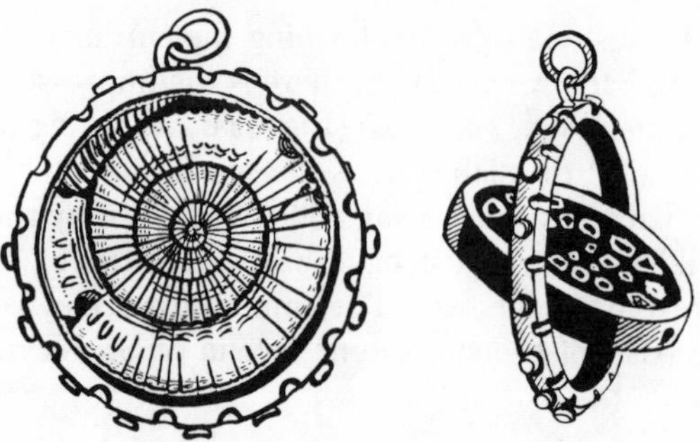

Fig. 12 Victorian silver watch-fob with ammonite from Lias of Whitby in swivelling annular mount. Diameter 3·2 cm. *Left*: outer surface of ammonite exposed in lateral view; spiral curve of the fossil has been accommodated within annular mount by insertion of tapering silver inlay. *Right*: ammonite in mount pivoted to expose polished median section with inner chambers filled by calcite crystals. E. J. Begg Coll., Pitt Rivers Museum, Oxford. Drawings by R. Powers.

work Department at the Victoria and Albert Museum, the watch-fobs with a swivelling bezel were popular in England during the eighteen-eighties.

During the British Museum expedition to the Upper Sepik river New Guinea in 1964. Mr. Bryan Cranstone found that fossils were commonly used as charms by members of the Tifalmin tribe, mainly as aids to hunting and gardening. One tribesman carried an impression of a Tithonian ammonite (Fig. 13) as protection against arrow wounds in battle or injury in pig-hunting.

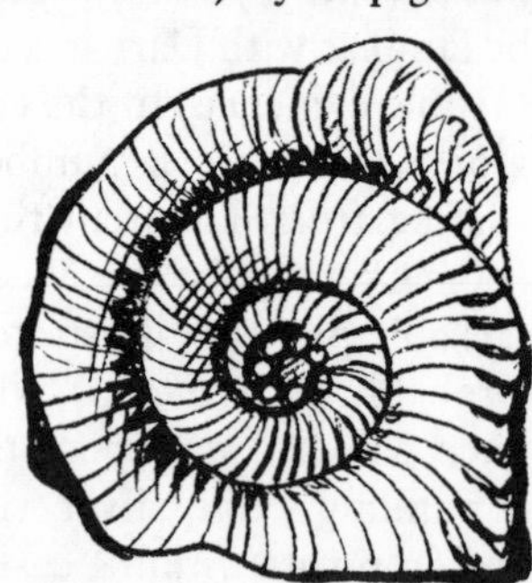

Fig. 13 External mould of Jurassic (Tithonian) ammonite used as charm believed to protect member of Tifalmin tribe, New Guinea, from injury in warfare or pig-hunting. Department of Ethnography, British Museum. Drawing by R. Powers.

Belemnites are also very notable fossils. They are the pointed guards of the chambered inner shells of extinct molluscs related to cuttlefish. They occur in Jurassic and Cretaceous rocks and always arouse great interest. They are most widely classed as thunderbolts but in some regions are known as Devil's Fingers or as St. Peter's Fingers—the ambivalent character of the symbolism is evident. It may be a matter for demographers to give an explanation of the fact that there are more folk names for belemnites in Germany than in any other country. Denys de Montfort recorded no less than seventeen German colloquial names for belemnites.[26] In Scotland they have been called botstones and water in which they have been steeped is believed to cure horses of worms. In many places there is a tradition that powdered belemnites will cure watery affections of the eyes of horses. Several 17th-century writers mention that when rasped, belemnites yield an odour like rasped horn, and so they identified the belemnite material with the *lapis lyncuris* of the ancients, an idea supported by its yellowish brown colour. Dr. László Vertés drew attention to two rounded (and apparently tooled) fragments of belemnite found in the Mousterian layer at Klein Peterwitzer,[27] because he thought these constituted some of the oldest known 'amulets'.

Professor P. I. Boriskovskii has described some perforated pieces of belemnite from an Upper Palaeolithic layer dated by C14 as 20,000 years old at the site known as Kostenki 17 on the Don.[28] The Gravettian hunters made these beads out of pieces of *Belemnitella* derived from the local equivalent of the Upper Chalk. The rich amber colour of this belemnite evidently made it seem unusually magical. It was no mean feat with primitive equipment to make a fine drill-hole through a tiny quadrangular cut piece of such brittle material. It is surely not stretching the meaning of 'charm' too far to include such ornaments in this category.

A smoothed belemnite was found with a female skeleton in a Bronze Age barrow on Langton Wold in Yorkshire. The figured specimen[29] is from a Bronze Age barrow in Dorset (Fig. 14). In his work of 1793 in which he figured this specimen, Douglas said that he thought prehistoric men probably occasionally used belemnites as arrow tips.

Although of course not fossils in the true sense, prehistoric arrowheads have a folklore similar to that of belemnites. Sickness in cattle has sometimes been attributed by country people to

Fig. 14 Belemnite from Bronze Age barrow, Dorset. After J. Douglas 1793.

prehistoric flint arrowheads which they believe have been shot into the animals by fairies. When the arrowheads are picked up in the fields they are collected as 'elf-shot', and preserved for use as a remedy. Water in which the arrowheads have boiled has widely been regarded as beneficial to diseased cattle. Arrowheads are sometimes mounted as charms for wearing as protection against being elfshot, or 'overlooked'.

The only fossil sponges which have been commonly reported from early sites are the small spherical calcareous sponges known as *Porosphaera*, occurring originally in the Chalk (Fig. 15). Many of them are perforated by a cylindrical hole, easily mistaken for an artificial drilling, but in fact a natural occurrence probably due to the sponge having grown around the stem of a seaweed. With the erosion of the Chalk large numbers of these sponges, many of them silicified, were washed out and re-deposited in river gravels, where they are sometimes found in 'nests', for example in gravel containing Acheulian hand-axes near Bedford, and others re-

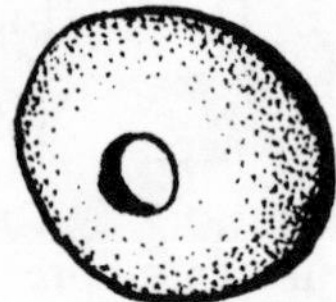 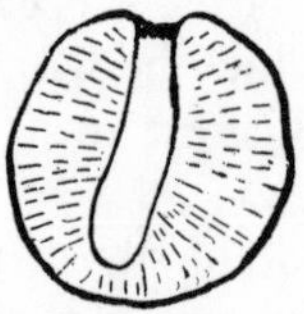 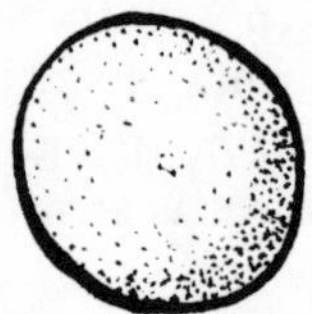

Fig. 15 Naturally perforated English specimens of the Chalk sponge *Porosphaera globularis* (Phillips). Drawings by R. Powers.

corded in the Somme gravels. It was formerly held that these 'nests' of *Porosphaera* represented necklaces of Acheulian man. However, similar 'nests' were found by Tom Shepperd in glacial gravels in Yorkshire, so there can be no doubt that the porosphaeras were brought together by the action of streams sorting their load according to size or weight. In later prehistoric, proto-historic and historic times these natural beads were frequently collected and used by man. A necklace of 79 *Porosphaera* beads[30] was found in a Bronze Age cist in Higham Marshes near Gravesend. The original is in the Anthropological Sub-Department of the British Museum (Natural History). Porosphaeras are particularly notable in Saxon grave groups (see Dr. Audrey Meaney's forthcoming book on *Saxon Amulets* in the Folklore Society's Mistletoe series).

At one time (1850–90) *Porosphaera* beads were collected on the beach at Brighton, strung together, and offered for sale as lucky necklaces. Half a century ago nearly every woman of the fishing and hawking class in Brighton wore a holed stone, usually a *Porosphaera* bead. There is an extensive folklore attached to naturally holed stones, known as hagstones, or witches' stones. They have been called 'adderstones' or 'adder-beads', which appears to be another version of the fabulous snakes' egg or *ovum anguinum* of classical writers.

One of the most interesting kinds of fossil from the archaeologist's point of view are the anchoring stems of the fossil 'sea-lilies' or crinoids. These animals are Echinoderms, and therefore related to star-fish, but attached to the sea-floor by a flexible stem with calcareous joints. The fossil crinoid stems are mainly found broken up in the geological source rock, which in Britain is commonly either Carboniferous Limestone, or one of the Jurassic limestones or clays.

Short lengths of crinoid stems were commonly used in the Bronze Age as beads. Those illustrated (Fig. 16, left) were found in barrows at Aldbourne, Normanton and Wilsford in Wiltshire, and were probably obtained from Carboniferous Limestone in the region of Frome. Were these crinoid stems the prototype of the segmented faience bead, or were they collected because Bronze Age men noticed their resemblance to the faience beads traded from Egypt (Fig. 16, right)?

Fossil crinoid stems are readily broken down into separate disc-

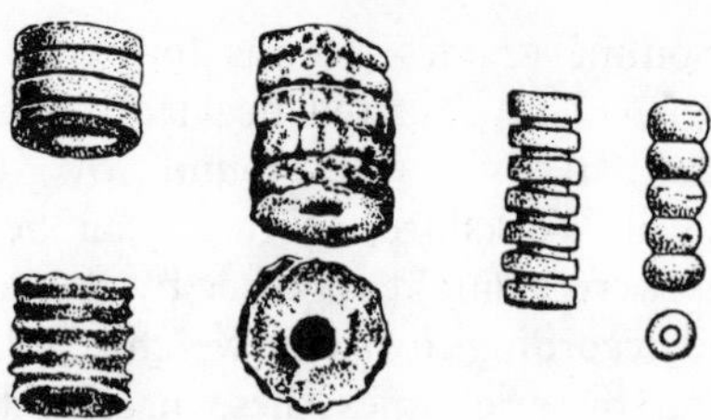

Fig. 16 Crinoid beads, i.e. silicified crinoid stem-joints from the Carboniferous Limestone, used as natural beads, compared with segmented faience beads. All Bronze Age. *L.* to *r*: two crinoid beads from Hoare's bowl barrow 156, Wilsford, Wiltshire (Devizes Museum); two views of crinoid bead from barrow at Aldbourne, Wilts. (British Museum); segmented faience bead from Carn Creis, Bosavern, Cornwall (British Museum); segmented faience bead from barrow on Tan Hill, Wilts. (British Museum). All natural size.

like joints. These may be round when they are from Carboniferous formations, or either star-shaped or round when they are of Jurassic origin; and they all have a central hole. Round crinoid stem-joints are known in Germany as *Bonifaziuspfennige* or St. Boniface's pennies,[31] and in many parts of this country as fairy money. In the north of England, particularly in Northumberland, they have been known at least since the 17th century as St. Cuthbert's beads. In Scott's Marmion (II.16) we read:

> But fain Saint Hilda's nuns would learn
> If, on a rock by Lindisfarne,
> Saint Cuthbert sits, and toils to frame
> The sea-born beads that bear his name:
> Such tales had Whitby's fishers told,'

Sir Cyril Fox[32] recorded that a bronze harness-fitting of lyre-form, dating from the Early Iron-age, found at Rainsborough hill-fort in Northamptonshire, was ornamented with round crinoid stem-discs from local Jurassic limestone (Fig. 17), perhaps because they were thought to have the magical effect of eyes.

Other Echinoderms with which most people are familiar are the sea-urchins (Echinoids). These animals are notable for their spiny exterior, hence their name which is based on the superficial similarity to hedgehogs (=urchins). There are several kinds of fossil sea-urchins that are the subject of folklore, the commonest in the south of England being endocasts in flint, derived from the

Chalk, of the heart-urchin *Micraster* (Fig. 18), and of the helmet-urchin *Echinocorys* (Fig. 19). Both of these, but more commonly the latter, are known to the country people as shepherd's crowns or fairy loaves. Formerly at least, the Essex labourer believed that so long as one of these fossil sea-urchins was kept in the house, his family would never go short of bread.[33] At a number of localities in southern England fossil echinoids are traditionally placed on dairy shelves to keep milk from going sour. This practice is clearly linked with the ancient idea that these fossils are thunderstones.

The best-known case of fossil echinoids being used in a ceremonial burial is in the Early Bronze Age tumulus on the Dunstable Downs, where nearly 100 shepherd's crowns, mainly *Micraster*, had apparently been arranged to surround the bodies of a woman and child. In the frontispiece of his well-known book,[34] Worthington Smith illustrated the skeletons as nearly encircled by the shepherd's crowns, but there is little doubt that the extreme

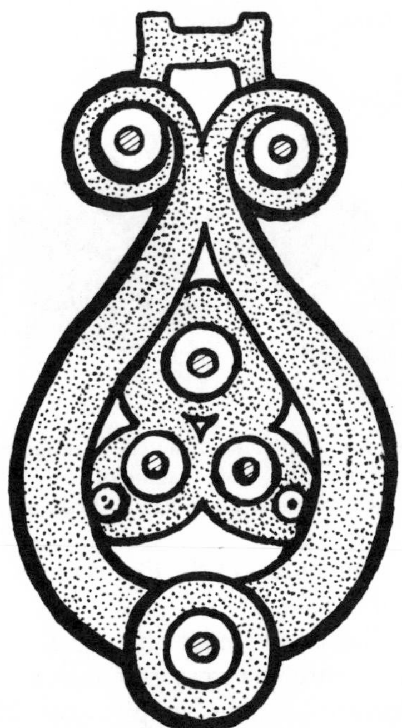

Fig. 17 Bronze harness fitting ornamented with Jurassic crinoid stem-discs from Early Iron Age hill-fort at Rainsborough, Northants. After C. Fox. National Museum of Wales.

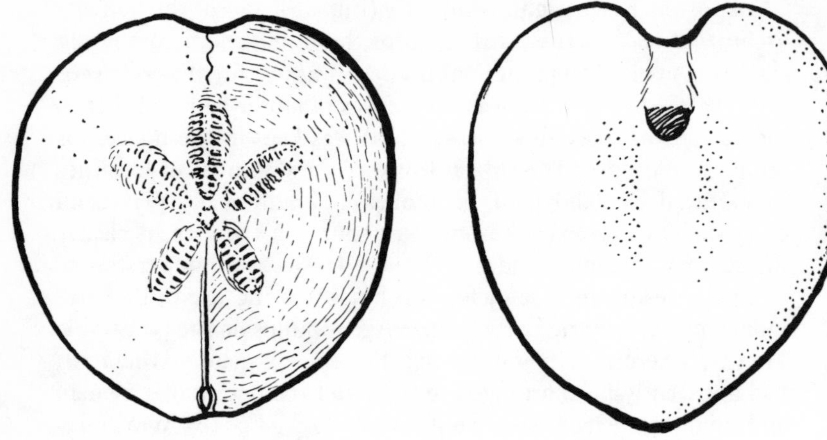

Fig. 18 *Left*: upper surface of flint endocast of the heart-urchin *Micraster*, from gravel derived from Upper Chalk, Bucks. Right: lower surface, showing mouth of *Micraster*, Upper Chalk, Norfolk. Natural size. Drawings by R. Powers.

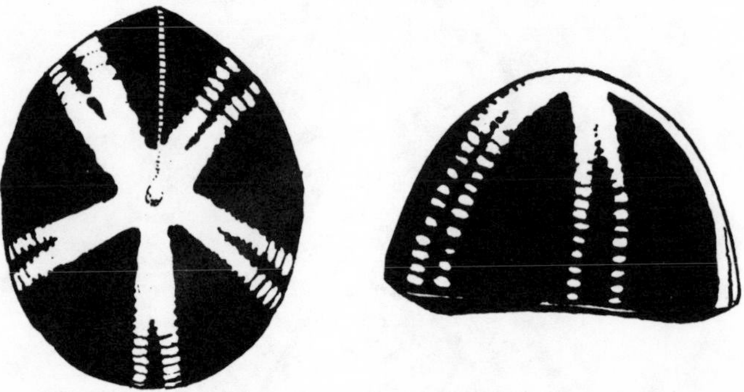

Fig. 19 Lateral and top views of water-worn flint endocast of the helmet urchin *Echinocorys*, from residue of Upper Chalk, Cromer beach, Norfolk. Drawings by R. Powers.

regularity of the arrangement of the fossils in this illustration owed something to artist's licence.

H. S. Toms collected evidence that up to the middle of the last century fossil sea-urchins were called thunderstones throughout Sussex, whereas they are now simply regarded as 'lucky' and if seen in the soil and not brought home, at least one should spit on the shepherd's crown and throw it over the left shoulder. Even the idea of luck being attached to sea-urchins found on the fields has disappeared latterly from many villages. As there were still scattered traces of the thunderstone beliefs in Sussex in 1930, it is probable that more than a century ago the thunderstone aspect was dominant there. This idea survived longer in West Sussex than in East Sussex and oral tradition can be traced back to 1860.

In the first decade of this century, Christian Blinkenberg collected in considerable detail ideas about thunderstones then current or recently current in Denmark.[35] The following are typical Danish records of which he published about eighty.

In the parts round Davbjerg and Mönstead, in the district of Viborg, people most frequently understood by thunderstones fossilized sea-urchins, or more seldom, flint axes. Both kinds acted as protection against thunder. The stone axes were kept on shelves in the sitting room; the fossils were laid on shelves in the pantry as they 'kept the milk fresh and caused plenty of cream'.

In one communication, a schoolmaster recorded that in his childhood it was believed that the thunderstone had really come down in a thunderstorm, and that it served as protection because 'where it had once struck it was not worth coming again'.

Another schoolmaster's account of the idea held in his childhood was remarkably specific: 'Only when a crashing thunderclap followed the lightning did we think that a stone had fallen, and it was precisely its fall and great speed which produced the crashing sound'.

An inhabitant of North Slesvig said that when the fossilized sea-urchins kept in various parts of the house 'sweated' it was always a sure sign that a storm was coming on.

This latter idea was probably a survival of a former belief that the fossil sea-urchin was animated by a god, and therefore was ideal as an amulet.

There is no doubt but that fossil sea-urchins were venerated in the Celtic world. One Gallo-Roman tumulus contained a stone cist enclosing no cinerary urn or human bones, but an isolated fossil sea-urchin foreign to the district.[36] They were sometimes worn as amulets during the Roman Iron Age (Fig. 20).

As Blinkenberg's study of thunderstone-lore showed, two kinds of stone picked up in the soil have been most commonly regarded by Danish people as thunderstones: namely fossil sea-urchins and Neolithic stone axes. A few years ago I came across a striking indication that this idea can be traced back in Britain to the time

Fig. 20 Flint endocast of the echinoid *Galeritea* mounted in bronze bands as a charm. From Bregninge, Lolland (Denmark). (Undated, but an almost identical mounted echinoid found in bronze vessel of Roman age at Broholm.) After Blinkenberg. Natural size. Original in National Museum, Copenhagen (Reg. no. C.14172).

when Early Iron Age culture entered this island. Digging at Southborough, on the outskirts of Tunbridge Wells, a workman unearthed a cremation burial which included a pottery bowl of Iron Age A type containing two objects: a flint sea-urchin (*Micraster*), and a weathered portion of a Neolithic flint axehead. These finds are preserved in the Tunbridge Wells Museum. That elements of the thunderstone-lore were ingredients in Roman-Celtic religious beliefs is suggested also by finding broken flint axes and fossil sea-urchins among the 'votive offerings' in temples.[37]

In Britain during the Early Iron Age the helmet-urchin was apparently used as a hut or horse charm, and this Celtic custom seems to have continued locally during the Roman occupation.[38]

There have been innumerable cases of fossils being used in folk medicine, and I have already touched briefly on this aspect of this subject, but the medicinal use of fossil sea-urchins in the Chalk of Kent is perhaps less well known. John Woodward[39] published the statement that *Echini marinae* dug out of the chalk pits at Purfleet, Greenhithe and Northfleet contain specially pure fine chalk, and that the diggers drive a trade with the seamen who pay good prices for these 'Chalk-eggs'. The fine clean chalk within these fossil shells was, he said, 'one of the finest remedies for subduing acrid humours of the stomach'. He wrote further: 'Those who frequent the sea, and are not apt to vomit at their first setting, fall frequently into loosenesses, which are sometimes long, troublesome and dangerous. In these they find *Chalk* so good a remedy that the experienced seaman will not venture on board without'.

Pliny[40] tells a story about an object called by the Druids an *ovum anguinum* (snake's egg). According to an ancient Celtic tradition innumerable snakes twining together at midsummer make a ball out of froth which they exude. If it could be stolen from the snakes it was an object of great magical power. It was said to be covered with a crust having excrescences like the suckers of a cuttle-fish. Its possession ensured success in battle and disputes. The object was identified, by 16th- and 17th-century writers as a fossil sea-urchin, but there remains doubt as to whether the objects classified as *ovum anguinum* in Roman times were necessarily fossil sea-urchins. The naturalist traveller de Boodt reproduced figures of two fossil sea-urchins,[41] saying that according to the tradition of his day these were *ova anguinum*, prized as antidotes against poison.[42] The sinuous ambulacral areas were construed as so many snakes attached to the surface. Curiously enough small fossil echinoids of the same 'regular'[43] kind, usually with a holed centre, were noticed and collected by Upper Palaeolithic peoples.

In later Prehistoric, Roman and Saxon times, flint moulds of fossil sea-urchins including occasionally *Cidaris* were used as artifacts such as hammer-stones, and if the centres were naturally perforated as spindle-whorls. Dr. Audrey Meaney called my attention to a decorated lead spindle-whorl of Roman Age from Woodhouse, Northumberland in the British Museum collection,[44] which closely resembles a fossil *Cidaris* (Fig. 21). There is little doubt that the pattern is based on a fossil cidarid, for it shows the characteristic fivefold symmetry and the nipple-like bases of the spines are represented by regularly spaced blobs. While this was going to press, Dr. W. M. S. Russell drew my attention to a pottery spindle-whorl from a Bronze Age site (c. 2300–2000 BC), seen in Limassol Archaeological Museum, Cyprus, which was clearly a copy of a fossil echinoid of the 'regular' kind.

The club-shaped spines of the fossil sea-urchin *Balanocidaris*, common in some Jurassic and Cretaceous limestones in the Middle East, have been used as talismans at least during the last three millennia.[45] It was therefore interesting when two of these 'jewstones' (Fig. 22) were discovered in 'Early Aurignacian'

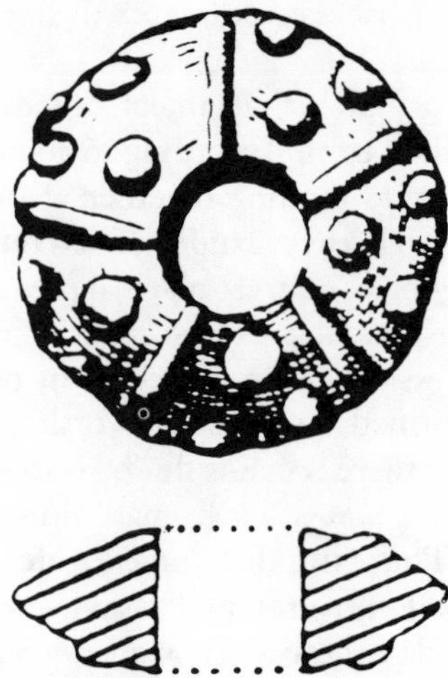

Fig. 21 Romano-British lead spindle-whorl from Woodhouse, Northumberland. Diameter 2·9 cm. Reproduced from British Museum *Guide to Roman Britain* (1951), Fig. 23, by permission of the Trustees. Pattern of ornamentation based on fossil echinoid (compare *Cidaris* in Fig. 22).

(=Antelian) occupation levels at the Ksar 'Akil rock-shelter in the Antelias Valley, Lebanon.[46]

Balanocidaris spines became known as jewstones simply because they were commonly obtained from Judea; but it was clearly their form (cf. glans) that suggested use in treatment of bladder troubles in accordance with the principle of sympathetic magic. John Woodward[47] wrote of them as follows: 'The bodies called *Tecolithi* by Pliny, *Lapidus Judaici* and *Syriaci* by other writers, so much celebrated by the ancient Physicians for their diuretic properties but reputed by all as no other than stones, have been at last publickly demonstrated to be only elevated spikes of *Echini ovarii*, brought forth of the sea at the Deluge....'

The Celtic distribution of belief in adderstones (see above p. 227) suggests that it was continuous in the time-dimension with the belief quoted by Pliny as current during his time in Druid Gaul. The 'snake's egg' is called *glain naidr* in Wales and *milprev* or *milpref* in Cornwall; while in both regions tradition tells that it was formed by a congress of snakes on Midsummer's Eve. The name *milprev* dates back at least to the 17th century, for it is mentioned

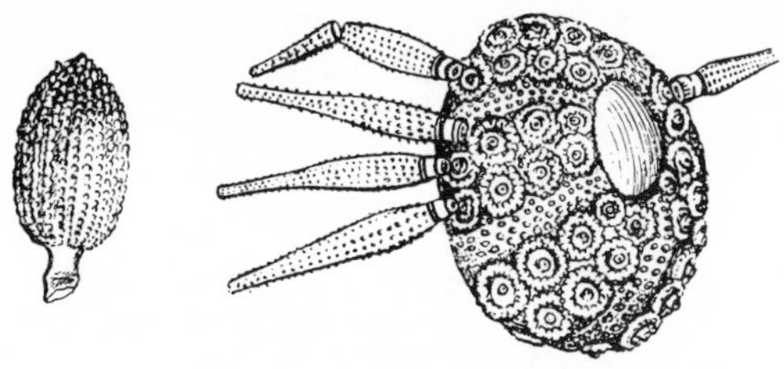

Fig. 22 *Left*: 'Jewstone', a spine of *Balanocidaris*. *Right*: Engraving by Imperato (1599) illustrating the fossil echinoid *Cidaris*.

in a letter from Edward Lhwyd, Keeper of the Ashmolean Museum, written in 1699.[48] Many quite different objects passed for adderstones, particularly fossils and stones whose markings suggested an intertwining of snakes.

According to tradition the adderstone usually has a central perforation. This applies to a number of fossils already treated (e.g. regular echinoids and the porosphaeras), but in folklore various objects that are *not* fossils have been included in this strange category. Thus, ancient spindle-whorls and Saxon glass beads with wavy lines have commonly been called *glain naidr* by country people, and are supposed to be valuable as a prophylactic against snake-bite or poison. Perforated stone hammers have also been classed sometimes as adderstones.

Sir Richard Colt Hoare figured a cylindrically perforated polished stone mace-head[49] found during excavation of Bush Barrow, near Wilsford, Wiltshire, and it is clear from his illustration that it was carved out of a fossil 'coralline'.[50] On examination the 'coralline' proved to be a Devonian stromatoporoid (*Amphipora*). The matrix of the fossil is calcareous, and fairly soft. As such rock is not very serviceable as a hammer-stone, it was justifiable to infer that its use at the time of the Wessex 'royal graves' (c. 1500 BC) was ceremonial. Pebbles of Devonian limestone containing corals and stromatoporoids are found in the New Red Sandstone pebble-beds of South Devon, and it seems very probable that this mace-head was made from a pebble picked up on account of its unusual appearance. What would it resemble in a primitive mind? In the adjoining county of Cornwall pebbles of coralline limestone showing markings of this same type are to this day called *milprev* (=1000 worms or small snakes). It is therefore not too far-fetched to suggest that the adderstone folklore originated from ideas current in Britain as far back as the Bronze Age.

In the John Evans collection at the Ashmolean Museum there are two polished stone axes from Troston near Bury St. Edmunds which have been carved out of a Jurassic serpulid limestone, probably obtained locally in the form of an erratic.[51] Serpulids are marine worms which construct calcareous tubes in which to live, usually attached to the sea-floor or to a shell. The Troston serpulid rock is an impure limestone. The resemblance of the rock to a congress of small serpents possibly accounts for its selection as the material for axe-heads in preference to harder rocks which are much commoner in the glacial drifts of Suffolk. An alternative explanation is possible and was suggested to me when my younger son, Giles, as a boy, looking at curling streaks of lightning, said that they made him think of *worms*. If the same idea formed in the minds of earlier men, serpulid rock may well have seemed suitable material for axe-heads as it would imbue them with celestial power.

Polished or transversely broken surfaces of many fossil corals of compound type also call to mind the night sky, for they have long been known to folklore as starrystones, notably the Jurassic massive coral *Isastraea* and the closely related *Pseudodiplocaenia* (Fig. 23). Humanly struck flakes of chert containing starry corals, one of them *Pseudodiplocaenia*, were found in the Middle Swanscombe Gravels in association with an Acheulian hand-axe industry. Geologically speaking these pieces of coralline chert count as 'far-travelled rocks' at Swanscombe. As the only two pieces recorded there are humanly struck flakes, I think it is not too speculative to suggest that starrystone was treasured by our Acheulian precursors and carried by them over a considerable distance from the place where they noticed it. The only known British provenance for chert containing *Pseudodiplocaenia* is in the Portlandian beds at Tisbury,[52] Wiltshire, over 120 miles from Swanscombe. There is also good evidence that a fossil coral of the starrystone type ('madrepore') was collected by Mousterian hunters at Grotte de Hyène, Arcy-sur-Cure (Yonne).[53]

An Ordovician trilobite perforated for suspension, was found in a Magdalenian occupation-layer in one of the rock-shelters at Arcy-sur-Cure (Fig. 24). The find was considered remarkable enough

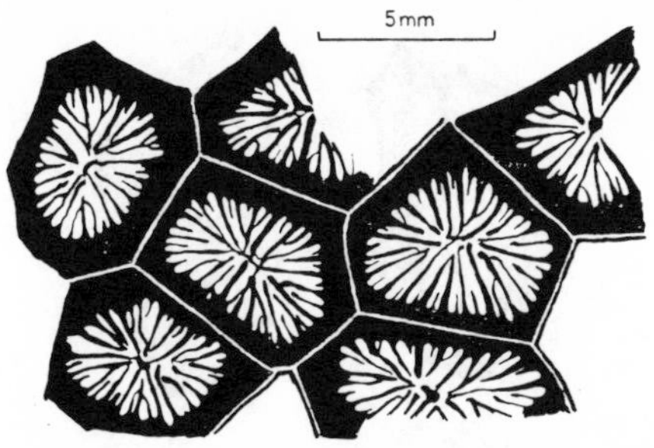

Fig. 23 Transverse section of the coral *Pseudodiplocaenia oblonga* (Fleming), highly magnified. Drawing based on specimen from Portlandian Beds, Tisbury, Wilts. Reproduced by courtesy of Dr. Ewa Roniewicz.

in the last century to give the name to the site: La Grotte du Trilobite.[54]

It almost goes without saying that a trilobite is likely to arouse a sense of wonder or beauty in the minds of people living in an age of enlightenment; but we might assume that to a Magdalenian hunter of 15,000 years ago it would be just another *objet trouvé*, an unusual pebble to be treasured perhaps as a curio, but something that occasioned no train of logical or speculative thought. Yet if we investigate the circumstances more closely, I believe we would find ourselves justified in giving the Magdalenian trilobite collector some credit for logic.

In the same layer which yielded the trilobite pendant at Arcy-sur-Cure there was a pendant carved out of lignite in the form of a buprestid beetle (Fig. 24). Both the carved beetle and the trilobite had been perforated for suspension in each case by a pair of holes drilled through lateral grooves.[55] The specimens were no doubt essentially amuletic in significance.

To the Palaeolithic craftsmen's eye, had the two pendants more in common than symmetry? There are other carvings of beetles at Magdalenian sites in France. There are several obvious reasons for Palaeolithic food-gatherers being interested in insects, so it is not unreasonable to infer that the trilobite would have appeared to the untutored yet observant Magdalenian mind as a kind of insect in stone.

We may be touching a deep-rooted human interest which has been manifested repeatedly and in different ways. We may recall,

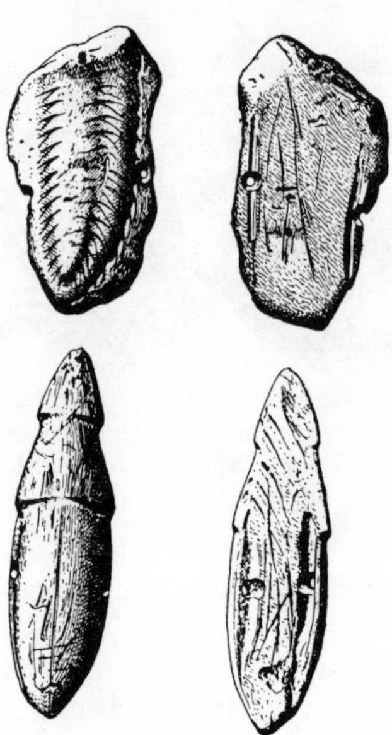

Fig. 24 *Above*: Ordovician trilobite (dalmanitid, probably *Kloucekia*); *below*: buprestid beetle carved in lignite. Both specimens show two perforations for attachment to a garment; from Magdalenian occupation layer, Grotte du Trilobite, Arcy-sur-Cure (Yonne). $\frac{3}{4}$ natural size. After Salmon.

for example, the persistent lore of the scarab beetle; and then again that the 19th-century jeweller Fabergé, working in the Russian court, produced many pendants in the form of a beetle.

According to Professor H. Douville, the trilobite used at La Grotte du Trilobite was a species of *Dalmanites* which had not been recorded in the rocks of France, but possibly had been carried from Central Germany. In 1973 Dr. R. A. Fortey at the British Museum (Natural History) examined high quality photographs of the specimen in question and came to the conclusion that it was probably a species of the Dalmanitid genus *Kloucekia*, which could have been collected in France. (The photographs were provided by l'Abbé Paul Gallet, at Ecole Saint Jacques, Sainte Thérèse, Joigny, where the original is preserved.)

One of the strangest facts in palaeontology is that the holotype of one species of Cambrian trilobite, *Lyriaspis alroiensis* (Etheridge fil.) lies in a piece of chert which had been chipped into an

Plate 2. Silurian trilobite, *Calymene blumenbachi* Brongniart from Wenlock Limestone, Dudley, Worcestershire, mounted in gold brooch (Victorian). Length of trilobite *c.* 4·3 cm. Formerly in collection of the late Miss E. J. Begg, now in Palaeontology Department, British Museum (Nat. Hist.), reg. no. In. 55371. Photograph reproduced by permission of the Trustees of the British Museum (Nat. Hist.).

implement by an Australian aborigine and carried far from the unrecorded locality where he obtained it.[56]

As soon as the Industrial Revolution increased the demand for limestone in the Black Country, mining of the Wenlock Limestone at Dudley frequently brought to light examples of the beautiful trilobite *Calymene blumenbachi* (Plate 2). This attracted widespread interest among collectors, and it became known to the quarrymen as the Dudley Locust or Dudley Insect.[57] Examples of this trilobite were occasionally mounted as brooches and tiepins, probably because it was fashionable to regard fossils either as 'Medals of Creation' or as evidence supporting Darwin's theory of evolution. If fossils were a kind of passport among the intelligentsia of Victorian society, they were in a sense serving as 'charms'.

NOTES

Notes

Historical Dragon Slayers — J. A. Boyle

1. J. G. Frazer, *The Magic Art and the Evolution of Kings* (London, 1911), II, 155.
2. E. S. Hartland, *The Legend of Perseus*, 3 vols., London, 1894–6. Curiously enough the Vedic and Avestan evidence was first cited by an earlier writer than Frazer or Hartland, the 'popularizer' Sabine Baring-Gould in his essay on St. George. See his *Curious Myths of the Middle Ages*, New Edition (London, 1888), pp. 304–6.
3. Hence *azhdahā*, the Persian word for 'dragon'. In the Avesta the serpent is described as having three mouths, three heads and six eyes; in the *Shāh-nāma* or '*Book of Kings*' of Firdausī Azhi Dahāka has become Ḍaḥḥāk, an Arab usurper and tyrant, but is still three-headed because of the two snakes that grow from his shoulders.
4. For a reconstruction of the original Aryan myth see Herman Lommel, *Der arische Kriegsgott* (Frankfurt, 1939), pp. 51–70; Geo Widengren, *Religionsphänomenologie* (Berlin, 1969), pp. 247–8.
5. *Pausanias's Description of Greece*, V, 44–5.
6. Leon Surmelian (transl.), *Daredevils of Sassoun* (London, 1964), pp. 46–7.
7. Mircea Eliade, *Patterns in Comparative Religion* (London, 1958), p. 291.
8. IV, 21. See B. E. Perry (ed. and transl.), *Babrius and Phaedrus* (London and Cambridge, Mass., 1965), pp. 332–5.
9. Michael Alexander (transl.), *Beowulf* (London, 1973), pp. 122–3.
10. R. G. Finch (ed. and transl.), *The Saga of the Volsungs* (London, 1965), p. 26.
11. James Ross (transl.), *Sadi: Gulistan or Flower-Garden*, Camelot Series (London, 1890), p. 221.
12. See the long list given by Alfred Maury, *Croyances et légendes du moyen âge* (Paris, 1896), p. 229, note 1.
13. This is the explanation offered by Maury, pp. 227–9.
14. Mircea Eliade, *The Myth of the Eternal Return* (New York, 1954), p. 43.

15. F. W. Hasluck, *Christianity and Islam under the Sultans* (Oxford, 1929), II, 649.
16. See William Henderson, *Notes on the Folk-lore of the Northern Counties and the Borders* (London, 1879), pp. 281–304; Katherine M. Briggs, *A Dictionary of British Folk-Tales*, IA, pp. 371–6, IB, pp. 159–72.
17. Robert Surtees, *The History and Antiquities of the County Palatine of Durham*, II (London, 1820), p. 171, quotes the following entry from a manuscript pedigree, formerly in the possession of the family of Middleton, of Offerton: 'Johan Lambton that slewe y[e] Worme was knight of Rhoodes and Lord of Lambeton and Wod Apilton [Wood Appleton] efter the dethe of fower brothers sans esshewe masle. His son Robert Lampton was drowned at Newebrigg.' Surtees comments that this statement that John Lambton succeeded to the family estates is contradicted by the 'proven Pedigree'. Indeed, according to that pedigree (see Surtees, p. 174) William Lambton of Lambton (born *ca.* 1390) was succeeded by his second son Thomas (d. 1473), John Lambton, his *fourth* son, being named in the will of his eldest brother Robert, 1442, when he was a Knight of Rhodes.
18. The following text, that used by the Manchester Morris Men, was kindly supplied me by their Archivist, my friend and colleague Mr. W. C. Brice, Reader in Geography in the University of Manchester:

1. On Sunday morning Lambton went a-fishin' in the Wear
And catched a Worm upon his hook he thought most awful queer,
But what 'na sort o' fish it was young Lambton couldna' tell,
And he wouldna' fash to tak it 'yam, so he hoyed it doon a well.

Chorus: Whisht lads an' hod yer gobs
an' I'll tell yer all an awful story;
Whisht lads and' hod yer gobs an'
I'll tell yer 'boot the Worm.

2. Now Lambton felt inclined to gan an' fight in foreign wars,
So he joined a group o' Knights that cared for neither wounds nor scars,
An' off he went to Palestine, where strange things him befell,
An' he very soon forgot aboot the queer Worm in the well.

Whisht, etc.

3. Now t'worm got fat an' grow'd and grow'd an grow'd an awful size,

Wi' great big teeth in a great big gob, an' great big goggly eyes,
An' when at night he'd crawl around to pick up bits o' news,
If he felt dry upon the road 'e'd milk a dozen coos.

Whisht, etc.

4. This fearful Worm would often feed on lambs an' coos an' sheep
An' swaller little bairns alive when they lay doon to sleep,
An' when 'e'd eaten all he could an' 'e 'ad 'ad 'is fill,
'E'd crawl away an wrap 'is tail ten times round Lambton Hill.

Whisht, etc.

5. Now news o' this most awful Worm an' is queer gannins-on
Soon crossed the seas an' reached the ears of brave and bold Sir John,
So back 'e came an' catched the Beast an' chopped 'im in twa 'alves,
An' that soon stopped 'im eatin' bairns an' lambs an' coos an' calves.

Whisht, etc.

6. So now you know how all the folks on both sides of the Wear,
Lost lots of sheep an' lots of sleep an' lived in mortal fear,
So let's 'ave one to bold Sir John, who saved the folks from harm,
Saved coos and calves by makin' 'alves of the awful Lambton Worm!

Whisht, etc.

For a full version of the story see the ballad reproduced in *The Wonderful Legend of the Lambton Worm*, a booklet published in Newcastle-on-Tyne *ca.* 1875. The ballad had appeared originally in an issue of *Tait's Edinburgh Magazine* (1832–46). I am grateful to Miss Theo Brown for lending me her copy of the 1968 facsimile reprint of the booklet. In the introduction (pp. 8–9*n*) a few lines are quoted from what is described as a 'Fragment of an Old Ballad'. These same lines are also quoted by Henderson, p. 290, where they are attributed to 'a local poet'.

19. I summarize the account given by Henderson, pp. 287–92. See also Surtees, p. 171, and Briggs, Part A, pp. 373–6.

20. See note 17.
21. Cf. the similar action by Alexander's dragon in its death throes. See p. 30 and note 26.
22. Razor blades in Surtees' version.
23. Stith Thompson motif S. 241 (Jephthah's vow).
24. E. A. Wallis Budge (ed. and transl.), *The History of Alexander, being the Syriac Version of the Pseudo-Callisthenes* (Cambridge, 1889), pp. 107–8. For a résumé of the account see J. A. Boyle, 'Alexander and the Turks' in *Tractata Altaica Denis Sinor Sexegario Optime de Rebus Altaicis Merito Dedicata*, ed. Walther Heissig, J. R. Krueger, F. J. Oinas, E. Schütz (Wiesbaden, 1976), pp. 107–17 (107–8).
25. i.e. the kingdom of Maghada on the Ganges.
26. See p. 27 and note 21.
27. Reuben Levy (transl.), *The Epic of the Kings* (London, 1967), pp. 263–9. For an earlier Middle Persian version of the story see Theodor Nöldeke (transl.), *Geschichte des Artachšîr i Pâpakân aus dem Pahlewi übersetzt* (Göttingen, 1879), pp. 49–57; also E. G. Browne, *A Literary History of Persia*, I (1902), 146–7.
28. Nöldeke, p. 49 and note 4, read the name Haftān-bōkht 'the Seven (Planets) have delivered', but see now Jean de Menasce, 'Haftvād ou Haftānbōxt' in *Yād-nāme-ye Irānī-ye Minorsky*, ed. Mojtaba Minovi and Iraj Afshar (Tehran, 1969), pp. 139–42.
29. The blood of cattle and sheep in the Middle Persian version.
30. See note 3.
31. Sir Peter Loschy, who slew the dragon of Loschy Hill (near East Newton in the parish of Stonegrave in the North Riding of Yorkshire), had the assistance of his dog, which carried away the fragments of the creature's body as Peter lopped them off and deposited them on a hilltop nearly a mile away near Nunnington church. See Briggs, Part B, p. 160.
32. *Bel and the Dragon*, vv. 23 ff.
33. Hasluck, p. 655.
34. Henderson, pp. 295–7, Briggs, IB, 164–5.
35. Quoted by Hartland, III, 87–8.
36. The very word 'worm' shows that the creatures were originally thought of as ophidians. In the nineteenth century it could still be seriously suggested that these legends were based on memories of the great lizards that roamed the earth in geological times. See Henderson, p. 282. Strangely enough there is evidence to show that fossils of the plesiosaurus discovered in the late Middle Ages did influence the iconography of the dragon, which had previously for the most part been depicted as a winged biped and which now appears as a wingless quadruped. See Emil Ploss, *Siegfried-Sigurd, der Drachenkämpfer* (Cologne, 1966), p. 56, note 160.

37. J. B. Pritchard (ed.), *Ancient Near Eastern Texts relating to the Old Testament*, 2nd. ed. (Princeton, 1955), p. 67b.

Animals as Threatening Figures in Systems of Traditional Social Control J. D. A. Widdowson

1. See, for example, E. C. Parsons, 'The Zuñi A'Doshlě and Suukě', *American Anthropologist*, new series, XVIII, 3 (1916), 338–47; O. F. Raum, *Chaga Childhood*, London, 1940; M. Mead, *Growing up in New Guinea*, Harmondsworth, 1942; B. B. Whiting, *Six Cultures: Studies of Child Rearing*, New York, 1963; J. W. M. Whiting, *Becoming a Kwoma*, New Haven, 1951; J. W. M. Whiting and I. L. Child, *Child Training and Personality*, New Haven and London, 1953; M. I. Hilger, *Chippewa Child Life and its Cultural Background*, Washington, 1951, *Arapaho Child Life and its Cultural Background*, Washington, 1952; F. Ranke, 'Kinderschreck, Popanz', *Handwörterbuch des deutschen Aberglaubens*, IV (1931–2), cols. 1366–74; F. Cramer, 'Galloromanischer Kinderschrecken', in *Volkstum und Kultur der Romanen*, IX (1936), 118–48; B. Tommola, *Yliluonnilliset Olennot Lastenpelotuksina*, Suomi, CVII, 2, 1955; J-P. Tijskens, 'Les Noms du Croquemitaine en Wallonie', *Enquêtes du Musée de la Vie Wallonne*, X (1954), 257–392, and XI (1966), 1–59; A. Taylor, 'Raw Head and Bloody Bones', *Kentucky Folklore Record*, VI (1960), 19–20; W. D. Hand, ed., *Popular Beliefs and Superstitions from North Carolina* in *The Frank C. Brown Collection of North Carolina Folklore*, VII (1904), 155.
2. H. Halpert, 'Raw Head and Bloody Bones' in 'Down Our Way', *Kentucky Folklore Record*, I, 1 (1955), 7–8; note to 'Old Wall-Eyes' in V. Randolph, *The Devil's Pretty Daughter and Other Ozark Folk Tales*, New York, 1955, p. 172; 'Some Observations on American Frightening Figures', unpublished paper presented at the meetings of the American Folklore Society, Toronto, 1967.
3. A. E. Green, 'Some Observations on Threatening Children', unpublished paper delivered at a meeting of the Folklore Society, London, 1970. J. D. A. Widdowson, 'The Bogeyman: Some Preliminary Observations on Frightening Figures', *Folklore*, 82 (1971), 99–115; 'Aspects of Traditional Verbal Control: Threats and Threatening Figures in Newfoundland Folklore', unpublished Ph.D. dissertation, Memorial University of Newfoundland, 1973; 'The Language of the Child Culture: Pattern and Tradition in Language

Acquisition and Socialization', in S. Rogers, ed., *They Don't Speak Our Language*, London, 1976, pp. 33–62.

4. J. Grimm, *Teutonic Mythology*, transl. J. S. Stallybrass, London, 1883–8; W. Mannhardt, *Wald und Feldkulte*, 2nd edn., Berlin, 1904–5; H. Ploss and B. Renz, *Das Kind in Brauch und Sitte der Völker*, 3rd edn., Leipzig, 1911; A. F. Chamberlain, *The Child and Childhood in Folk Thought*, New York and London, 1896, pp. 140–2; D. Kidd, *Savage Childhood*, London, 1906, esp. pp. 131–42.
5. C. W. von Sydow, *Selected Papers on Folklore*, Copenhagen, 1948, esp. No. 4, 'The Mannhardtian Theories about the Last Sheaf and the Fertility Demons from a Modern Critical Point of View', pp. 89–105, and No. 8, 'Comparative Religion and Popular Tradition', pp. 166–88.
6. See for example J. C. Foster, *Ulster Folklore*, Belfast, 1951, pp. 106–7, and Widdowson, *Aspects*, esp. pp. 137–49.
7. For example, M. M. Firestone, *Brothers and Rivals: Patrilocality in Savage Cove*, St. John's, 1967, pp. 122–3; J. F. Szwed, *Private Cultures and Public Imagery: Interpersonal Relations in a Newfoundland Society*, St. John's, 1966, pp. 79–82; J. C. Faris, *Cat Harbour: A Newfoundland Fishing Settlement*, St. John's, 1966, pp. 100–2, 132; Widdowson, *Aspects*; *Child Culture*.
8. The imperative structures offer interesting parallels and contrasts with Bernstein's 'imperative modes' and indeed threats as a whole are particularly relevant to his discussion of positional and personal orientations in social control. See B. Bernstein, 'A Sociolinguistic Approach to Socialization: With Some Reference to Educability', chapter 3 of R. Williams, ed., *Language and Poverty: Perspectives on a Theme*, Chicago, 1971, pp. 25–61.
9. For a discussion of these linguistic patterns see Widdowson, *Aspects*, esp. pp. 62–97; *Child Culture*, pp. 57–9.
10. This material, in manuscript and taperecorded form, is deposited in the Memorial University of Newfoundland Folklore and Language Archive in St. John's.
11. See J. D. A. Widdowson, 'S.L.F. Research Projects: Systems of Social Control. Project I: Threats and Other Verbal Constraints Used in Controlling Children', *Lore and Language*, I, 4 (1971), 2–3.
12. See, for example, S. Rachman, *The Meanings of Fear*, Harmondsworth, 1974, esp. pp. 44, 46, 48–9, 52, 81, 84. Rachman's lucid discussion of many aspects of fear has particular relevance for the choice of figures, especially animals, used in the threatening of children.
13. The authenticity of this reference is confirmed in 2 Kings, 2, verses 23 and 24, describing Elisha's cursing of children who mocked him:

'And he went up from thence unto Beth-el: and as he was going up by the way, there came forth little children out of the city, and mocked him, and said unto him, Go up, thou bald head; go up, thou bald head. And he turned back, and looked on them, and cursed them in the name of the LORD. And there came forth two she bears out of the wood, and tare forty and two children of them.'

I am indebted to my colleague, Dr. D. J. A. Clines, Department of Biblical Studies, University of Sheffield, for locating these references.

14. I have been unable to confirm my suspicion that moles and weasels are not indigenous to Newfoundland. Their use in threats may therefore be a folk memory from the British Isles.
15. See Rachman, p. 81.

The Black Dog in English Folklore — Theo Brown

1. *Folklore* LXIX (1958), pp. 175–92.
2. *Journal*, Society for Psychical Research, XIII (1908), pp. 256–61.
3. Kathleen Wiltshire, *Ghosts & Legends of the Wiltshire Countryside*, Salisbury, 1973, pp. 8 and 12.
4. Ruth L. Tongue, *Somerset Folklore*, London, 1965, pp. 109–10.
5. E. H. Rudkin, 'The Black Dog', *Folklore XLIX (1938)*, pp. 111–31.
6. Theo Brown, 'The Black Dog in Devon', *Transactions*, Devonshire Association, XCI (1959), pp. 38–44.
7. Barbara C. Spooner, 'The Dog in the Lane', *Old Cornwall*, I (1925–1930) Pt. xii, pp. 25–8; and 'The Dog called Darley', *ibid.* Pt. viii, pp. 23–6.
8. Hesiod, *Theogony*, Ll. 767–74; Virgil: *Aeneid*, VI, Ll. 416–27; M. Gaster, *Roumanian Bird & Beast Stories*, 1915, p. 243.
9. William Howells, *The Heathens*, 1949, pp. 143–4; G. C. Vaillant, *The Aztecs of Mexico*, 1950, p. 171.
10. P. Mag, Par. 1432 pp., p. 80W, cit. by Erwin Rohde, *Psyche*, tr. 1925, p. 324, Note 99 to Ch. IX.
11. K. Kerényi, *The Gods of the Greeks*, 1958, pp. 128–9; Marija Gimbutas, *The Gods & Goddesses of Old Europe, 7000–3500 BC*, London, 1974, pp. 190–200; Erich Neumann, *The Origins & History of Consciousness*, New York, 1949, 1954 Tr., pp. 94–5.
12. Theo Brown, 'The Triple Gateway', *Folklore* LXXVII (1966), pp. 123–31.

13. Marija Gimbutas, *op. cit.*, Pl. 144, 147–53 etc.
14. G. R. Levy, *The Gate of Horn*, London, 1948, p. 19 and Figs. 11, 12 on p. 18.
15. A. B. Cook, 'The European Sky-God', *Folklore* XVI (1905), p. 299.
16. Marija Gimbutas, *op. cit.*, p. 199.
17. H. R. E. Davidson, 'Mithraism & the Gundestrup Bowl', *Mithraic Studies*, ed. John R. Hinnells, Manchester, 1975, p. 502.
18. Christiane Desroches-Noblecourt, Letter dated 3 Nov. 1969.
19. F. E. Zeuner, *A History of Domesticated Animals*, London, 1963, p. 31 and Ch. IV.
20. S. Bökönyi, *History of Domesticated Mammals in Central & Eastern Europe*, Budapest, 1974, pp. 313–33.
21. S. Bökönyi, *op. cit.*, p. 313.
22. Lidio Cipriani, *The Andaman Islanders*, London, 1966. Note also the observations on pariah dogs in India by Lockwood Kipling, *Man & Beast in India*, 1891/2, pp. 267–8.
23. Theo Brown, 'Living Images', *Folklore*, LXXII (1962), pp. 25–40.
24. Barbara Hannah, *The Religious Function of the Animus in the Book of Tobit*, Guild of Pastoral Psychology, London, Guild Lecture No. 114, 1961.
25. James Hope Moulton, *Early Zoroastrianism*, London, 1913, pp. 250, & 333–4.
26. H. R. Ellis (Davidson), *The Road to Hel*, 1943/69, pp. 127–30.
27. C. Desroches-Noblecourt, *Tutankhamen*, 1963/5, p. 188.
28. *Ibid.*, Letter dated 3 Nov. 1969.
29. F. B. Jevons, ed., *Plutarch's Romane Questions*, trans. 1603 by Philemon Holland, London, 1892, pp. l–liii.
30. A. B. Cook, *Zeus*, Vol. II, Appendix pt. II, H, 1940, pp. 1059–65.
31. W. Warde Fowler, *The Roman Festivals of the Period of the Republic*, 1895/1925, p. 144 fn. and p. 306 fn.
32. J. Wentworth Day, *Here are Ghosts & Witches*, 1954, p. 31.
33. Sir Arthur Waugh, Letter dated 12 Jan. 1959.
34. *Proceedings*, Society for Psychical Research, X (1894), pp. 155–6.
35. Margaret A. Murray, *The Witch Cult in Western Europe*, 1921/62, Ch. VIII, §3, p. 225.
36. Carmen Blacker, *The Catalpa Bow*, London, 1975, pp. 51–61.
37. A. C. Fox-Davies, *A Complete Guide to Heraldry*, 1909/50, pp. 326–7.

Animal Lore and the Evil-eye in Shepherd Sardinia — Alexander Lopasic

1. A. Pigliaru, *Il Banditismo in Sardegna*, Varese, 1970, p. 120.
2. R. Marchi, 'Le maschere barbaricine', *Il Ponte*, Florence, 1951, pp. 1359–60.
3. P. Moretti, 'Mamutones e Maimones', *Lares*, XX, Fasc. III, Florence, 1954, pp. 179–80.
4. M. L. Wagner, *Dizionario Etimologico Sardo*, II, Heidelberg, 1962, p. 61.
5. F. Alziator, *Il Folklore Sardo*, Bologna, 1957, p. 80. See also: P. Massajoli, 'I Mamutones', *L'Universo*, Novara, 1972, No. 4, pp. 777–94.
6. R. Marchi, 'Il Boe muliache della Barbagia e "l'Essere fantastico" di Nule'. *Atti del Convegno di Studi religiosi Sardi*, Cagliari, 1962, Padova, 1963, pp. 295–6.
7. For the word *Musca Macedda* see: M. L. Wagner, *Dizionario Etimologico Sardo*, II, Heidelberg, 1962, p. 143; G. Vidossi, 'Musca macedda', Catania, 1934, *Folklore Italiano*, IX, pp. 119–23.
8. G. Vidossi, *op. cit.*, pp. 121–3.
9. G. Bottiglioni, *Leggende e tradizioni di Sardegna*, Geneva, 1922.
10. J. W. Tyndale: *The Island of Sardinia*, London, 1849, III, pp. 192–7. For a recent study on Tarantism in Sardinia with special emphasis on Oristano see: C. Gallini, *I Rituali dell' Àrgia*, Padova, 1967.
11. M. L. Wagner, 'Il mallochio e credenze affini in Sardegna, *Lares*, II, 1913, Rome, pp. 129–50.
12. M. L. Wagner, *op. cit.*, pp. 139–41, 145–7.
13. The reference is about Lucca. See E. de Martino, *Sud e magia*, Milan, 1966.
14. M. L. Wagner, *Dizionario* ..., II, p. 571.
15. G. Reichel-Dolmatoff, *The People of Aritama*, Chicago–London, 1961, pp. 284–5, 402–3.
16. H. Schoeck, *Der Neid. Eine Theorie der Gesellschaft*, Freiburg, 1966. (English Translation, *Envy. A theory of Social Behaviour*, London, 1969.)
17. *Der Neid und die Gesellschaft*, Freiburg, 1974, pp. 104–12.
18. C. Gallini, *Dono e Malocchio*, Palermo, 1973, discusses the rôle of reciprocity and gifts in relation to 'evil-eye' and modern changes both in Sardinia and mainland Italy.

Witchcraft and Magic in the Old Testament, and their Relation to Animals J. R. Porter

1. G. Parrinder, *Witchcraft: European and African*, 1958, p. 121.
2. *Op. cit.*, p. 125.
3. *Op. cit.*, 1938, p. 263.
4. *Op. cit.*, p. 12.
5. *Op. cit.*, p. 27.
6. Cp. E. Evans-Pritchard, *Witchcraft, Oracles and Magic among the Azande*, 1937, p. 21.
7. *Op. cit.*, p. 122.
8. Cp. Is. iii, 1–3.
9. For this, reference may be made to such works as J. G. Frazer, *Folklore in the Old Testament,* 1919; F. S. Bodenheimer, *Animal and Man in Bible lands*, 1960, pp. 214ff; T. H. Gaster, *Myth, Legend and Custom in the Old Testament*, 1969.
10. Cp. John Garstang, *Joshua Judges*, 1931, pp. 258–60.
11. Cp. in general, W. Robertson Smith, 'Animal Worship and Animal Tribes among the Arabs and in the Old Testament' in *Lectures and Essays of William Robertson Smith*, ed. J. S. Black and G. Chrystal, 1912, pp. 455–83.
12. Cp. the essay by A. Lopasic in this volume, p. 59
13. On might instance the occurrences of frogs, maggots, flies and locusts among the plagues of Egypt in Exod. vii–xi, a narrative which contains many folklore elements, cp. F. Dumermuth, 'Folkloristisches in der Erzählung von den ägyptischen Plagen', *Zeitschrift für die Alttestamentliche Wissenschaft* 76, 1964, pp. 323ff. Whether the divine name *Baal-zebub* in 2 Kings i indicates a deity who was actually known as 'Lord of the Flies' is very doubtful. The original form of the word, in the light of Canaanite evidence, appears to be *Baal-zebul*, meaning something like 'prince Baal': cp. John Gray, *I & II Kings*, 2nd edn., 1970, p. 463.
14. Cp. most recently Karen Randolph Joines, *Serpent Symbolism in the Old Testament: A Linguistic, Archaeological and Literary Study*, 1974.
15. For Lilith, cp. T. H. Gaster, *Orientalia* 11, 1942, pp. 41–76.
16. For Mowinckel's original position, cp. his *Psalmenstudien I*, 1921, and for his later modification of his views, cp. his *The Psalms in Israel's Worship*, 1962, Vol. II, pp. 250f.
17. For Resheph, cp. A. Caquot, 'Sur quelques démons de l'Ancien Testament', *Semitica* VI, 1956, pp. 53–68.
18. Cp. T. H. Gaster, *Myth, Legend and Custom in the Old Testament*, 1969, p. 769.
19. For these, cp. Geo Widengren, *The Accadian and Hebrew Psalms of Lamentation as Religious Documents*, 1937.

20. Compare also the frequent expression of the psalmist's desire that his enemies may go down to the realm of the dead—e.g. Ps. xxxi, 18; iv, 15, 24—with the following passage from an Assyrian text, referring to Nergal, the god of the dead:

> May they be taken to him,
> may they go down to him,
> to the land without return.

Animals and Witchcraft in Danish Peasant Culture — Joan Rockwell

1. Evald Tang Kristensen, *Danske Sagn*, *Ny Række* (New Series) VI (published posthumously in 1936), §31. In the following notes, sources are indicated briefly, with fuller details in the list of references that follows the notes.
2. *Op. cit.*, §74; and many other examples of the practice quoted: see e.g. *ibid.*, §§553–63.
3. Mauss, p. 36.
4. Gaardboe, p. 18.
5. Kristensen (1936), §497.
6. *Ibid.*, §523.
7. Mauss, p. 12.
8. Kristensen (1936), §346.
9. Kristensen (1899), §72.
10. Mauss, p. 33.
11. Kristensen (1899), §1.
12. Kristensen (1936), §93.
13. Lewis, p. 9.
14. Steensberg, p. 11.
15. Kristensen (1899), §§775–84; Hals-Præst was not a pastor: he is named for the town of *Hals* and for being able to imitate any sermon he heard, and generally improvise rhetoric. With education, he certainly *could* have been a minister.
16. *Op. cit.*, §380.
17. Kristensen (1891), §251.
18. *Ibid.*, §§261, 262, 264, 266.

References

Gaardboe, Anton, *Det sidste Natmandsfolk i Vendsyssel*, Copenhagen, 1968 (first published 1900).

Kristensen, Evald Tang, *Jyske Almueliv* (Gamle Folks Fortællinger af det Jyske Almueliv, som det har blevet f⌀rt i Mands Minde), Copenhagen, 1891, VI.

Kristensen, Evald Tang, *Danske Sagn, som de harlydt i folkemund*, Aarhus, 1899, VI.

Kristensen, Evald Tang, *Danske Sagn, Ny Række*, Copenhagen, 1936, VI.

Lewis, Norman, *The Sicilian Specialist*, Collins, London, 1973.

MacFarlane, Alan, *Witchcraft in Tudor and Stuart England*, Routledge and Kegan Paul, London, 1970.

Mauss, Marcel, *A General Theory of Magic* (first published Presses Universitaires de France, 1950), transl. Robert Brain, Routledge and Kegan Paul, 1972.

Steensberg, Axel, 'Folkeskik og Folketro', in *Dagligliv i Danmark i den syttende og attende aarhundrede 1720–1790*, (ed. Axel Steensberg), p. 11, Nyt Nordisk Forlag, Arnold Busch, Copenhagen, 1971.

The Role of Animals in Witchcraft and Popular Magic

Kathryn C. Smith

1. Stith Thompson, *Motif Index of Folk Literature*, Academia Scienarum Fennica, 6 vols. 1932–6. See G. 211–211.4. Also G. 241.2.1.
2. *Ibid.*, G. 225.0.3, G. 225.3.4, D. 1766.4.2.
3. *Ibid.*, D. 1605.2, D. 2083.2.1, G. 265.4, G. 265.6.3.
4. Apuleius (2nd century AD), *The Golden Ass*, tr. Robert Graves 1950, pp. 88–93; Gervase of Tilbury, *Otia Imperalia*, iii, 92.
5. *Malleus Maleficarum* (1486), tr. Montague Summers 1948, quest. 1, cap. 9; John Webster, *The Displaying of Supposed Witchcraft*, 1677 fol.5^{v}. See also Joseph Glanvil, *Sadducismus Triumphatus* (1681), 1726 ed. p. 304, dealing with the 1664 examination of Alice Duke.
6. Edward Fairfax, *Daemonologia* (1622), Ackrill, Harrogate, 1882, ed. Wm. Grainge, pp. 95, 97.
7. Stith Thompson, *op. cit.*, G. 252.
8. G. Ewart Evans & D. Thompson, *The Leaping Hare*, Faber and Faber, 1972, p. 165.

9. See Institute of Dialect & Folk Life Studies, Leeds University fieldwork in Wetwang, J. S. Chamberlain. My thanks are due to the Director of the Institute for permission to quote from archive holdings.
10. Calvert MS. pp. 41–2. I am indebted to the late J. Fairfax-Blakeborough for permission to use this MS.
11. Fieldwork for doctoral thesis by the present writer, 1974.
12. This tale was originally collected by Richard Blakeborough in *Yorkshire Wit, Character, Folklore & Customs*, London, Frowde, 1898, pp. 173, 193–4.
13. *Yorkshire Evening Post*, 15th Feb. 1926, 'Witches of Goathland' J.B.B.
14. G. E. Evans and D. Thompson, *op. cit.*, p. 42.
15. Bodleian Library 13th-century MS. Digby 86f. 108.[v] For translation see Ross in *Procs. of Leeds Phil.Soc.Lit. and Hist.Section*, sect. 3, 1935, pp. 347–77.
16. R. Burton, *Anatomie of Melancholie*, 1621, rep. 1893, London, ed. Shillitoe.
17. This is the outline of a story given to me by J. Fairfax-Blakeborough in 1973, but also given by his father in *op. cit.*, 196–7 (see note 12).
18. Fairfax, *op. cit.*, pp. 32, 33, 34 and subsequently. Tewhit is a Yorkshire dialect word for lapwing.
19. *Sunday Chronicle*, 9th Sept. 1928. Redcap is a common witch name in Essex folklore.
20. F. Cobley, *On Foot through Wharfedale*, 1882, pp. 240–1.
21. W. Henderson, *Notes on the Folklore of the Northern Counties of England and the Borders*, pub. for Folklore Society, London, 1866, p. 202. Blakeborough, *op. cit.*, p. 203.
22. An unpublished MS. I am again indebted to the late J. Fairfax-Blakeborough for permission to use this material. The account was probably written c. 1890 to his father Richard Blakeborough, referring to events about 40 years earlier.
23. Richard Blakeborough, *op. cit.*, p. 162; J. G. Hall, *A History of South Cave and of Other Parishes in the East Riding*, Hull, 1892, pp. 132–3, quoting T. Jackson, 'Recollections of My own life and times'; Henderson, *op. cit.*, p. 223.
24. P. Shaw Jeffrey, *Whitby Lore and Legend*, Stockton, 1923, p. 184.
25. W. D. Wood-Rees, *A History of Barmby Moor from Pre-historic Times*, Pocklington, Firth, 1911, pp. 59–61.
26. J. Nicholson, *The Folklore of East Yorkshire*, London, Hull & Driffield, 1890, pp. 91–2.
27. *Essex Herald*, December 1890.
28. Blakeborough *op. cit.*, p. 186; Shaw Jeffrey, *op. cit.*, p. 180.

29. Borthwick Institute of Historical Research, York.v.1590–1/CB1 f. 61.
30. *Ibid.* v.1633/CBI f. 427.ᵛ
31. Tale recorded in 1965 by A. E. Green, Institute of Dialect and Folk Life Studies, Leeds University.
32. *Yorkshire Evening Post*, 15th Feb. 1926, *op. cit.*
33. Fieldwork in Goathland by R. J. Green, 1963, Institute of Dialect & Folk Life Studies, Leeds University.
34. *Poll for the Knights of the Shire*, May–June 1807, p. 214. The Church-wardens Accounts are in North Riding Record Office. The envelope is now in the Whitby Literary & Philosophical Society, Pannett Park. My thanks are due to the Whitby Literary & Philosophical Society for permission to quote from their archive holdings.
35. J. Atkinson, *Forty Years in a Moorland Parish*, London, Macmillan, 1891, pp. 124–5.
36. Keith Thomas, *Religion & the Decline of Magic*, Penguin University Books, 1973, for instance, considered that earlier wise men in the trials period tended to blame anything inexplicable on witchcraft. From later evidence this is not entirely satisfactory, see p. 247.

The Snake Woman in Japanese Myth and Legend — Carmen Blacker

1. See for example Joseph Fontenrose, *Python: a study of Delphic myth and its origins*, Berkeley, 1959.
2. *FF Communications No. 209*, Helsinki, 1971.
3. See F. J. Daniels, 'Snakes as Wives and Lovers in Japanese Myth and Legend', *Bulletin of the Japan Society of London*, No. 75, February 1975. Hiroko Ikeda classifies monkey and snake husbands under Type 312, and dog husbands, *inu-muko*, under Type 411D. Snake, crane, fish, fox and frog wives are Type 413, while *Ryūgū-nyōbo*, wives from the Dragon Palace, appear under Type 470B.
4. Hiroko Ikeda's Type 470. The tale is also found in the 8th-century chronicle *Nihon Shoki*, described as a historical event for the year AD 478. See W. G. Aston, *Nihongi*, p. 368.
5. Seki Keigo treats the folktale types and motifs which deal with communication between the water world and the world of men in his *Nihon Mukashibanashi Shūsei*, Vol. 3, pp. 997–1034. This version of the tale, Hiroko Ikeda's Type 470A, is often known as *Ryūgū-dōji*, Boy from the Dragon Palace. This miraculous child is Yanagita's

celebrated 'small hero', discussed very helpfully by C. Ouwehand in his *Namazue and their Themes*, Leiden 1964, pp. 146–62.

6. Yanagita Kunio, *Nihon Mukashibanashi*, p. 43.
7. The oldest recorded version of this legend again goes back to the 8th century. It appears in the chronicle *Kojiki*, chapter 45.
8. Daniels, *op. cit.*, p. 14.
9. 'Mrs. White' is in Arthur Waley's *The Real Tripitaka*, 1952, p. 183. For an excellent treatment of the snake woman in China, see Edward H. Schafer, *The Divine Woman: Dragon ladies and Rain Maidens in T'ang Literature*, Berkeley, 1973. De Visser's otherwise very useful *Dragon in China and Japan*, Amsterdam, 1913, is curiously reticent on dragon-women.

   Gervase of Tilbury's story is quoted in E. S. Hartland's *Science of Fairy Tales*, pp. 272–3.

   For the cup or chalice as a life-giving symbol, see Emma Jung and Marie-Louise von Franz, *The Grail Legend*, 1971, chapter 7.
10. In the Nō play the story has become a local legend of Shizuoka prefecture. The theme of the Celestial Wife has been treated by Usuda Jingorō in his *Tennin Nyōbo sono Ta*, 1973.
11. I have discussed the *wankashi-densetsu*, Ikeda's Type 730, in my *The Catalpa Bow; A Study of Shamanistic Practices in Japan*, 1975, pp. 76–8. Kitami Toshio analysed nearly 150 surviving bowl-lending legends in 1954, finding the highest proportion of them in Nagano prefecture in regions by rivers, lakes or deep pools 'Nihonjin no ikyō-kannen no ichi-dammen, wankashi-densetsu wo megutte', *Nihon Minzokugaku*, No. 4, 1954, pp. 111–18. See also Yanagita's 'Kakurezato', *Yanagita Kunio Shū*, Vol. 5, pp. 230–50.
12. Hartland, *op. cit.*, p. 145. See also Keightley's *Fairy Mythology*, pp. 255–6, 284–5.
13. A full and helpful English study of the tale by Seki Keigo, 'The Spool of Thread; a subtype of the serpent-bridegroom tale', may be found in Richard Dorson (ed.), *Studies in Japanese Folklore*, Bloomington, Indiana, 1963. Ikeda classes the Snake Paramour stories under Type 411C.
14. *Heike Monogatari*, book 8. Utsumi's edition pp. 446–7.
15. Nakayama Tarō, *Nihon Fujoshi*, pp. 248–9; *Minzokugaku Jiten*, pp. 490–1; Yanagita, *Imōto no Chikara*, *Yanagita Kunio Shū*, Vol. 9, pp. 108–9.
16. Yanagita Kunio, 'Tamayorihime-kō', *Yanagita Kunio Shū*, Vol. 9, p. 54.
17. Nakayama, *op. cit.*, pp. 248–9.
18. Matsumura, *op. cit.*, Vol. 3, pp. 196–218.
19. See *The Catalpa Bow*, pp. 115–26, 169–70.
20. *Heike Monogatari*, Utsumi's edition, pp. 372–4.

Shape-changing in the Old Norse Sagas

H. R. Ellis Davidson

1. *Hrôlfs Saga Kraka*, p. 50.
2. In the history of Saxo Grammaticus (Bk. ii, 64) Bjarke declares that he won the name *belliger* (warlike) from a previous exploit. This is presumably Saxo's Latin translation of *boðvar*, genitive of *bǫð*, a poetic word for battle.
3. M. Barbeau, 'Bear Mother', *Journal of American Folklore* 59 (1946), pp. 1ff.
4. J. Turi, *Turi's Book of Lapland*, ed. E. D. Hatt, translated from the Danish by E. G. Nash (1931), p. 124.
5. E. Topsell, *The Historie of Foure-Footed Beastes* (1607), p. 27.
6. Barbeau (note 3 above), pp. 4ff.
7. H. Vierck, 'Zum Fernverkehr über See im 6 Jahrhundert', in K. Hauck, *Goldbrakteaten aus Sievern* (Munich, 1970), p. 385.
8. M. Danielli, 'Initiation Ceremonial from Norse Literature', *Folklore* 56 (1945), pp. 229–45.
9. A. Irving Hallowell, 'Bear Ceremonialism in the Northern Hemisphere', *American Anthropologist* (N.S.28), 1926, pp. 2ff.; R. Karsten, *The Religion of the Samek* (Leiden, 1955), and references there given.
10. *Ibid.*, p. 114; cf. Hallowell (see above), pp. 104, 132.
11. *Ibid.*, pp. 104, 130; A. V. Ström, 'Die Hauptriten des Wikingert zeitlichen nordischen Opfers', *Festschrift Walter Baetke* (Weimar, 1966), p. 336.
12. Hallowell (note 9 above), p. 149.
13. Turi (note 4 above), pp. 123, 125.
14. *Ibid.*, p. 245, note 41*.
15. *Landnámabók* (Isl.Forn., Reykjavik, 1968), S. 350, I, ii. pp. 355–6.
16. *Örvar-Odds Saga*, 5; cf. *Faereyinga Saga*, 12, where the bear is propped up after being killed, and a piece of wood put between its jaws to keep them open.
17. Hallowell (note 9 above), p. 85.
18. G. Müller, *Studier zu der theriophoren Personennamen der Germanen* (*Niederdeutsche Studier* 17, Vienna, 1970); cf. H. Beck, *Das Ebersignum im Germanischen* (*Quellen u.Forschungen zur Sprach- und Kulturgeschichte der Germ. Völker*, N.F. 16, 1965), pp. 70ff.
19. E. Noreen, 'Ordet Bärsärk', *Arkiv f. Nord Filologi* (series 3) 4 (1932), pp. 242–54.
20. Also known as *Haraldskvæði* (F. Jonnson, *Den Norsk-Islandske Skjaldedigtning* (Copenhagen, 1912), p. 23, verse 8; p. 25, verse 21; cf. N. Kershaw, *Anglo-Saxon and Norse Poems* (1922), pp. 76ff.).
21. E.g. The dies from Ölund (H. R. E. Davidson, *Pagan Scandinavia*,

1967, pl. 41). Cf. P. Paulsen, *Alamannische Adelsgräber von Niederstotzingen* (Stuttgart, 1967), pp. 96ff.

22. N. Lid, 'Til Varulvens Historie', *Trolldom* (Oslo 1950), pp. 82–108, esp. pp. 91ff.
23. H. R. E. Davidson, 'The Significance of the Man in the Horned Helmet', *Antiquity* 39 (1965), pp. 23ff.
24. H. R. E. Davidson, *The Viking Road to Byzantium* (1976), pp. 113ff.
25. *Egils Saga*, chapters 27, 40, 57, 65.
26. *Völsunga Saga* 8.
27. Turi (note 4 above), pp. 130ff.
28. G. Turville-Petre, 'Dream Symbols in Old Icelandic Literature', *Festschrift Walter Baetke* (Weimar, 1966), pp. 348ff.; cf. *Folklore* 69 (1958), pp. 93ff.
29. *Flateyjarbók* (Christiania, 1860) I, pp. 205, 253.
30. O. Pettersson, *Jabmek and Jabmeaimo* (*Lunds Univ. Aarskrift* N.F.1, 52) (1956), pp. 64ff.
31. H. Falk and A. Torp, *Etymologisk Ordbog* (Oslo, 1903), *fylgje*; cf. Turville-Petre, 'Liggja Fylgjur þinar til Islands', *Viking Society Saga Book* 12 (1940), pp. 119–26.
32. J. Jonasson, *Islenzkir Þjoðh ættir* (Reykjavik, 1934), p. 261.
33. A. Hultkranz, 'Spirit Lodge', *Studies in Shamanism*, ed. Edsman (Stockholm, 1967), pp. 59–60; cf. Karsten (note 9 above), pp. 76ff.
34. *Ibid.*, p. 79.
35. *Sturlaugs Saga Starsfsama* 12; *Hjálmðérs Saga ok Olvés* 20; cf. H. R. E. Davidson, 'Hostile Magic in the Icelandic Sagas', *The Witch Figure*, ed. Newall (1973), pp. 29ff.
36. Beck (note 18 above), pp. 41ff.
37. H. R. E. Davidson, *Gods and Myths of Northern Europe* (1964), pp. 98ff.
38. *Þorskfirðinga Saga* 10, 17; cf. *Harðar Saga* 26; *Eyrbyggja Saga* 20.
39. In Snorri Sturluson's account of the building of a wall round Asgard, in the *Prose Edda*, Loki becomes a mare in order to lure away the giant's horse which had been acting as his helper.
40. The fullest study of the practice of *níð* is B. Almqvust, *Norrön Niddiktning* (Uppsala, 1965); cf. F. Ström, 'Níð, ergi and Old Norse moral attitudes', Dorothea Coke Lecture, University College, London, 1973 (1974).
41. J. Werner, 'Tiergestaltige Heilsbilder und germanische Personennamen', *Deutsche Vierteljahrsschrift f. Literaturwissenschaft* 37 (Stuttgart, 1963), pp. 379ff.

The Social Biology of Werewolves — W. M. S. Russell and Claire Russell

References are to the bibliography that follows these notes, the numbers referring to pages. Where more than one work by the same author are used, the particular work is simply identified, usually by the publication date in brackets. Montague Summers's *History of Witchcraft* and *Geography of Witchcraft* are referred to as 'Summers (1956)' and 'Summers (1958)', respectively; his *Werewolf* is referred to simply as 'Summers'.

Section	*Paragraph*	*Notes*
1	2	Petronius, *Satyricon*, Sections 61–2, transl. W. M. S. Russell. See also Heseltine and Warmington, 134–9; Smith, 5–7.
	3	Petronius: Heseltine and Warmington, ix–x, xxv–xxvii, xxxv, 132–5. Bordelon: Smith, 42; Summers, 262. Royal Society: Summers, 252–3. Ansbach: Hamel, 65.
	4	Werewolf story revival: Frost, 23. Radio: J. Harmon in Huebel, 116. Films: McNally and Florescu, 232–47. Marryat: Frost, 24; Bleiler, xiv. Other episodes: Anderson; De Camp and Pratt; Williamson. Bibliographical: Smith; Summers; Bleiler, xiv; Frost. Quotation: Davidson (1975).
	5	Campbell and Tarrant, 28–33; Frost, 48.
	6	Derleth, I, i; IV, 273; III, 165–88.
	7	Frost, 48; Stableford, personal communication.
	8	Campbell and Tarrant, 75–95 (quotation, 79); Boucher.
	9	Reynolds: Bleiler, xiv, 150, 155. Ernst: Schneede, 137–40.
	10	Bleiler.
	11	Bill.
	12	B. M. Catalogue; Endore (1956, 1974); Frost, 43.
	13	Summers, 264; Baring-Gould, 255–60; Fort, 68; Frost, 43.
	14	Endore (1974). Incest: *ibid.*, 171. Versailles: *ibid.*, 233. Priests' bastards: Summers, 232, 241 note 23. Mass-murder: Russell and Russell (1968), 276.
	15	*Olalla*: Stevenson, VIII, 123–67. *Jekyll and Hyde*: Stevenson, V, 1–74. *Chapter on Dreams*: Stevenson, XXX, 41–53. Dreams and folklore: Davidson (1975). *Jekyll and Hyde* and werewolf:

Section	*Paragraph*	*Notes*
		Smith, 42. Stevenson and Brodie: Hennessy, 115; Russell and Russell (1961), 353. *Jekyll and Hyde* dream: Mackay, 144–6; L. Osbourne in Stevenson, V, ix–xi; F. Stevenson in Stevenson, V, xv.
2	1	Etymology: Summers, 6–10. Slavs and Greeks: Summers, 15–18, 147–52; S. Runciman in Baynes and Moss, 339–40; Finlay, 283–5. King John: Summers, 189; Smith, 32.
	2	Woodcut: Huxley (1974), 61. Eschenbach: Mustard and Passage, xvii.
	3	Believers: Summers, 73, 77, 81, 90, 118; Illis, 26. Trial records; e.g. Summers, 226–7. Stump: Summers, 253–9.
	4	Franche Comte: Summers, 228. Trials used for analysis: Summers, 103, 105, 112, 122–3, 223–35, 252–9. 1590s: Russell and Russell (1968), 27.
	5	Summers, 225–8.
	6	Summers, 114.
	7	Eyebrows: Summers, 118, 131 note 160, 192; Baring-Gould, 75, 110. Palms: Baring-Gould, 107. Ears and gait: Summers, 116. Boucher and Quinn: Stableford, personal communication; Frost, 33. Drake: Ditmas.
	8	Moonlight: Summers, 163–4, 241 note 23. Spells: Summers, 109. Clothes: Summers, 104; Baring-Gould, 73. Ointment: Summers, 104ff., 224, 229, 231, 233. Skin: Summers, 112, 232. Girdle: Summers, 110–12, 255. Other methods: Summers, 112–13. Urination: Summers, 155–6, 176; Smith, 8–9; Huxley (1974), 57.
	9	Return to human form: Summers, 113, 255; Baring-Gould, 79. Repercussion: Summers, 156, 225, 228, 235. Cure: Summers, 116, 164–6. Lupins: Summers, 237, frontispiece. Recent folklore: Summers, 162, 192, 238. Summers's views: Summers, 119–24; F. Morrow in Summers (1956), xiii.
	10	Herodotus: Summers, 133; transl. Selincourt, 276. Daneau: Summers, 128 note 73.
3	2	Possession of wolf: Summers, 78, 80–81, 120. Glamour: Summers, 23, 57 notes 115–16, 89–90, 119–20. Summers's views: Summers, 119–24.

Section	*Paragraph*	*Notes*
3	3	Wolf quotations: Matheson, 11; Pollard, 15. French institution: Matheson, 15–16. Bounties: Matheson, 14. Gevaudan: Matheson, 12–13; Clarke, 173–4; Pollard, 48–55. Tsaritsin: Matheson, 11. Karelia, Dent, 127. Wolves killing human beings: Matheson, 11–13, 17; Clarke, 171–6; Pollard, *passim*; *The People* (1929).
	4	Fire-arms: Dent, 121; Matheson, 12; see also R. O. Stephenson and R. T. Ahgook, in Fox, 288. War and wolves, quotation: Matheson, 11. Paris: Matheson, 11; Pollard, 23–5. Later French history: Matheson, 11–12, 16. Ireland: Fitzgibbon, 37. Finnish data: E. Pullainen, in Fox, 299. Reduction of wolves, quotation: Matheson, 17.
	5	Isengrin: Varty, 21–4; Ellis, vii–viii. Folk tale types: Aarne and Stith Thompson, 50, 125. Fenrir: Davidson (1964), 37–8. Wolf-month: Summers, 180; Dent, 111. *Pierce*: Summers, 7. Laws of Cnut: Summers, 4. Montgomerie: Summers, 8, 53 note 28. Hunting books: Summers, 11–12, 52 note 10. Geiler: Baring-Gould, 261–6. Gevaudan story: Summers, 236.
	6	Extinctions: Matheson, 15–17; Rockwell, 411; Dent, 99–100 (quotation), 128, 130–34. Effect on werewolf belief: Illis, James VI quotation: G. B. Harrison, 61–2. Labout: Hughes, 184.
	7	Dogs, quotation: Scott. Jarmo figures: S. Cole, in Brodrick, 24, 29. 'Tween dog and wolf: Frost, 25, 56; Dent, 114.
	8	'Wild dogs': Dent, 115. Llywelyn: Pollard, 79–80; Aarne and Stith Thompson, 65.
	9	Taillessness: Smith, 41; Summers, 89, 229. Transformation rules: Briggs, 80 (quotation); Summers, 121. Grenier case: Summers, 231–2.
	10	Dogs in folklore: Brown, this volume. Rabies in antiquity: Merlen, 70–81. Soranus: Robinson. Wolf-bite cases: Matheson, 13–15; Pollard, 57–68. Pasteur: Compton, 222; Williams, 52–4; de Kruif, 174.
	11	Rabies in the present: Genower and Ranger; Robinson (quotations).
	12	Pasteur at nine: Compton: 195; de Kruif, 58–9. Quotation: Robinson.

Section	*Paragraph*	*Notes*
	13	Medical writers of Roman Empire: Merlen, 70–81. Salius: Summers, 41, 46. Summers's views: Summers, 46, 61.
4	1	Werewolves and mass murder: Baring-Gould, 130–41, 181–237 (on Gilles de Rais).
	2	Mass-murderers: Bolitho, *passim*; Russell and Russell (1968), 274–7. Harpe gang: Wellman, 65–6. Hitler: Russell and Russell (1968), 277, 286–7. Rumour of Nazi 'werewolves': W. M. S. Russell, personal recollection. HQ *Werewolf*: Shirer, 1094.
	3	De Rais: Benedetti, 31, 109, 112, 180, 196–200; Penrose, 111, 119. Bathory: McNally and Florescu, 149, 153; Penrose, 8, 12, 14–16, 50, 79, 94, 106, 140, 142, 152.
	4	Smith, 27, 41; Summers, 187.
	5	Cannibalism: Russell and Russell, Animal, Vegetable, Mineral. 1315–17 famine: Lucas, in Carus-Wilson, 57–8.
	6	German cannibals: Bolitho, 180 (quotation); Hogg, 204–5.
	7	Kirkland report: Rawcliffe, 263–4. Ergot: Kavaler, 92–3, 102; Fuller, 2–3, 65, 85–6, 96, 112–16, 139, 141–3, 159–60, 182, 207–13, 277–8, 286, 300–301.
	8	Ointment cases: Summers, 224, 226, 229, 231, 233. Werewolf and witch ointment: Summers, 104; Forbes, 119; for Weyer, see Summers, 19, 56 note 88, 130 note 106; Summers (1958), 129. Hallucination idea: Russell and Russell (1968), 199; Summers, 98–9, 106, 108; Forbes: 119–20; for Cardano, see Wykes, *passim*. Recipes: Summers, 98, 106, 108; Forbes, 119–21. Ingredients: Forbes, 120–21; Heiser, 2, 154–6. Experiments: Forbes, 122; Heiser, 154–6; Barnett, 443.
	9	James VI quotation: G. B. Harrison, 61. Webster quotation: Symonds, 219.
	10	Padua case (sometimes mistakenly located at Pavia): Summers, 41, 74, 127 note 48, 160–61; Baring-Gould, 64–5. The other case: Baring-Gould, 65–6. Pont-Saint-Esprit case: Fuller, 112. Bernard de Gordon: Summers, 22, 57 note 109. 1852 case: Summers, 50–51. Scot: Summers, 13; Summers (1958), 128. Camden: Summers, 210–11; Dorson, 2.

Section	Paragraph	Notes
		Cotgrave: Summers, 12, 295. Assam case: Rawcliffe, 270.
4	11	Marcellus of Side: Summers, 38. Other medical writers on lycanthropy: Summers, 39–46, 49–50. Werewolves and porphyria: Illis. Dry eyes: Summers, 49. Garnier: Summers, 226; Illis.
5	1	Were-animals: Hamel, *passim*. Were-tigers, were-hyenas: Summers, 21. Were-coyotes: Oakes, 170–74. Were-lizards: Masters, 30–31.
	2	Totemism: Russell and Russell, Social Biology of Totemism; Lindsay, *passim*.
	3	Russell and Russell, Social Biology of Totemism.
	4	Apollo: Summers, 143–4. Arcadian stories: Summers, 134–43; Levi, 307–8, 372–3. Ridgeway: Summers, 141, 173 note 35. Addaura: Armstrong, 16–17, Plate 4 facing p. 33. Catal Huyuk: S. Cole, in Brodrick, 38–9. Urubu and Tupinamba: Huxley (1956), 9–12, 251–9 (quotations, 256, 259). Giraldus: Summers, 207, 216 note 99.
	5	Turks: Russell (1967), 127. Roman she-wolf: Russell (1975), 128; Grant, 109–18 (quotation, 114); E. B. Harrison, Plate 14; Rossiter, 123.
	6	*Lupa*: Grant, 117.
	7	Celtic wolves: Ross, 426–7; Mabinogion story: Jones and Jones, ix, xx, 61–3. Burgot and Verdun: Summers, 224.
	8	Summers, 4–6, 251.
	9	Summers, 207–10, 216 note 99.
	10	Isengrin: Varty, 22. Quotation: Smith, 5. Romances: Smith, 12–13; McKeehan, 789, 793–4, 797 ff:. *William of Palerne*: McKeehan, 786–9, 801; Oakden, 38–40; Noble, personal communication.
	11	Swedish tale: Thorpe, 5–15. Surnames: Russell and Russell (1968), 247. Werewolves and silver: Smith, 34. Folklore and sympathetic werewolves: Summers, 113–14; Smith, 21.
	12	*Jungle Books*: Carrington, 259. Irish bounties: Fitzgibbon, 37.
	13	Kipling and Scouts: Carrington, 484. Wolf conservation movements: Dent, 134. Totemism and Spencer: Russell and Russell, Social Biology of Totemism. Lapp children: Marsden.

Section	Paragraph	Notes
	14, 15	The Wolf-Man: Gardiner, 5, 7, 21, 98–106, 192, 198, 286–9.
	16	Kinship symbols: Russell, Symbols of Kinship; Russell and Russell, Kinship in Monkeys and Man.
	17	Quotation from Freud: Gardiner, 198.
	18	The Moghul miniature is printed on the cover of Richard Lannoy's *The Speaking Tree* (University Press, Oxford, 1971). It dates to about 1650.
	19	Initiation: Miller, *passim*. Parental behaviour under stress: Russell and Russell (1968), 163–9.

Bibliography

A. Aarne and Stith Thompson *The Types of the Folktale* Academia Scientiarum Fennica, Helsinki, 1961.

P. Anderson *Three Hearts and Three Lions* (Avon edn.) Avon Books, New York, 1962.

E. A. Armstrong *The Folklore of Birds* (2nd edn.) Dover, New York, 1970.

S. Baring-Gould *The Book of Werewolves* (Causeway edn.) Causeway Books, New York, 1973.

B. Barnett, Witchcraft, Psychopathology and Hallucinations *British Journal of Psychiatry 111* 439–45, 1965.

N. H. Baynes and H. St. L. B. Moss (ed.) *Byzantium* (Paperback edn.) Clarendon Press, Oxford, 1961.

J. Benedetti *Gilles de Rais* Peter Davies, London, 1971.

A. H. Bill *The Wolf in the Garden* (Centaur edn.) Centaur, New York, 1972.

E. F. Bleiler (ed.) *G. W. M. Reynolds: Wagner, the Wehr-wolf* Dover, New York, 1975.

W. Bolitho *Murder for Profit* (Travellers' Library edn.) Cape, London, 1933.

A. Boucher *The Compleat Werewolf and Other Stories* Ace Books, New York, 1969.

K. M. Briggs *Pale Hecate's Team* Routledge and Kegan Paul, London, 1962.

A. H. Broderick (ed.) *Animals in Archaeology* Barrie and Jenkins, London, 1972.

T. Brown, The Black Dog in English Folklore: this volume.

J. W. Campbell and C. Tarrant (ed.) *From Unknown Worlds* Atlas, London, 1952.

C. Carrington *Rudyard Kipling* (Pelican edn.) Penguin Books, Harmondsworth, 1970.

E. M. Carus-Wilson (ed.) *Essays in Economic History. II* Edward Arnold, London, 1962.

J. Clarke *Man is the Prey* (Panther edn.) Panther, London, 1971.

P. Compton *The Genius of Louis Pasteur* (Bay Tree edn.) Bay Tree Books, London, n.d.

H. R. Ellis Davidson *Gods and Myths of Northern Europe* Penguin, Harmondsworth, 1964.

H. R. Ellis Davidson, Folklore and Literature *Folklore 86* 73–93, 1975.

L. Sprague de Camp and F. Pratt *The Castle of Iron* (Pyramid edn.) Pyramid Books, New York, 1962.

P. de Kruif *Microbe Hunters* Albatross, Hamburg, 1935.

A. Dent *Lost Beasts of Britain* Harrap, London, 1974.

A. Derleth *Solar Pons. I, III and IV* (Pinnacle edns.) Pinnacle Books, New York, 1974–5.

E. M. R. Ditmas *The Legend of Drake's Drum* Toucan Press, St. Peter Port, Guernsey, 1973.

R. M. Dorson *The British Folklorists. A History* Routledge and Kegan Paul, London, 1968.

F. S. Ellis (transl.) *The History of Reynard the Fox* David Nutt, London, 1897.

G. Endore *King of Paris* Cresset-Gollancz, London, 1956.

G. Endore *The Werewolf of Paris* (Sphere edn.) Sphere Books, London, 1974.

G. Finlay *History of the Byzantine Empire* (Everyman edn.) Dent, London, 1906.

C. Fitzgibbon *Red Hand: the Ulster Colony* Michael Joseph, London, 1971.

T. R. Forbes *The Midwife and the Witch* Yale University Press, London, 1966.

C. Fort *Wild Talents* (Ace edn.) Ace Books, New York, n.d.

M. W. Fox (ed.) *The Wild Canids* Van Nostrand Reinhold, London, 1975.

B. J. Frost (ed.) *Book of the Werewolf* Sphere Books, London, 1973.

J. G. Fuller *The Day of St. Anthony's Fire* Hutchinson, London, 1969.

M. Gardiner (ed.) *The Wolf-Man and Sigmund Freud* (Pelican edn.) Penguin, Harmondsworth, 1973.

P. Genower and C. Rangers, Mad Dogs and Englishmen *TV Times London* 19th–25th July 1975.

M. Grant *Roman Myths* (2nd edn.) Penguin, Harmondsworth, 1973.

F. Hamel *Human Animals* (University Books edn.) University Books, New Hyde Park, N.Y., 1969.

E. B. Harrison *Ancient Portraits from the Athenian Agora* American School of Athens, Princeton, 1960.

G. B. Harrison (ed.) *King James the First: Daemonologie (1597); Newes from Scotland (1591)* John Lane The Bodley Head, London, 1924.

C. B. Heiser *Nightshades* Freeman, San Francisco, 1969.

J. Pope Hennessy *Robert Louis Stevenson* Cape, London, 1974.

M. Heseltine and E. H. Warmington (ed. and transl.) *Petronius* Heinemann, London, 1969.

G. Hogg *Cannibalism and Human Sacrifice* (Pan edn.) Pan Books, London, 1961.

H. E. Huebel *Things in the Driver's Seat: Readings in Popular Culture* Rand McNally, London, 1972.

P. Hughes *Witchcraft* (Pelican edn.) Penguin, Harmondsworth, 1965.

F. Huxley *Affable Savages* Hart-Davis, London, 1956.

F. Huxley *The Way of the Sacred* Aldus-Jupiter, London, 1974.

L. Illis, On Porphyria and the Aetiology of Werewolves *Proceedings of the Royal Society of Medicine 57* 23–6, 1964.

G. Jones and T. Jones (transl.) *The Mabinogion* (2nd edn.) Dent, London, 1974.

L. Kavaler *Mushrooms, Moulds and Miracles* Harrap, London, 1967.

P. Levi (transl.) *Pausanias: Guide to Greece. II* Penguin, Harmondsworth, 1971.

J. Lindsay *A Short History of Culture from Prehistory to the Renascence* Studio Books, London, 1962.

M. Mackay *The Violent Friend: the Story of Mrs. Robert Louis Stevenson* Dent, London, 1969.

W. Marsden *The Lemming Year* Chatto and Windus, London, 1964.

A. Masters *The Natural History of the Vampire* (Mayflower edn.) Mayflower Books, St. Albans, 1974.

C. Matheson, The Grey Wolf *Antiquity 17* 11–18, 1943.

I. P. McKeehan *Guillaume de Palerne*: a Medieval 'Best Seller' *Publications of the Modern Language Association of America 41* 785–809, 1926.

T. McNally and R. Florescu *In Search of Dracula* (Warner Paperback edn.) Warner Books, New York, 1973.

R. H. A. Merlen *De Canibus: Dog and Hound in Antiquity* J. A. Allen, London, 1971.

N. Miller *The Child in Primitive Society* Kegan Paul, Trench, Trubner, London, 1928.

H. M. Mustard and C. E. Passage (transl.) *Parzifal: by Wolfram von Eschenbach* Random House, New York, 1961.

P. S. Noble, personal communication.

J. P. Oakden *The Poetry of the Alliterative Revival* University Press, Manchester, 1937.

M. Oakes *The Two Crosses of Todos Santos* (Paperback edn.) University Press, Princeton, 1969.

V. Penrose *The Bloody Countess* (transl. A. Trocchi) (NEL edn.) New English Library, London, 1972.

The People 10th February 1929.

J. Pollard *Wolves and Werewolves* Robert Hale, London, 1964.

D. H. Rawcliffe *Occult and Supernormal Phenomena* Dover, New York, 1975.

D. A. Robinson, Rabies *Update 12* 649–54, 1976.

J. Rockwell, The Danish Peasant Village *Journal of Peasant Studies 1* 409–61, 1974.

A. Ross *Pagan Celtic Britain* (Cardinal edn.) Sphere Books, London, 1974.

S. Rossiter (ed.) *Greece* (2nd edn.) Ernest Benn, London, 1973.

C. Russell, Symbols of Kinship, in preparation.

C. Russell and W. M. S. Russell *Human Behaviour: a New Approach* Deutsch, London, 1961.

C. Russell and W. M. S. Russell *Violence, Monkeys and Man* Macmillan, London, 1968.

C. Russell and W. M. S. Russell, The Social Biology of Totemism *Biology and Human Affairs 41* 53–79, 1976.

C. Russell and W. M. S. Russell, Animal, Vegetable, Mineral *Biology and Human Affairs* in press.

C. Russell and W. M. S. Russell, Kinship in Monkeys and Man *Biology and Human Affairs* in press.

W. M. S. Russell *Man, Nature and History* Aldus, London, 1967.

W. M. S. Russell, Saints, Tribes and Ancestors *Biology and Human Affairs 40* 118–30, 1975.

U. M. Schneede *The Essential Max Ernst* (transl. R. W. Last) Thames and Hudson, London, 1972.

J. P. Scott, Dog *Encyclopaedia Britannica* 1964.

A. de Selincourt *Herodotus: the Histories* Penguin, Harmondsworth, 1954.

W. L. Shirer *The Rise and Fall of the Third Reich* (Pan edn.) Pan Books, London, 1964.

K. F. Smith, An Historical Study of the Werewolf in Literature *Publications of the Modern Language Association of America 9* 1–42, 1894.

B. M. Stableford, personal communication.

R. L. Stevenson *Works. V, VIII, XXX* (Tusitala edn.) Heinemann, London, 1924.

M. Summers *The History of Witchcraft and Demonology* (Dell edn.) Lyle Stuart, Secaucus, N.J., 1956.

M. Summers *The Geography of Witchcraft* (University Book edn.) University Books, Evanston and New York, 1958.

M. Summers *The Werewolf* (University Book edn.) University Books, New Hyde Park, N.Y., 1966.
J. A. Symonds (ed.) *Webster and Tourneur* Ernest Benn, London, 1948.
B. Thorpe (ed.) *Yule-Tide Stories* George Bell, London, 1904.
K. Varty *Reynard the Fox* University Press, Leicester, 1967.
P. I. Wellman *Spawn of Evil* (Corgi edn.) Transworld, London, 1966.
H. Williams *Masters of Medicine* Pan Books, London, 1954.
J. Williamson *Darker than You Think* (Berkley Medallion edn.) Berkley Publishing, New York, 1969.
A. Wykes *Doctor Cardano: Physician Extraordinary* Frederick Muller, London, 1969.

Acknowledgements

We should like to thank Peter Noble for information about the early versions of *William of Palerne* and for referring us to the valuable paper by McKeehan, and Brian Stableford for information about James Blish, Anthony Boucher and Seabury Quinn.

Birds and Animals in Icon-Painting Tradition — Venetia Newall

1. Anne Ross, *Pagan Celtic Britain* (London, 1967), p. 297.
2. The Dismissal Hymn for the Feast of the Archangel on November 8th, quoted by Timothy Ware, *The Orthodox Church* (Harmondsworth, 1963), p. 261.
3. Ernst Benz, *The Eastern Orthodox Church* (Chicago, 1963), p. 16.
4. William Addis and Thomas Arnold, *A Catholic Dictionary* (St. Louis, 1960), p. 23.
   Joan Hussey, 'Irene', *Encyclopaedia Britannica* (Chicago, 1972), XII, p. 587.
5. Ross, p. 234.
   A. D. Howell-Smith, *Thou Art Peter* (London, 1950), p. 69.
6. For other examples of the genre see:
   Richard Hare, *The Art and Artists of Russia* (London, 1965), Plate 24.
   H. P. Gerhard, *The World of Icons* (London, 1971), Plate 21.
   J. Leussink, *De Heilige Ikonen* (Heemstede, 1941), Plate 10.
   Thorvi Eckhardt, *Engel und Propheten* (Recklinghausen, 1976), Plate 14.

S. I. Maslenitsyn, *Jaroslavian Icon Painting* (Moscow, 1973), Plates 35, 69.

7. Hare, p. 37.
8. Maslenitsyn, Plate 33.
9. R. M. Dawkins, *The Monks of Athos* (London, 1936), p. 114.
   C. E. Clement, *Christian Symbols and Stories of the Saints* (Boston, 1871), p. 16.
10. An example of this genre is illustrated in:
    John Stuart, *Ikons* (London, 1975), Plate 396.
    Heinz Skrobucha, *Meisterwerke der Ikonenmalerei* (Recklinghausen, 1975), Plate 57.
    Ikonen Museum Recklinghausen (*Catalogue*) (Recklinghausen, 1976), Plate 94; see p. 185.
    For a further example see:
    Walter Felicetti-Liebenfels, *Geschichte der Russischen Ikonenmalerei* (Graz, 1972), Plate 334.
11. Gerhard, pp. 181–2.
    G. H. Hamilton, *The Art and Architecture of Russia* (Harmondsworth, 1954), p. 102.
12. *Ephesians*, V.6.
    Skrobucha, pp. 277–8.
13. Nicholas Zernov, *Eastern Christendom* (London, 1961), pp. 284–5.
14. For other examples of the genre see:
    Gerhard, Plate 61.
    Felicetti-Liebenfels, Plate 349.
    Galerie Ilas Neufert: Katalog (Munich, 1972), Plates 35, 62.
    Ikonen: 13 bis 19 Jahrhundert, Haus der Kunst (*Catalogue*) (Munich, 1970), Plates 251, 262.
15. Donald Attwater, *The Penguin Dictionary of Saints* (Harmondsworth, 1965), p. 312.
    The Book of Saints (London, 1966), p. 652.
16. Personal observation, December 1976.
17. J. S. Roucek (ed.), *The Slavonic Encyclopaedia* (New York, 1949), p. 63.
    Recklinghausen Catalogue, Plates 138–9; 188–9.
18. Venetia Newall, *The Folklore of Birds and Beasts* (Tring, 1971), pp. 39–40.
    A. M. Prokhorov (ed.), *Bol'shaia Sovetskaia Entsiklopediia* (Moscow, 1970), Vol. 1, p. 1305.
19. M. G. Wosien, *The Russian Folk-Tale* (Munich, 1969), pp. 109–10, 117.
    W. R. S. Ralston, *The Songs of the Russian People* (London, 1872), pp. 107, 109–11, 118, 216.

Dictionary of Folklore, Mythology and Legend, ed. M. Leach (New York, 1949), Vol. 1, p. 456.
See A. N. Afanas'ev, *Narodnye russkie skazki*, ed. V. Propp (Moscow, 1958), Vol. II, No. 265.

20. Ralston, p. 111.
Raffaele Pettazzoni, *Essays on the History of Religions* (Leiden, 1954), p. 163.
21. Howell-Smith, p. 70.
22. A. Grabar and G. Oprescu, *Rumania: Painted Churches of Moldavia* (Paris, 1962), pp. 7, 17; Plates 24, 25, 26.
Attwater, pp. 199–200.
Book of Saints, pp. 385–6.
M. V. Alpatov, *Early Russian Icon Painting* (Moscow, 1974), p. 185.
Kurt Weitzmann and Fred Anderegg, 'Mount Sinai's Holy Treasures', *National Geographic* (Washington, D.C., January 1964), p. 115.
23. Cecil Roth (ed.), *Encyclopaedia Judaica* (Jerusalem, 1971), XI, p. 733.
24. L. C. Sheppard, 'Devil', *Britannica*, VII, p. 328.
25. *Isaiah*, xiii. 21.
26. *Ibid.*, xxxiv. 14.
27. Augustine, ed. David Knowles, *City of God* (Harmondsworth, 1972), II. x. 58.
28. Robert Hughes, *Heaven and Hell in Western Art* (London, 1968), pp. 234–42.
J. A. MacCulloch, *Medieval Faith and Fable* (London, 1932), p. 59.
29. Vladimir Lossky, *The Mystical Theology of the Eastern Church* (London, 1957), p. 129.
30. Zernov, p. 282.
31. Lossky, p. 129.
32. Grabar and Oprescu, p. 13, Plate 4.
V. N. Lazarev, *Freski Staroye Ladogi* (Moscow, 1960), Plate 11.
Alpatov, Plate 40.
A Celebration of St. Nicholas: Temple Gallery Catalogue (London, Summer 1970), pp. 10, 22.
Dmitrij Tschizewskij, *Der Hl. Nikolaus* (Recklinghausen, 1957), Plate 16.
Ikonen Museum Recklinghausen: Catalogue (Recklinghausen, 1976), No. 435.
33. Skrobucha, *Meisterwerke*, pp. 39, 251–4.
Ibid., *Icons in Czechoslovakia* (London, 1971), Plates 15, 23, 44, 55.
Dezanka Milošević, *Das Jüngste Gericht* (Recklinghausen, 1963), *passim*.

G. and M. Sotiriov, *Icones du Mont Sinai* (Athens, 1956), Plates 150–1.
Alexander Frický, *Ikony* (Košice, 1971), p. 67.
Petru Comarnescu, *Voroneţ* (Bucharest, 1959), pp. 16–21.
Alpatov, p. 113.
There is an example in the Tretyakov Gallery, Moscow. Personal observation, Spring 1959.

34. Hughes, p. 178.
35. E. K. Chambers, *The Medieval Stage* (Oxford, 1903), Vol. II, pp. 137, 861.
36. André Degeur, *Ikonen* (Ramerding, 1976).
P. Dale-Green, *Dog* (London, 1966), p. 180.
37. Dawkins, pp. 194–5.
38. *Ibid.*
A Celebration of St. Nicholas, p. 39.
39. Zofia Ameisenowa, '*Animal-headed Gods, Evangelists, Saints and Righteous Men*', *Journal of the Warburg and Courtauld Institutes* (London, 1949), XII, p. 42.
40. *Ibid.*, pp. 42–5.
41. *Ibid.*, p. 42.
42. Personal observation, December 1976.
43. *Ibid.*
44. *A Celebration of St. Nicholas*, p. 39.
45. *Ikonen Museum Recklinghausen*, p. 202.
46. Attwater, p. 243.
Book of Saints, p. 501.
C. Mulock and M. Langdon, *The Icons of Yuhanna and Ibrahim the Scribe* (London, 1946), p. 16.
47. Information kindly supplied by the Rev. Richard Hayes.
48. Ameisenowa, p. 33.
49. Cecil Roth, *Jewish Art* (London, 1961), pp. 397–8.
Chaim Raphael, *A Feast of History* (London, 1972), pp. 110–11.
50. Roth, *Encyclopaedia Judaica*, XI, p. 732.
51. *Ibid.*, VIII, p. 1267; XI, pp. 731–3.
52. V. Kotov, *The State Museum of Palekh Art* (Moscow, 1975), Plate 117.
53. Wosien, p. 122.
54. Attwater, pp. 132–3.
Book of Saints, p. 280.
A Celebration of St. Nicholas, p. 34.
Ikonen Museum Recklinghausen, Plates 71, 115.
Alpatov, pp. 310, 314, Plates 119, 120, 143, 144, 148.
E. Smirnova and S. Yamshchikov, *Old Russian Painting* (Leningrad, 1974), Plates 17, 18, 60.

N. E. Mneva, *Iskusstvo Moskovskoye Rusi* (Moscow, 1965), p. 57.

55. L. Ouspensky and V. Lossky, *The Meaning of Icons* (Boston, 1952), p. 141.
K. Onasch, *Icons* (London, 1963), pp. 356–8.

56. Corina Nicolescu, *Icônes Roumaines* (Bucharest, 1971), Plates 78, 79.

57. Kosta Balabanov, *Icons from Macedonia* (Belgrade, 1969), p. 44.

58. Cornel Irimie and Marcela Focşa, *Romanian Icons Painted on Glass* (Bucharest, 1969), p. 15.

59. Alpatov, p. 144.
Smirnova and Yamshchikov, Plate 17.

60. W. Kolarz, *Religion in the Soviet Union* (London, 1961), p. 86.

61. *A Celebration of St. Nicholas*, pp. 40–1; Plate 29.
Constantin de Grunwald, *Saints of Russia* (London, 1960), p. 72.
C. G. Loomis, *White Magic* (Cambridge, Mass., 1948).

62. Dawkins, pp. 367–71.

63. Mulock and Langdon, pp. 21, 54–5.

64. David Talbot Rice, *The Icons of Cyprus* (London, 1937), p. 166.

65. Personal observation, Moscow, 1959.

66. Dawkins, p. 99.
Attwater, pp. 150–1.
Leach, I, p. 55.
Loomis, pp. 58–9.
Alpatov, Plate 193.

67. Attwater, *Dictionary*, pp. 176–7.
Attwater, *Saints of the East* (London, 1963), pp. 16–17.
Ikonen 13 bis 19 Jahrhundert, Plate 387.

68. Alpatov, Plate 87.

69. *Temple Gallery Exhibition Catalogue* (London, 1969), No. 25.

70. Otto Demus, *Byzantine Art and the West* (London, 1970), pp. 53–6, Plates 59, 61.

71. *Ikonen Museum Recklinghausen*, p. 198.

72. *Galerie Ilas*, Plate 36.

73. *New Grecian Gallery: Catalogue. Russians Icons: 16th to 18th century* (London, 1972), Plate 2.

74. Irimie and Focşa, p. 19.
Ouspensky and Lossky, p. 141.
Attwater, *Dictionary*, p. 148.

75. e.g., *Ikonen Museum Recklinghausen*, p. 204.

76. Tamara Talbot Rice, *Russian Icons* (London, 1963), Plates 15, 26, 31, 34.

77. Talbot Rice, *Icons of Cyprus*, p. 85.

78. MacCulloch, p. 61.

79. Wosien, p. 144.
For some examples of the genre, see: Gerhard, Plates 14, 40, 42.
Mneva, Plates 25, 63.
Felicetti-Liebenfels, Plates 251–6.
Skrobucha, *Czechoslovakia*, Plate 52.
István Rácz, *Suomen Ortodoksisen Kirkon Taideaarteita*, (Helsinki, 1971), Plates 44, 45.
Hamilton, Plate 42.
Cyril Bunt, *Russian Art from Scythes to Soviets* (London, 1946).
A. Papageorgiou, *Icons of Cyprus* (Geneva, 1969), p. 107.
Galerie Ilas, Plates 96, 104, 161, 169, 170.
Ikonen 13 bis 19 Jahrhundert, Plates 51, 202.
Irimie and Focşa, *Icoane pe Sticlă* (Bucharest, 1971), Plate 40.
80. Irimie and Focşa, *Icoane*, Plate 48.
Ibid., *Romanian Icons*, p. 19.
81. Alpatov, *Altrussische Ikonenmalerei* (Dresden, 1958), Plate 7.
82. Loomis, p. 65.
83. Gerhard, Plate 28.
84. Zernov, p. 284.
85. *Ibid.*, pp. 281–4.
See, for example, *Temple Gallery Exhibition Catalogue*, Plate 4.
86. Gerhard, pp. 181–2.
87. Sandro Chierichetti, *Ravenna* (Milan, 1960), pp. 24–5.
88. *Ikonen Museum Recklinghausen*, p. 77.
89. Dawkins, p. 208.
90. Lazarev, pp. 7–8; Plate 6.
91. Grabar and Oprescu, p. 17; Plate 22.
Comarnescu, Plates 73–5.
Also personal observation, Autumn 1963.
92. Skrobucha, *Meisterwerke*, pp. 251–2.
93. Leussink, Plate 12.
94. Dorothy Spicer, *The Book of Festivals* (New York, 1937), p. 4.
95. M. Ilyin, *Russian Decorative Folk Art* (Moscow, 1959), p. 102.
Eckhardt, Plate XI.
96. Benz, p. 17.
97. Stuart, p. 21.
98. Ilyin, pp. 108–9.
O. S. Popova, *Russkoye narodnoye iskusstvo* (Moscow, 1972), pp. 15–21.
G. V. Zhidkov, *Pushkin v iskusstve Palekha* (Moscow–Leningrad, 1937), pp. 16–17.
99. Kotov, Plate 44.
100. M. Friedberg, *Russian Classics in Soviet Jackets* (New York, 1962), p. 153.

101. A. E. Alexander, *Bylina and Fairy Tale* (The Hague–Paris, 1973), pp. 52, 60.
102. N. M. Zinov'yev, *Iskusstvo Palekha vtoroye izdaniye* (Leningrad, 1975), pp. 177–80, Plate 38.
103. A. N. Afanas'ev, *Narodnye russkie skazki* (Moscow, 1914), No. 68.
104. For other examples of the genre see:
Eckhardt, Plate 12.
Mneva, P. 74.
Rácz, Plate 43.
Ikonen: 13 bis 19 Jahrhundert, Plate 65.
Irimie and Focşa, *Icoane pe Sticlă*, Plates 13, 20, 49, 53, 56.
Alpatov, *Early Russian Icon Painting*, p. 312; Plates 129, 181.
Skrobucha, *Meisterwerk*, Plate 42.
Kotov, Plate 10.
105. Zinov'yev, pp. 188, 190, Plate 42.
106. de Grunwald, p. 18.
107. *A Celebration of St. Nicholas*, p. 12.
108. Zhidkov, pp. 146–8, Plate 47.
109. Efim Vikhrev, *Paleshanye* (Moscow, 1934), pp. 241–7.
A. V. Bakushinsky, *Iskusstvo Palekha* (Moscow–Leningrad, 1934), Plate 1.
110. Example in the author's collection, painted by V. Petrov (1958).
111. Hare, pp. 31–2.
Hamilton, pp. 153–4.
Bunt, pp. 96–7.
112. Kotov, Plate 24.
See, for example, the prominent and elaborate representations of animals, including a large red dragon, in 'John the Baptist in the Wilderness', Maslenitsyn, Plate 70; also Alpatov, *Early Russian*, p. 201.
113. Kotov, Plate 38.
Zhidkov, Plate 17.
114. Gerhard, p. 74.
115. Hare, p. 31.
116. cf. Kotov, Plate 117. See Plates 99–105, 118, 123, 137–8, 156 for work by women artists. The same author in his earlier book (*Iskusstvo Palekha*, Moscow, n.d., 47) discusses a slightly earlier work (1944) by Anna Kotukhina, one of these artists.
117. Hare, pp. 38–9.
118. *Ibid.*, pp. 33–4.
119. Zinov'yev, pp. 138, 141, Plate 22.
120. *Ibid.*, p. 142.
121. *Ibid.*, p. 64.
122. *Ibid.*, p. 65.

123. *Ibid.*, pp. 65–6.
124. *Ibid.*, pp. 68–9.
Vikhrev, pp. 53–4, 97–8, 211–14.
Zhidkov, pp. 94–5.
P. Solonin, *Zdravstvui Palekh!* (Yaroslavl, 1974), pp. 34–9.
125. Kotov, Plate 121.
Janko Lavrin, *From Pushkin to Mayakovsky* (London, 1948), pp. 77–81.
Michael Lermontov, *The Demon* (London, 1875), II.XV; pp. 78–9.
126. Zhidkov, 26–7.
127. *Ibid.*, p. 66. Plates 3–15.
128. *Ibid.*, pp. 21, 37–43, Plates 1, 2.
Kotov, Plate 60.
Zinov'yev, p. 70.
129. H. B. Cotterill, *A History of Art* (London, 1922), I, pp. 218–19.
130. *Ausstellung Kroatischer Kunst* (Berlin, 1943), pp. 5–30, Plates 1–32.
131. Oto Bihalji-Merin, 'Naive Art in Yugoslavia', *Jugoslavija* (Belgrade, 1959), XII, pp. 17–18.
132. *Ibid.*, p. 18.
Stefka Cobelj, 'Icons Painted on Glass', *IXth International Congress of Anthropological and Ethnological Studies*, (Chicago, 1973), p. 2.

Animal Fossils as Charms — Kenneth P. Oakley

1. E. D. Gill 1957; F. W. Whitehouse 1958.
2. L. Vértes 1964, pp. 141–2.
3. The associated flint industry appears to be transitional between Mousterian and Szeletian.
4. In 1967 J. C. Vogel and W. T. Waterbolk (*Radiocarbon*, 9, p. 118) reported the C14 dating of charred bone from the culture layer at Tata as 33,300 ± 900 years before (Sample No. G & N 2023).
5. P. Fischer 1876, pp. 352–5.
6. H. Breuil 1949, Scene 22, p. 74: 'Trading with ornamental shells'.
7. P. Fischer 1876, p. 335.
7A. K. P. Oakley 1965, p. 10, fig. 1*c*.
7B. 'Screwstone', endocast of *Cerithium* from Great Oolite, Bath, reproduced from Walcott by Oakley 1965, p. 15. fig. 6*b*.
8. Replicas of Miocene marine gastropods from 'Neolithic' (really Copper Age) temples in Malta are figured in K. P. Oakley 1965, Pl. I.

8A. Reconstructed necklace of Miocene marine shells from Upper Palaeolithic site at Dolní Věstonice, Moravia, drawing by Rosemary Powers, based on a photograph by K. Absolon. Illustrated by Oakley 1965, p. 11, fig. 2.
9. R. C. Hoare 1812, p. 61.
9A. Fossil bivalve mollusc shells probably used as charms, are figured by Oakley 1965, p. 12, fig. 3*a*: natural endocast of Corallian *Protocardia* from Bronze Age Barrow, Aldbourne, Wilts; fig. 3*b*: Pliocene *Pectunculus* shell perforated for suspension, from Magdalenian layer in rock-shelter near Les Eyzies, Dordogne.
9B. *Gryphaea*, the Jurassic 'Devil's toe-nail' oyster, illustrated by Oakley 1965, p. 12, fig. 4.
10. E. M. Clifford 1952, p. 61.
11. F. D. K. Bosch 1960.
12. J. E. Jude 1960.
13. O. Abel 1939, p. 56.
14. O. Abel 1939, p. 55.
15. J. Needham 1959, p. 615.
16. M. G. Bassett 1971, pp. 14–16.
17. E. D. Gill 1957, p. 96.
18. J. G. Jackson 1966, p. 76.
19. C. W. King 1860, p. 254.
20. T. F. Kehoe 1965, p. 212.
21. Note in Warne's Albion Edition of W. Scott's *Marmion*.
22. Jurassic ammonites are common about the village. 'This gave rise to a fabulous legend, which says that St. Keyna, from whom the place takes its name, resided here in a solitary wood, full of venomous serpents, and her prayers converted them into stones, which still retain their shape'. These are the words of the Rev. J. Mitford, quoted in White's *Natural History of Selbourne* (1789), 1876 edition, revised by J. E. Harting, p. 9, footnote 2. The first published record of the Keynsham 'snakestones' is by W. Camden (1586) who is quoted by W. N. Edwards 1967, p. 8 as referring to them as 'little sporting miracles of nature', a description indicating more enlightened thought on the part of this Elizabethan historian.
23. W. W. Skeat 1912, pp. 58–60.
24. D. T. Donovan on the geology of Stony Littleton long-barrow, *Antiquity*, forthcoming number.
25. J. Walcott 1779, p. 30, pl. 40 (XL).
26. Denys de Montfort 1808, p. 834.
27. L. Vértes 1964, p. 141.
28. P. I. Boriskovskii 1956.
29. J. Douglas 1793.
30. H. S. Toms 1932.

31. O. Abel 1939, pp. 28–9.
32. C. Fox 1958, pl. 66 *c*.
33. W. Johnson 1908, p. 147.
34. W. G. Smith 1894, frontispiece, pp. 335–40.
35. C. Blinkenberg 1911.
36. C. Chauvet 1900, p. 283.
37. R. E. M. Wheeler 1928, p. 314.
38. N. H. Field 1965.
39. *The Naturall Historie of C. Plinius Secondus*, II, p. 629.
40. J. Woodward 1729, pp. 7–8.
41. A. de Boodt 1609.
42. *Ova anguinum*, as figured by de Boodt 1609, after Gesner 1565, reproduced by Oakley 1965 pl. XXIII*b*.
43. Zoologists and palaeontologists recognize two main groups of sea-urchins: 'Irregular' in symmetry such as the heart-urchin *Micraster*, and 'Regular' about a centre as in *Cidaris*.
44. Romano-British antiquities, British Museum reg.no. 1883.7–5.110.
45. O. Fraas 1878.
46. C. O. van Regteren Altena 1962, p. 96.
47. J. Woodward 1728, pp. 11–12.
48. H. Rowlands 1766, p. 318; see also R. T. Gunther 1945, p. 464.
49. R. C. Hoare 1812, pl. xvii, fig. 3. This specimen (Devizes Museum 175) was examined in the Department of Palaeontology, British Museum (Nat. Hist.) in March 1949. The 'coralline' proved to be *Amphipora ramosa* (Phillips). Pebbles of Devonian limestone containing this species occur in the New Red Sandstone pebble-beds of South Devon, for example around Plymouth.
50. The 'coralline' macehead from Bush Barrow is illustrated by Oakley 1965 p. 120, fig. 10 and pl. XXIII*a*.
51. Neolithic axehead of serpulid rock, Troston, Suffolk, illustrated by Oakley 1965, p. 120, fig. 11.
52. E. Roniewicz 1970.
53. A. Leroi-Gourhan 1964.
54. A. Ficatier 1886.
55. P. Salmon 1883.
56. F. M. Whitehouse 1958.
57. The first scientific account of the Dudley trilobite (Plate 2) was by Charles Lyttleton (1750), who called it the Dudley Insect. The common colloquial name for it at that time and onwards was Dudley Locust (Mantell 1844, p. 555).

Bibliography

Abel, O. (1939). *Vorzeitliche Tierreste im Deutschen Mythus, Brauchtum und Volksglauben*, Jena 304 pp.

Altena, C. O. van Regteren (1962). 'Molluscs and Echinoderms from Palaeolithic deposits in the rock shelter of Ksar'Akil, Lebanon', *Zool.Med. Rikjsmus*, 87–99.

Bassett, M. G. (1971). 'Formed Stones' Folklore and Fossils', *Amgueddfa, Bulletin of the National Museum of Wales*, VII (17 pp.).

Beck, H. C. and Stone, J. F. S. (1935). 'Faience beads of the British Bronze Age', *Archaeologia*, LXXXV, 203–52.

Blinkenberg, C. (1911). *The Thunderweapon in Religion and Folklore.* Cambridge University Press. 122 pp.

Boodt, A. de (1609). *Gemmarum et Lapidum historia.* Hanover. 294 pp.

Boriskovskii, P. I. (1956). 'Belemnity v drevnem kamennom veke', *Priroda*, XI, 113–14.

Bosch, F. D. K. (1960). *The Golden Germ: an introduction to Indian Folklore.* 'S-Gravenhage. 264 pp.

Breuil, H. (1949). *Beyond the bounds of History.* London. 100 pp.

Camden, W. (1586). *Britannia.* London. 556 pp.

Chauvet, G. (1900). 'Ovum anguinum', *Revue archeologique* (3), XXXVI, 201–85.

Clifford, E. M. (1952). 'The Ivy Lodge Round Barrow', *Trans. Bristol & Glos.Arch.Soc.*, LIX, 59–77.

Douglas, J. (1793). *Nenia Britannica: Sepulchral history of Great Britain.* London. 197 pp.

Edwards, W. N. (1967). *The Early History of Palaeontology.* London: British Museum (Nat.Hist.) 58 pp.

Ficatier, A. (1886). *étude paléolithique sur la grotte magdalenienne du Trilobite à Arcy-sur-Cure (Yonne).* Auxerre. 24 pp.

Field, N. H. (1965). 'Fossil Sea-urchins from a Romano-British Site', *Antiquity*, XXXIX, 298.

Fischer, P. (1876). 'Sur les coquilles récentes et fossiles trouvées dans les Cavernes du Midi de la France et de la Ligurie', *Bull. Soc. Géol. Fr.*, IV, 329–42.

Fox, C. (1958). *Pattern and Purpose: A Survey of Celtic Art in Britain.* Cardiff: National Museum of Wales. 160 pp.

Fraas, O. (1878). 'Geologisches aus dem Libanon', *Jb. Ver. Vet. Nat. Wurttemburg*, XXXIV, 257–81.

Gesner, C. (1565). *De Rerum Fossilium, Lapidum et Gemmarum.* Zurich. 169 pp.

Gill, E. D. (1957). The Australian Aborigine and Fossils, *The Victorian Naturalist*, LXXIV, 93–7.

Gunther, R. T. (1945). *Early Science in Oxford*, 14, 464 (letter from E. Lhwyd, written 1701).

Hoare, R. C. (1812). *The ancient history of South Wiltshire*. London. 259 pp.

Jackson, J. S. (1966). Stone Head from near Newcastle West, *North Munster Ant. Journ.*, X, 76–7.

Johnson, W. (1908). *Folk Memory*. Oxford. 416 pp.

Jude, P. E. (1960). 'La Grotte Rochereil, Station magdalenienne et Azilienne', *Archs. Inst. Paléont. Hum.* mem. 30.

Koenigswald, G. H. R. von (1956). *Meeting Prehistoric Man*. London. 216 pp.

Kehoe, T. F. (1965). 'Buffalo Stones': an Addendum to 'The Folklore of Fossils', *Antiquity*, XXXIX, 212–13.

King, C. W. (1860). *Antique Gems*. London. 498 pp.

Leroi-Gourhan, A. (1964). *Les Religions de la Prehistoire* (*Paleolithique*). Paris. 154 pp.

Lyttleton, C. (1750). 'A letter ... concerning a nondescript petrified Insect', *Phil. Trans. R.Soc. Lond.*, XLVI, pp. 598–9.

Montfort, D. de (1808). *Conchyliologie Systematique et classification methodique des Coquilles*, I. Paris.

Mortimer, J. R. (1905). *Forty Years Researches in British and Saxon Burial Mounds*. London. 452 pp.

Mantell, G. A. (1844). *Medals of Creation*, II, 457–1016.

Needham, J. (1959). *Science and Civilization in China*, III, esp. 'Palaeontology', 611–23.

Oakley, K. P. (1965). 'Folklore and Fossils', *Antiquity*, XXXIX, 9–16, 117–25.

Oakley, K. P. (1975). 'Decorative and Symbolic Uses of Vertebrate Fossils', Pitt Rivers Museum, University of Oxford, *Occasional Papers on Technology*, 12, (60 pp.).

Pliny (C. Plinius Secundus). *The Naturall Histoire of C. Plinius Secundus* (Trans. by Philemon Holland into English, 1634), II, 629.

Roniewicz, E. (1970). Scleractinia from the Upper Portlandian of Tisbury, Wiltshire, England, *Acta Palaeontologica Polonica*, XV, 115–31.

Rowlands, H. (1766). *Mona Antiqua Restaurata*. London. 2nd edition. 357 pp.

Salmon, P. (1183). *In* M. Bertillon *et al.*, *Dictionnaire des sciences anthropologique*. Paris. (Pp. 1075–6).

Skeat, W. W. (1912). 'Snakestones and Thunderbolts as subjects for systematic investigation', *Folklore*, XXIII, 45–80.

Smith, W. G. (1894). *Man, the Primeval Savage*. London. 349 pp.

Toms, H. S. (1932). 'An Early Bead Necklace found at Higham', *The Rochester Naturalist*, VI, 125–32.

Vertes, L. (1964). Tata: *Eine Mittelpaläolithische Travertin-Siedlung in Ungarn*. Budapest. 253 pp.

Walcott, J. (1779). *Petrifications near Bath*. 51 pp.

Wheeler, R. E. M. (1928). 'A Roman Celtic Temple near Harlow, Essex', *Antiq. J.*, VIII, 300–26.

Whitehouse, F. W. (1958). 'The Australian Aboriginal as a Collector of Fossils', *Queensland Naturalist*, XIII, 100–2.

Woodward, J. (1728). *Fossils of all kinds digested into a method, suitable to their mutual relation and affinity*. London. 56 pp.

Woodward, J. (1729). *An attempt towards a natural history of the fossils of England*, I. London. 243 pp.

Acknowledgements

I wish to express my gratitude to members of the staff of the Department of Palaeontology, British Museum (Natural History) who were kind enough to let me bother them to identify some of the invertebrate fossils described in this paper: Dr. C. G. Adams, Dr. R. A. Fortey, Dr. M. K. Howarth, Dr. R. P. S. Jefferies, Dr. C. P. Nuttall, Mr. E. F. Owen and Dr. H. G. Owen. I am specially indebted to Mr. E. F. Owen because he drew my attention to the painted wooden beads from India, and allowed me to quote his identification of the brachiopod species replicated by the example shown in the Frontispiece. My warm thanks are also due to Miss Christine Court for drawing the Stony Littleton long barrow on the basis of advice kindly provided by Mr. L. V. Grinsell. Miss Rosemary Powers generously undertook to prepare the majority of the line-drawings, illustrating nautiloids, ammonites, crinoids, echinoids and porosphaeras. With such a wide-ranging subject as I chose to deal with in this paper, it was necessary to seek advice and help from friends and colleagues, and I would like to say how much I appreciated the willingness of the following to spare time to aid me in the task I had set myself: Mrs. Shirley Bury, Mr. B. L. Cranstone, Prof. D. T. Donovan, Mrs. Ellen Ettlinger, Mr. Basil Greenhill, Miss Sheila Hönigsberg, Mr. John Irwin, Dr. Desmond Morris, Miss Dorothy Norman, Miss Bridget O'Connor, Mrs. Eileen Sliwa, Mr. G. L. L'E. Turner, Miss Elizabeth Woods and Dr. V. Zwalf. Finally I would like to record my thanks to all those who allowed me to use line-blocks based on their published figures, including Mr. J. G. Jackson, Prof. G. H. R. von Koenigswald, Dr. Ewa Roniewicz and Dr. C. Teichert. The publication of the colour photograph forming the frontispiece of this book was made possible by a generous award from the British Academy to the Folklore Society.

Index